THE FIRE OF PERU

THE FIRE OF PERU

RECIPES AND STORIES FROM MY PERUVIAN KITCHEN

RICARDO ZARATE

& JENN GARBEE

Photography by Ed Anderson

HOUGHTON MIFFLIN HARCOURT

BOSTON / NEW YORK / 2015

Food and prop styling by Valerie Aikman-Smith

Design by Laura Palese

For information about permission to reproduce selections from this book, write to Permissions, Houghton Mifflin Harcourt Publishing Company, 215 Park Avenue South, New York, New York 10003.

www.hmhco.com

Library of Congress Cataloging-in-Publication Data

Zarate, Ricardo.
  The fire of Peru : recipes and stories from my Peruvian kitchen / Ricardo Zarate & Jenn Garbee.
     pages cm
  Includes index.
  ISBN 978-0-544-45430-9 (hardcover) — ISBN 978-0-544-45329-6 (ebook)
1. Cooking, Peruvian. I. Garbee, Jenn. II. Title.
  TX716.P4Z37 2015
  641.5985—dc23   2014044522

Printed in the United States of America

DOW 10 9 8 7 6 5 4 3 2 1

FOR MIGUEL:

Brother, friend, business partner, mentor, and drill sergeant, who always pushed me to do more, in the way that only true *hermanos* can do. *Te extraño mucho.* You will always be in my heart.

AND FOR OUR *PAPÁ*:

For bringing and keeping the Zárate-Choy families together, and dedicating your life and love equally to all thirteen of your kids. *¡Echa Muni!*

CONTENTS

INTRODUCTION

THE ROOTS OF PERUVIAN CUISINE

What is truly authentic Peruvian food? It is a question I am asked often, and one that I always find difficult to answer. *¿Sabes este sentimiento?* (Know the feeling?) Some people compare the food of my country to modern fusion cuisine. That always surprises me. Fusion cuisine is a modern concept. It centers on the idea of intentionally layering unexpected flavors and textures together and often happens in a sophisticated dining setting. Peruvian cooking is the opposite. It is very humble, honest cooking. The flavor combinations are sophisticated, yes. But they are also rooted in long-standing traditions, the result of dozens of cultures' cooking styles and ingredients merging together over many years. I often refer to the food of my homeland as one big *estofado*, or stew, that has been simmering for five hundred years and is finally ready to serve. It is Peruvian cuisine's finest hour.

Understanding what makes Peruvian food so relevant today begins with its history, *mi pasión secreta*. An incredible number of foods—thousands of varieties of potatoes, quinoa, chile peppers, and so many other vegetables and fruits—trace their roots to Peru's ancient *costa, sierra, y selva* (the coast, mountains, and jungle, as we call each region of my country) and our neighbors. Two civilizations in particular built incredible empires around those foods: the Moche, who flourished in northern Peru from the early second to around the eighth century, and the Incas, who spoke Quechua (a dialect still spoken today), who dominated the coast of northern and central South America from the thirteenth century until they were conquered by the Spanish in the late sixteenth century. When the Spanish embarked on a voyage around the world in the late fifteenth and early sixteenth centuries, hoping to find a faster route to Asia for the spice trade, they landed smack in the middle of a whole world of new ingredients. It would take a while for people elsewhere to appreciate them, but many truly changed world history.

That's not to say it was a one-way street. The Spanish brought many ingredients that locals had never tasted: olives and olive oil, wheat flour, beef and different types of cheeses, garlic and herbs like cilantro, new fruits and vegetables, and "exotic" spices. (I still get excited, like a little kid doing something sneaky, when I throw star anise and cinnamon sticks, two of my favorite Asian spices brought from the Spanish Spice Trade stash, into so many of my savory and sweet dishes.)

Even more important were the people who made Peru their new home and who became an essential part of developing Peruvian *cultura* into what it is today. Some of Peru's most famous dishes have African roots from the cooking styles of the slaves the Spanish brought along with them, like *anticuchos*, grilled meats and poultry in a tangy sauce (traditionally, organ meats, leftovers that the slaves were given, were and are still used on the streets of Peru). In 1821, after finally winning independence from Spain, the door to Peru opened for immigrants from all over the world. Like the United States, Peru has citizens with German, British, Arabic, and so many other roots. Italians were particularly influential to Peruvian cooking and brought pasta, Parmesan cheese, and more, but probably most important to modern Peruvian cooking was an influx of Chinese, Japanese, and other Asian immigrants in the nineteenth and twentieth centuries. They opened up a

whole new world of Eastern flavors (beyond the spices the Spanish had already brought), from soy sauce to stir-fries and dumplings. Local ingredients merged with those of European, African, and Asian cultures.

That melting pot was a big mix, or stew, of cultures, yes, but probably the most significant of those new influences on Peruvian cooking was southern Chinese. After slavery was abolished in the 1850s, southern Chinese contract laborers arrived in Peru to fill the labor void. They were almost entirely Cantonese men who came to work on Peru's sugar and cotton plantations. It was hardly better than slavery, but when the contract laborers finally paid back their travel and labor contracts after years of hard work, they started setting up their own businesses. Until recently, *el Chino de la esquina*, literally "the Chinese on the corner," was slang for our neighborhood grocery stores, now filled with ingredients like soy sauce and *kión*, or ginger, which is indigenous to southern China. Ginger is usually called *jengibre* in Spanish, but we use the Cantonese root word. In the new *Chino-Latino* culture, we didn't follow the same grammar rules as other Spanish-speaking countries— what's the fun in that? Even the Chinese-Peruvian restaurants you find on almost every other block in Lima are known as *chifas* instead of *restaurantes chinos*.

What is so amazing to me is how all of those global influences didn't stay locked up in each culture, but merged to create an entirely new style of cooking—that's the true fusion of Peruvian cuisine. A good example is *carapulcra* (page 160), one of the oldest dishes still made by home cooks everywhere in Peru. The base of the stew is *papas secas*, traditional dried potatoes, with a good number of European, Asian, and African flavors coming from ingredients like garlic, peanuts, and spices. As I often tell people, I am not the creator of the food of my country. I simply polished the rough edges and took Peruvian food, so rich with history, where it always wanted to go. Yes, as a chef I add my own touches and incorporate more modern influences (particularly Japanese, as I spent many years working in some of the best sushi restaurants), but honoring the integrity of the ingredients and traditional dishes of my homeland is still most important to me.

The Lima of My Memories

To understand my style of cooking, you should also know something about my personal history. Lima was a very different city when I was growing up in the 1970s and 1980s, without all of the fancy hotels and cosmopolitan restaurants. The tiny, shoebox-shaped cement houses with tin roofs that you still find in the poorest neighborhoods of the city were everywhere. I grew up in one of those houses.

We learned at a young age that you had to work hard for your *soles*, the currency in Peru, but hard work wasn't a bad thing. Peruvians are very proud people who want to earn their wages, not be given handouts. You see that today in the street performers in Lima doing quick magic tricks and juggling shows at stoplights, and in the villagers at small Amazon markets scaling the river fish they caught that morning or selling their backyard chickens. But mostly, people sell whatever they made in their own kitchens or cook up to order on the streets: anticuchos (grilled meat and poultry), *rosquitas* (braided anise cookies), *marcianos* (ice pops), and so many other handmade foods. I made, and sold, every single one of those at one point as a little kid or when I was older, and my first pop-up restaurant was on those streets. As a teenager, I'd grill anticuchos whenever I needed a little extra cash.

Rímac, the district in northern Lima where I grew up, is the oldest district in Lima, just north of downtown and across a little river by the same name. Sometimes, when my friends and I told a cabdriver that we wanted a ride home late at night, he would shake his head and drive off. It wasn't exactly Beverly Hills (where I later opened a restaurant). Back then, it was a lot harder to piece together a living in Lima than it is today. Inflation was a huge problem. Your *soles* were likely going to be worth less when you went to the produce market than they were worth the day you got paid. Terrorists were also a part of daily life. It was very real, not something you heard about on television. The two most powerful groups, Shining Path and Tupac Amaru, would blow up entire buildings full of innocent people,

simply to make a point. I knew several people who were killed, point blank, for no reason. Even as a little kid, you learned to always look in every direction around you in case they were hiding nearby. One of the rival groups that was powerful at the time put bombs in the home of one of my sisters. Her house was above a bank. I was there visiting when the bombs exploded. I remember her toilet breaking into thousands of pieces, with the shards flying everywhere. We had to dive onto the floor to avoid being hit, like in a Hollywood movie. We were so lucky that no one was hurt, but those memories always live with you.

It's probably not going to be a surprise when I tell you that no one really vacationed or came for work to Lima or elsewhere in Peru like they do today. The rare times when my school friends and I spotted *turístas*, with their skinny legs poking out of short little pants in the winter (often summer in other countries), it was usually in the Plaza Mayor, also known as the Plaza de Armas, where my friends and I used to hang out. We would point and stare like we'd just seen a flamingo at the zoo for the first time. They looked so funny! Now, the historic government palace and cathedral in the center of the city are always packed with tourists. When I go back to visit today, I'm so *orgulloso*, proud, to see Lima's success and how much it has changed.

My Family

Some things were very difficult, *sí*—but we saw it as just part of life, and we had a very happy life, and one that I am very proud is my own. I come from a big *católico*, Catholic, family, and nine of my brothers and sisters have Chinese roots. Peruvian *cultura* wouldn't be what it is today without the influence of immigrants from all over the Asian continent, my family included. After my mom and her first husband separated, she married my father and had four more children, including me, to make thirteen. I guess you would call my dad a native Peruvian, but like our food, that means a mix of so many cultures.

Suddenly we were all part of this fantastically giant family. There was never any thought that we might be apart and live like two separate families. To my father, all thirteen of us were his children. The youngest among us called my father *Papá*, and the oldest, already teenagers, would call him *Chochera*, the nickname for "best friend." When I go back to my neighborhood, some of my father's old friends still call me *chocherita*, or "little best friend"—a nickname I secretly love. When the papá of my brothers and sisters came by our house, he was family, too. I was too little to understand, so my parents introduced him to me as my *akun*, the Cantonese word for "grandfather." I was always so excited when my akun came over to visit that I'd run into his arms. Like all of my brothers and sisters, I really loved him, even when I was old enough to understand that we weren't related by birth.

My older brothers still like to joke that I got off pretty easy as the second youngest. By the time I came along, they had finished building our little house in the backyard, or courtyard, really, behind another small home in Rímac. For years our floor had been a patchwork of cement and the *tierra*, earth. My brothers poured one section at a time, depending on how much cement our father could afford at the time. (It was finished before I was born, but like any kid brother, I used to give my older *hermanos* a hard time about one section of a wall that curved like a llama's neck—

couldn't they build a straight wall?) Our father worked as carpenter, a cabdriver, or in any odd job he could find to make a few extra soles. He really hustled. Anything he could do to bring home another fifty-kilo bag of potatoes. You needed a lot of *papas fritas*, fried potatoes, to feed a family the size of ours.

The one thing my father always wanted to do was open a restaurant. He had a small café for a while and had invested his meager savings in it, but the economy in Lima at the time was very bad. He had to shut his beloved little place down pretty quickly, but he never complained. It's one of the many reasons that as a teenager, I started going by Ricardo, my first name, when my family had always called me Martín, my middle name. Ricardo was my father's name. I dreamed of opening my own restaurant someday—in honor of *mi papá*.

The Dirty Dishes

My parents came up with a pretty clever system to give us opportunities beyond the walls of poverty in Lima in the 1970s and 1980s. With thirteen kids and a tight budget, there was a limit on how much my parents could do financially. When one of my older brothers or sisters got a full-time job, they were to give one of their younger siblings help jump-starting his or her career. Sometimes, that meant covering tuition at school, other times pitching in to buy a plane ticket abroad. Each of us would repay *el favor* to the next siblings in line.

For me, the "favor" from my older brothers and sisters included both my culinary school tuition at the Instituto de las Américas, Lima's culinary college, where I enrolled at seventeen, right after graduating from secondary school (the equivalent of high school), and a plane ticket abroad after I graduated. This was back in the early 1990s, when most restaurants in Lima really weren't trend-setting like today. One of my brothers, Miguel, and my cousin Arturo were working and living together in London, comparatively a much better restaurant city at the time. They had a couch

where I could crash, so I applied to Westminster Culinary College. (Hey, a second three-year culinary degree couldn't hurt—especially when it came with a student visa that meant I could apply for restaurant jobs at the same time.) Small problem: I didn't speak more than a few words of English.

This is the part of the story where some chefs might tell you that they landed a *stage* (essentially a culinary internship) at a famous restaurant like The Fat Duck or back then, The River Café. Those places are great, but I'm very proud that my career didn't work out that way. I started out a little further down the kitchen pecking order: the dishwashing station at a chain restaurant. Actually, I almost didn't even get to London. A woman on my layover in Florida thought I was trying to illegally immigrate to the United States and called the police. I was detained by immigration security (to a petrified twenty-year-old, they looked like a SWAT team), and I missed my flight. After several hours, it became clear that they were trying to put me on a flight back to Peru. Good luck convincing an immigrations officer that you really *are* going to London (and didn't buy the ticket with a layover in Florida intentionally) and have all of *cero*, zero, interest in illegally immigrating to the United States. (How times change. I am so proud to be an American citizen today.) More than twenty-four hours later, after desperate phone calls to my family and finally convincing immigration they couldn't pay me to stay in Florida, I was able to get on another flight.

When I finally got to London, the first job I found was working the early morning janitorial shift at an office building. I was happy for the work, but I wanted a kitchen job—any kitchen job. I also needed the extra cash. My cousin Arturo worked in the kitchen at Benihana, the American chain restaurant known for its Japanese-style grilled hibachi dishes. Arturo convinced his boss to give me a shot as a dishwasher, the position where he had started in the kitchen. I was so grateful for the work, even if my schedule was a little crazy. On weekdays, after my office cleaning rounds, I would run across town to wash dishes for the lunch rush before making a brief appearance at the culinary school (sure, I skipped a lot of classes since I already had a culinary degree, but for the record, I *did* graduate). After class, I would go back to the restaurant to wash dishes again until past midnight, and then crawl home to crash for a few hours, exhausted.

I'd be lying if I said I adjusted to my new life seamlessly. It was like I had woken up from a really good dream and suddenly been slapped into *realidad* in a foreign culture very different from where I had grown up. I loved Lima, and loved my family and friends. I probably would have stayed, had there been good work opportunities, as there are today, but that wasn't an option back then. The night after my first full day of the dawn-to-dusk work-and-school schedule, I laid in my bed and cried. I didn't think I would make it. (I still think about that night whenever I face a very difficult situation. I say, "I'll make it happen" so often, my friends now always laugh when they hear it.) I think my cousin sensed I was struggling. Arturo told me that if I wasn't promoted to hibachi chef within six months, as he had been, he and my brother were kicking me out and putting me on a plane back home. I didn't realize it then, but he and Miguel were trying to give me the confidence I desperately needed to be successful.

Six months later, I was standing in front of my first customers behind the restaurant's steel *teppanyaki* cooking tables and hardly understanding a word anyone said to me. I was so worried that customers would complain about the language barrier, until I figured out that all you had to do was ask, "How's the weather?" and people in London would talk on and on among themselves for what seemed like hours. All I had to do was smile, nod, and focus on what I did best—cooking.

My First Kitchen

It may not have been a five-star restaurant, but I will always be grateful for that first chain restaurant kitchen gig. Two years later, I landed a position at Aykoku-Kaku, one of London's oldest and most respected sushi restaurants. Not that it was all smooth sailing from there. This was back when there was a lot of discrimination in London toward Latinos. The owner looked me up and down and assumed I had been hired as a new dishwasher, not a line cook. I once made her favorite sashimi plate. She took one bite and said it was the best she'd ever had—who made it? When she found out that I had, the owner sent the plate immediately back to the kitchen, the rest of the food untouched. *El jefe del infierno*—the boss from hell.

But the master sushi chefs (who had hired me), all from Japan, respected the hard work and dedication I gave them. They also showed the same *respeto*, respect, for every single ingredient on the plate. Peruvian food has plenty of Japanese influence, but learning to truly appreciate that unfussy way of cooking—what I call "clean" cooking—was the most important lesson in my culinary career. You can really see that heightened Japanese influence in my style of modern Peruvian cooking today. I spent the next twelve years working my way up in several of London's best Asian fusion and modern European restaurants at the time. They were all incredible opportunities to hone my cooking style, but after thirteen years, I needed a change. And I'm not going to lie: I needed sunshine.

When I got a call to revamp the menu at a Cal-Asian restaurant in downtown Los Angeles, I jumped on it. L.A. reminds me a lot of Lima, with people from so many different cultural backgrounds, a true *mezcla*, mix. There is also an energy in Hollywood that you can almost feel in the air—the idea that anyone can do anything, no matter what his or her background or personal story. After getting the restaurant going, I returned to London for a while for work, but I knew I would be back very soon.

I was—by 2009, I had taken over the stoves at Wabi-Sabi, an Asian-fusion restaurant in Venice Beach.

Recomendaciones Para Hoy

Musciame de Pato S/30

Chilcanos de

Hierba Buena
Coca
Kion

S/15

Restaurants were closing right and left because of the recession, but that didn't bother me. I had waited long enough to go out on my own. I saved up what I could, basically what amounted to one week's rent for many high-end restaurants, only I needed it to last my first few months. It was just enough to rent a tiny little corner in Mercado La Paloma, a communal marketplace in downtown Los Angeles stuffed with taco stands and Oaxacan pottery shops. I called the humble little lunch stand Mo-Chica, after the Moche people, whom I've always admired (see sidebar, page 154). In the beginning, working at two cross-town restaurants was more than a little crazy based on the notorious L.A. commute time alone. Every morning before the sun came up, I shopped for Mo-Chicha ingredients at the fresh fish market downtown, then prepped the ceviches and other dishes before working the lunch shift. In the late afternoon, I would drive back across town to Wabi-Sabi in time for the dinner shift. (Fortunately, I lucked into finding an aspiring Peruvian chef in Los Angeles who could manage the dinner shift at Mo-Chica.) The double-time work schedule was almost identical to what I'd been doing fifteen years earlier, when I was just starting out in London, but I'd learned by then that sometimes that's just how life works out. And, I could finally bring *my* style of cooking, my little corner of modern Peruvian food, to people.

You may know how this story ends, or continues, as I like to think. The best compliment came from critic Jonathan Gold when I landed on the cover of a fancy food magazine's Best New Chefs issue. He described my nomination in reference to Mo-Chica as "an honor not generally awarded to lunch counters, even great ones." It was such an honor to me, to my takes on classic dishes like *lomo saltado* (beef stir-fry, page 140) and *seco de cordero* (a traditional lamb stew, page 150). It was also life changing. Suddenly, Mo-Chica was on the Los Angeles food map, and I had enough regular business to keep paying rent and my (all of two) loyal staffers.

Mo-Chica soon moved to a bigger space downtown, and several other Los Angeles–area restaurants followed. Picca, a modern Peruvian cantina on the edge of Beverly Hills, I based loosely on the Queirolo, one of the oldest cantinas in Lima. It was there that I perfected my Anticucho Sauce (page 112), still one of the foundation recipes of my cooking. Paichẽ, which can best be described as a Japanese izakaya-style Peruvian seafood restaurant, was where all of the years working in Asian restaurants, especially those with a Japanese focus, really came through with my riff on *tiraditos*, *causas*, and *ceviches*. I have since moved on from these restaurants, and have opened Suave Riko in Los Angeles. It is more of a laid-back kind of place, an open-"fire" Peruvian rotisserie featuring local ingredients. It's an incredibly exciting time to be sharing my take on modern Peruvian cuisine with people who may never have tasted anything like it, and my personal estofado has certainly had plenty of time to simmer.

I hope with this book, you will become as excited as I am about the food of my country. If you are new to Peruvian cooking, then maybe start by trying some of the slow-braised meats and poultry, called estofados, and sauces—my anticucho sauce—the next time you grill steak or fish. If you're familiar with Peruvian cuisine and ceviches, lomo saltado, or pisco sours are your thing, I hope you'll have fun with my versions, or be inspired to come up with your own.

And, if you are working your way through the book, as you finish those last few rosquitas (page 254)—which, now that I think about it, were one of my first forays into the food business when I was nine or ten years old—I hope you will have a better understanding of and love for Peruvian culture. There are always so many new flavors and traditional dishes to explore. I still get excited about playing around with different flavor combinations and adding my own twists. But the true *fuego*, or fire, behind each and every one of the dishes in this book comes from the Peruvian home cooks, including *mi madre*, who cooked the most amazing dishes long before I could even reach the stove. To them, we must all say *gracias*.

THE KITCHEN

The kitchen was the center of my mom's *reino*, kingdom, the place all of thirteen of us kids gathered when we weren't off doing things she probably wasn't supposed to know about. Our house was small, truly built one sack of cement at a time, with the eight boys stacked in one room, the five girls in another, and a living room nook where we all could hang out. *La cocina* was my favorite room in the house.

The kitchen had a whole row of restaurant-size pots, always lined up and ready to go, and a cranky, old industrial kerosene stove that took some muscle to light. When I went to friends' houses, I thought their moms were just pretending, playing house with their tiny pots and pans. You only had to turn a dial and *tímido* little flames spat out. (What could you cook on that?) Each morning, one of my older brothers would hand-crank the pump, over and over, until there was a loud *whoosh!* and a giant, half-foot-tall blue flame finally leapt out of our stove's belly. Then *Mamá* was ready to start her twelve-hour shift.

Mom ran a very tight ship. With so many kids, she had to. There were *no excusas* when it came to chores. Although my father loved cooking, men in Peru didn't usually spend much time in the kitchen. It was a very traditional culture, but my mom refused to discriminate when it came to

kitchen chores. I always wanted to be in the kitchen, but most of my older brothers would have rather helped our dad fix anything around the house, even haul junk off the street in the summer heat. I thought I'd won the lottery when Carlos, one of my older brothers, offered me the equivalent of a quarter to chop onions when it was his turn. I was too small to reach the counter, so I'd stand on a chair when our mom wasn't looking and put a plastic bag over my head with sunglasses so I wouldn't cry (note to my kids: definitely *not* a good idea).

When I was finally old enough to take care of the "dailies," meaning do some of the produce and meat market shopping, I would plan out a few of my own menus for the family for the week ahead. I was so proud that I would carefully write them out on our refrigerator in my ten-year-old script. Being in charge of the kitchen (at least in my head, as my mom was really in charge) also came with a bonus: When one of my older brothers would give me a hard time, his least favorite entrée would suddenly show up on the dinner menu. *Dulce venganza*—sweet revenge.

Ingredients

Sometimes, creative cooking is simply about looking in a new way at ingredients that have been right under our noses. Most of the staple ingredients I cooked with when I was growing up I still use today. Some you probably know well, like potatoes; others, like certain Peruvian ají chile peppers, maybe not. I hope you will be as excited as I still am to try them all. Most aren't very expensive and are pretty easy to find. Those that aren't everywhere yet, like the pepper pastes, you can order online and keep in your pantry or refrigerator for months.

AJÍ (CHILE PEPPERS)

Like most Peruvians, I'm pretty sure my blood is spiced with ají peppers. People from my country have been eating native wild and cultivated peppers, both spicy and sweet, since at least 7500 BC, and hundreds of varieties were later cultivated, worshipped as religious icons, and eaten in every fresh, roasted, and dried form (my money would have been on the Incas to win any ancient chile pepper–eating contests).

What's really amazing to me is how those peppers were adopted all over the world. It's hard to imagine eating Thai food without fiery bird's-eye chiles, Indian food without cayenne pepper, or Spanish food without sweet, red pimientos. I would have loved to have seen the looks on people's faces when they tasted those peppers for the first time.

AJÍ AMARILLO, AJÍ PANCA, AND ROCOTO PEPPERS AND PASTES

I'm always surprised that many of the peppers that we use aren't typically household names outside of Peru. I'm biased, but the people from the land where thousands of varieties of peppers first grew probably know a thing or two about choosing the best ones to grow. Fortunately, you really only need a few varieties of chile peppers to make most Peruvian dishes, and all of the dishes in this book: *ají amarillo*, *ají panca*, and *rocoto*. Most of my recipes use the first two, amarillo and panca, considered the yin and yang opposites of Peruvian cooking. Ají amarillo are spicy but light and subtly sweet, while ají panca have a big, smoky flavor but aren't too hot.

In Peru, we like to turn the peppers we use the most into pastes. It is both convenient for cooking and concentrates the peppers' flavors. I make my own "fresh" pepper pastes from frozen, blanched ají amarillo and rocoto peppers (it can still be hard to find the fresh peppers in the United States). Look for them in a well-stocked Latin market (some focus more on Mexican or other Latin products, not yet Peruvian) or online. Most of the jarred, store-bought pastes are very good quality, so I have adapted all of the recipes in the book to use them. I always keep jars

of all three pastes in my fridge at home. With some peppers, like dried ají panca, I think the jarred paste is actually preferable over making your own paste. If you do luck out and find fresh or frozen ají amarillo or rocoto peppers (or whole, dried ají panca) and want to make your own pastes, I included a recipe on page 34. For frozen pepper and jarred paste sources, see the Resources (page 261).

Ají Amarillo

These sunny orange peppers have an almost fruity flavor with a back heat that hits your throat, not the tip of your tongue. I really love that, as the spiciness doesn't mask the other flavors in whatever you are eating. Ají amarillo are very versatile peppers, from the flavors and spiciness down to the skin, which changes colors like a *camaleón*,

chameleon, from yellow to vibrant orange as the peppers mature (the sun-dried version is called *ají mirasol*, or "look into the sun"). The paste, made from blanched peppers, almost melts into slow-cooked sauces and stews, and yet is still bright enough for raw dishes like ceviche.

Ají Panca

More smoky-sweet than hot, ají panca paste is used most often in slow-cooked stews and sauces (many times along with spicier ají amarillo paste) to lend smokiness and depth of flavor. We use ají panca almost like tomato paste, to add flavor complexity. The paste also works well when grilling meats and poultry, as the dried pepper's bigger flavors aren't covered up by the smoke and char. If you find the dried, whole peppers (see Resources, page 261), you could make

PERUVIAN HEAT

Ají panca peppers are more smoky than hot, while ají amarillo and rocoto peppers are highest on the Scoville scale, a measure of the heat index of peppers. Both are used in small quantities in most dishes. Though they register the same Scoville units as ají amarillo peppers, rocoto peppers taste much hotter to me. (For comparison, jalapeños are 2,500 Scoville units.)

	AJÍ PANCA	AJÍ AMARILLO	ROCOTO
HEAT INDEX	Mild to Medium	Hot	Very Hot
SCOVILLE	1,000–1,500 units	30,000–50,000 units	30,000–50,000 units
FLAVOR PROFILE	Smoky and slightly sweet	Bright and fruity	Spicy and aromatic, like a hot green pepper
USES	Deepens the flavor of cooked dishes Sauces, stews, and roasts	Most versatile, works well with other flavors in both fresh and cooked dishes Salad dressings, cocktails, salsas, dressings, ceviches	Usually added at the end of cooking or to raw dishes for a kick of heat Ceviches, salsas, sauces
LOOK FOR	Jarred paste Dried peppers (to make a paste)	Jarred paste Fresh or frozen peppers (to make a paste or chop)	Jarred paste Fresh or frozen peppers (to make a paste or chop)

your own paste (page 36), but it's a lot of work. I almost always use the store-bought panca pastes. The quality is usually really good, and you can't beat the price, usually less than five dollars per jar from a Latin market or online.

Rocoto

For some reason, the bright red rocoto pepper goes by the shortened nickname *rocoto* without the *ají* in front (maybe all that extra heat it holds scared off the *ají*). The peppers have an almost green bell pepper flavor followed by a pretty intense heat. Like ají amarillo peppers, the fresh peppers can be tough to find. I hear they're becoming popular with chile pepper buffs in the United States, who are growing their own. As with ají amarillo, I use frozen, blanched peppers to make my own paste (page 34), but the more widely available jarred pastes are usually very good quality. Don't substitute powdered rocoto peppers for the paste— *terrible*.

PAPAS Y CAMOTES (POTATOES AND SWEET POTATOES)

The two places I've lived outside of Peru, the United States and England, are almost as obsessed with potatoes as my native country. I'm pretty sure that's not a coincidence, but if you really want to get to know potatoes, you need to go to where they originated: the Andean highlands.

Papas is the Quechan word for "tuber." Potatoes, sweet potatoes, and related tubers were grown—or tamed, really, as most wild potatoes are poisonous—by early Andean civilizations some seven thousand years ago. As Western explorers later learned, potatoes are hearty and, even better, grow underground, so they are relatively easy to grow in different climates. When Andean growers learned how to dry and preserve them (*chuño* and *papas secas*, page 27, are good examples), potatoes became an even more important part of the Peruvian diet.

Peru is still home to hundreds of varieties of edible tubers in all different sizes, shapes, and colors. Some are smooth and shiny, almost like pearls; others are so gnarled and twisted that they remind you of the hard work they had

to do growing up. But even in Peru, you usually only see a handful of varieties at most markets today. You'd probably have to hike high up in the Andes to taste those with some of my favorite traditional Quechua names: Like a Deer's White Tongue, Makes the Daughter-in-Law Cry, and Like an Old Bone (what I'm pretty sure my line chefs will call me from now on).

Fresh Potatoes

In a home kitchen, you really only need three types of potatoes to cover all of your cooking bases: a solid starchy variety, a versatile waxy variety, and sweet potatoes. (Most other Latin American countries refer to sweet potatoes as *batatas*, but in Peru, we call them *camotes*.) I also like some nice little guys for roasting, which usually fall under the waxy umbrella.

Waxy. Though not universally, smaller potato varieties (therefore, most potato varieties) tend to fall more on the waxy side of the potato kingdom to varying degrees. Because they hold their shape well and have a creamy texture, waxy potatoes are good in chilled salads, stews, and stir-fries, and for roasting. In Peru, we also use them for mashing. To make *causas*, a chilled potato casserole, I use the everyday, medium-size, red-skinned potatoes you find at most grocery stores. The mashed potatoes get a nice, creamy texture when you knead them, almost like pasta dough, and they hold their form when cut into different causa shapes.

You can use any potatoes for roasting, but I really like small potatoes like fingerlings, nubby purple Peruvian potatoes, or whatever small potato variety I can find at the farmers' market. Most tend to be waxy, but when you get into specialty varieties, some are starchier. When roasting such little potatoes, the starch content really doesn't matter. If you leave the skins on (cut larger potatoes in half), they get nice and crispy on the outside and so tender inside.

Starchy. With little water and a high starch content, the flesh of starchy potatoes is very tender inside but will get nice and crispy on the outside. I know people in the United States love their russets for mashed potatoes, but I really only use them to make french fries. They turn out too fluffy for causas, the closest thing to mashed potatoes in Peru. For fries, if you luck into Kennebecs, an American variety that looks like a russet, grab them. They have a lower water content, so they fry up super golden brown and crispy. Starchy potatoes are not the best for roasting, as they tend to fall apart.

Sweet. Camotes (sweet potatoes) come in varieties from starchy to waxy, with cream-, carrot-, or purple-colored flesh. The most common varieties in the States are the orange potatoes. Those are usually pretty starchy, but still hold up well, so they are good for mashing or roasting, make great fries, and are so good just boiled, which is how we serve them with ceviche and so many other dishes in Peru.

Sweet potatoes versus yams. We tend to use yams and sweet potatoes interchangeably and serve them boiled or in stews. True yams, which go by the same Spanish name as sweet potatoes in Peru, are not related to potatoes or sweet potatoes. They are a different tuber that has been cultivated in Asia, Africa, and the Americas for thousands of years.

Dried Potatoes

Chuño (South American freeze-dried potatoes) have a very distinct flavor and are definitely worth trying, but I mainly cook with papas secas (boiled and dried potatoes). They add an unexpectedly rich potato flavor to soups, stews, and similar slow-cooked dishes. For dried potato sources, see Resources (page 261).

Chuño. The process of naturally freeze-drying potatoes originated in Peru and Bolivia at least five hundred years ago, probably much earlier. Freeze-drying makes the uniquely bitter variety of potatoes that grow at high altitudes in the mountains edible (the process eliminates most of the bitter flavor) and also makes them shelf-stable and lightweight, so they are easy to transport. The dried potatoes are soaked in water and used in stews, or ground into a starchy flour to use as a thickener for sauces or in baked goods.

To make black chuño, the potatoes are left outside at night to freeze, then thawed by the mountain sunshine. After several days, the freeze-dried potatoes are smashed underfoot to remove the skins and break the potatoes into small pieces. During the process, the chuño turns dark brown to purple or almost black, resembling little lumps

of charcoal. To make white chuño, the potatoes are freeze-dried in a similar process (left outside to freeze), and then soaked in icy-cold rivers or misted with water for a few days or as long as a month. Soaking turns the potatoes so chalky-white they almost look like powdered sugar–covered fritters.

Papas Secas. When preserved by boiling and drying, "everyday" (non-bitter) potato varieties become not only shelf-stable and lightweight to transport, but they develop a very interesting, chewy, almost al dente pasta–like texture. You can boil papas secas to use in potato soups or to make carapulcra (page 160), a traditional dried potato stew. If you're going camping, think like an Andean mountain man and pack the dried potatoes along with *cancha* (page 46), dried corn used for toasting and popping.

MAÍZ (CORN)

In Peru, corn is as much of, if not more than, a daily presence as potatoes. In Lima, the giant, chewy cobs used to make *choclo* poke out of bubbling pots of water on street vendors' anticucho grills, and the chilled cooked kernels are almost always spooned up alongside ceviche. My uncle Lucio, a man from, and truly of, the mountains, taught me how to make cancha (page 46), the oldest known version of popped corn, which dates back to around 4700 BC. The snack is still so popular, you can count on seeing empty little bowls and the salt remnants scattered on almost every restaurant table in Peru.

That's not to say that corn is uniquely Peruvian. *Maíz* has been central to Mesoamerican culture for thousands of years. Corn was probably domesticated farther north, in Central America, around the same time as or a little earlier than potatoes, and was also considered sacred by both the ancient Moche and Inca civilizations.

Today, people all over Latin America grow everyday-looking stalks that open up to reveal corn the color of ivory, gold, and copper, or the deepest purples of the night sky. Some varieties are incredibly sweet and as juicy as a peach; others are starchy, like bread, with an almost earthy flavor. The diversity is incredible.

Fresh & Frozen Corn

I haven't yet convinced my local farmers in southern Calfornia to grow fresh choclo, or had much luck with exporters when I go back to Peru. Fortunately, frozen imported choclo is usually very good quality. (I really don't recommend the canned version.) For frozen corn sources, see Resources (page 261).

Choclo. The name *choclo* (also known as Peruvian or Cuzco corn) refers to the starchy varieties of large-kernel corn that are available fresh at virtually every market in Peru. It is used as the traditional side dish for ceviche and anticuchos. The nickname "Cuzco corn" refers to the Incas' capital city in southern Peru, Cuzco, where the dietary staple was cooked into a porridge. For an authentic flavor and texture, look for the frozen kernels at Latin markets. The fresh corn varieties available in the United States are very different, with smaller and sweeter kernels. They are a suitable substitute when steaming or boiling choclo as a side dish, but will taste very different. In dishes like *tamalitos verdes* (page 64), the starchiness of the authentic choclo is essential for the tamales to hold their shape.

Dried Corn

With dried corn, stock up when you find it at a Latin market or online. For dried corn sources, see Resources (page 261).

Maíz Chulpe. These large corn kernels are dried and then fried in oil to make cancha (page 46), a popular salty, crunchy snack that dates back to at least Moche times. Today, cancha is served almost like bread, in the center of the table. Sometimes you are also served bread, a Spanish addition (or rice, in Lima especially, with such a large Chinese-Peruvian population), so the old and new, or at least newer, influences are right there together on the table. I know many people refer to cancha as the Peruvian version of corn nuts, but it's really the other way around. In the 1930s, after tasting them on a business trip, an American businessman began importing the dried kernels from Peru. He tinkered around with his recipe and gave the cancha a more marketing-friendly name. The real deal is lighter, with a softer, more popcornlike center and an extra-crunchy dried kernel "shell" on the outside. Several different varieties of maíz are used to make cancha, including *serrana*, with bigger kernels, but I really like the *maíz chulpe*. It's just the right size for grabbing by the handful.

Maíz Morado. Dried, dark purple (*morado*) varieties of corn have a subtle, earthy flavor. Long used to make natural fabric dyes, the corn also turns drinks like *chicha morada* (corn punch, page 224) and dishes like *mazamorra morada* (purple corn pudding, page 243) an inky, Cabernet-like color. The corn is easy to cook with, since it is dried and sold on the cob, and you just throw everything into the pot. Like blueberry pie filling, the purple corn juice stains whatever it touches dark purple, so save your best white T-shirt for another day.

Maíz Mote or Mote. To make the Peruvian version of hominy, large, starchy varieties of corn are dried and nixtamalized, meaning treated with mineral lime. This variety is so big, it is known as *maíz mote gigante del Cusco*, "giant hominy from Cusco." Like dried beans, you need to soak the corn for a really long time to soften the kernels up

before cooking. One of my favorite preparations is the very simple, comforting, stewlike side dish that goes by the same name as the dried corn (page 220). Don't substitute canned hominy. The dried corn has a distinct chewy texture that is very different.

GRANOS Y FRIJOLES (GRAINS & BEANS)

Peruvians have a long relationship with beans, going back to ancient cave dweller times and on through the Moche and other ancient societies. Indigenous Andean "grains," really seeds like quinoa and amaranth, were just as central to the local diet, if not more so, and became powerful religious symbols (see pages 200 to 201). The Spanish brought barley, also some rice, with more to come later from the large Asian population that settled in Lima and surrounding areas.

In some ways, that eclectic mix of grains and beans, all still very important to the local culture, is very much what modern Peruvian cuisine is all about. The old and new work together at most meals, not separately.

Grains

Good-quality rice, quinoa, and similar seedlike grains, and barley are pretty easy to find these days at well-stocked grocery stores. For grain sources, see Resources (page 261).

Arroz (**Rice**). In Peru, we eat rice with enough *emoción*, excitement, you would think it is native to our soil. To fuel my huge family's taste for rice, my dad would cart home 50-kilo (about 110-pound) bags at a time. In the smaller towns and villages, most people buy their rice from outdoor markets. You can scoop up as much rice as you want from giant sacks filled with a dozen different varieties, usually the medium- to long-grain rice used in Chinese cooking. I also cook with a lot of Japanese-style sushi rice. I love the sticky texture.

Kinúwa (**Quinoa**) and *Kiwicha* (**Amaranth**). Quinoa and amaranth have been staples in the Peruvian diet for thousands of years. Quinoa was considered the sacred "mother grain" (really a seed) by the Incas and is a key export crop for Peru and Bolivia today. Quinoa's much smaller cousin, amaranth, has also been cultivated in the Andes and throughout Central America for thousands of

years. Both are incredibly versatile and can be used cold in salads or hot, like rice, in stews or stir-fries.

Trigo (**Barley**). The Spanish brought barley (also called *mote de trigo*, *trigo pelado*, or *cebada*) to Peru by way of the Middle East. It was originally used mainly to make *emolientes*, grain-and-herb-based teas that street vendors still sell claiming many health benefits. Barley has a nutty, slightly chewy texture that also works well in risottos (see page 214) and other dishes. I'm partial to those from Peru, but you can use any barley that you find.

Beans

So many different beans are native to Central and South America, while nonnative pulses like lentils are just as popular. These are the ones I use most in my cooking. For bean and pulse sources, see Resources (page 261).

Lentejas (**Lentils**). Lentils aren't native to South America, but they are so affordable, filling, and tasty, they have become very popular in Peru. My mom used them as the base for *tacu tacu*, savory cakes make from various leftover beans and rice (page 211), or just cooked up big, steaming pots for the middle of the table. There are many varieties to try, but if you find them, beluga lentils, the black "caviar" of the bean world, are worth the price (see page 219).

Pallares (**Lima Beans**). In Peru, we call lima beans *pallares*, but the English name "lima" stuck after they were first shipped abroad (see sidebar, page 212). The nickname "butter beans" refers to their flavor. Lima beans are fairly firm and hold their shape well. Fresh, green limas are good in salads like *solteritos* (page 173), and I really like the dried white beans simply boiled in plenty of water with a few stock-friendly vegetables and a good shake of salt.

Canario (**Mayocoba Beans**). Despite the nickname *Peruano* beans, these medium-size beige beans (also called canario, or canary beans, even in Peru) are native to Central America. They have a mild flavor and a creamy texture that makes them versatile in so many dishes (see page 212), but I really like canarios in simple stews or boiled up the same way as lima beans. You could substitute great northern or similar beans.

LA DESPENSA (THE PANTRY)

Along with the ingredients on the previous pages, I always keep these staple Peruvian ingredients in my pantry and produce drawers.

Ajo (Garlic) and Kión (Ginger)

Other than ají peppers, garlic and ginger are probably the most important ingredients in my kitchen. Garlic brings in the Spanish influence, ginger the Asian kick. Like peppers, we usually grind them up individually into pastes (see page 37). Unlike the minced or pressed versions of garlic, or grated ginger, the pastes almost melt into meats and sauces and don't brown too quickly when cooked at high heat. Having the purees around also cuts down on prep time, since all you have to do is spoon out a dollop. You can also freeze them. I've had people tell me that, both flavor- and convenience-wise, the garlic paste in particular has changed their daily cooking lives. I'm not going to go that far, but just promise me you won't substitute the jarred garlic pastes found at many grocery stores. The homemade version is on a whole other level. If you can't make the pastes, you can finely grate the ginger and garlic (see page 37) as an alternative, if you must.

Cebollas Rojas (Red Onions)

In Peru, you never hear anyone say they don't like onions, I think partly because we use red onions almost exclusively. The fresh onions are sliced or chopped up to use in *salsa criolla* (page 44), probably the most important condiment in Peruvian cooking, while the cooked onions are the base of so many stir-fries and stews. The varieties in Peru tend to be smaller and sweeter than the giant red onions widely available in the United States, but the ones you find here are still good, and I use them at my restaurants. To temper the acidity, especially if you are using the onions raw, soak freshly chopped or sliced red onions for a few minutes in ice water. A quick ice water soak also makes the onions extra-crispy.

Culantro (Cilantro), Sacha Culantro (Jungle Cilantro), and Huacatay (pronounced "wah-kah-tie")

It probably goes without saying that shortly after arriving with the Conquistadors, cilantro was adopted into pretty much every Central and South American cuisine. If you ever get to Peru, look for our wild version called *sacha culantro*, or jungle cilantro. The plant, native to the Amazon, has small, pointy leaves and a stronger cilantrolike flavor that I like to use as a garnish when I can. Peruvian cooks also use a lot of *huacatay*, an herb native to the Andes known as "Peruvian black mint" that looks like a small, bushy fern with thin, spear-shaped leaves. It lends an almost aniselike mint flavor to traditional Andean dishes. Unlike cilantro, huacatay can be difficult to find fresh in the United States outside of a handful of growers at some farmers' markets. I substitute smaller amounts of frozen huacatay (see Resources, page 261), which has a more concentrated flavor. You could also substitute equal parts fresh mint and basil. The flavor won't be as intense, but the combination works.

Harina de camote (Sweet Potato Starch) and Katakuriko (Japanese Potato Starch)

In Peru, starches are derived from locally grown crops like potatoes (rather than wheat) and are used as thickeners. In Japanese cooking, the starch of regular (not sweet) potatoes is often used as a coating for fried foods because it creates a very light, crispy crust. I use both in my cooking. I recommend looking for both at specialty Latin and Asian markets, but you can substitute any potato starch. Don't substitute potato flour, a very different derivative of potatoes. Cornstarch is often a suitable substitute, especially when frying.

The most traditional Peruvian starch, harina de camote (sweet potato starch), gives puddings like mazamorra morada (page 243) an almost silky texture. It doesn't leave the off-taste that corn and some wheat starches sometimes can, so it's worth seeking out for desserts like the pudding that call for a large quantity of starch (alternatively, substitute regular potato starch). Potato starches also gelatinize at lower temperatures than corn starches. Like other starches, add the potato starch toward the end of cooking (prolonged high heat can cause the starches to break down and separate), and mix the powder into a little water or other liquid first.

Katakuriko (Japanese potato starch) gives fried foods a "lighter" crust than purely flour batters. I really prefer

the texture of katakuriko, which is incredibly light, but you can substitute any regular potato starch for the fried recipes in this book. They all work well. When I don't have potato starch, I use cornstarch for frying, which also works. Any katakuriko or potato starch is also a good stand-in for harina de camote in baking recipes.

Limón Peruano (Peruvian Limes)

Peruvian limes have a reputation for being more acidic than the Persian variety in most American grocery stores. They are, but in an aromatic and very balanced way. Persian limes are a good stand-in, and I use them for most dishes at my restaurants. The one exception is when I'm making a Pisco Sour (page 226). The cocktail really is top notch with Peruvian limes, but a mix of equal parts lime and lemon juice gives you a close approximation to the real deal.

Salsa de Soya (Soy Sauce) and Tamari

Most people refer to soy sauce as just *Sillao* in Peru, the name of the most popular brand there (based on the Cantonese word for soy sauce), and the one I grew up with. It's so popular, the fermented-soybean-and-wheat-based sauce is a staple in both home kitchens and on tables at chifas, Peruvian-Chinese restaurants, all over Lima. It's used not just for saltados, or Peruvian-style stir-fries, but on anything that needs a splash of bold, salty flavor. I use soy sauce to wake up everything from the simplest bowl of leftover rice to the most elegant-looking tiraditos, Peruvian-style sashimi. After working at sushi restaurants in London, I must admit I can't go back to the Peruvian version and switched to good-quality Japanese brands like Yamasa. It is so much more balanced, and less salty, than the everyday soy sauce I grew up eating.

Unlike soy sauce, most tamari does not contain wheat, so it is a little thicker and has a slightly stronger flavor. Tamari is also usually gluten-free (check the label; a few brands contain a tiny amount of wheat). If you are avoiding gluten, you can substitute tamari for the soy sauce in any of the recipes in this book. The flavor will be a little stronger, so decrease the amount slightly.

Yuzu Kosho

Peruvian cooking has many Asian influences, but I had never tasted the Japanese condiment yuzu kosho until I worked in Japanese restaurants. The paste is a tongue-awakening combination of fermented green or red chile peppers, yuzu peel, and salt. I use the more *picante* green chile pepper version that you can find at most Asian markets on grilled seafood and meats, often delivered by way of what I call my "Peruvian pesto" (page 117), an olive oil–based sauce packed with global flavors: yuzu kosho, ají amarillo peppers, garlic, ginger, lemongrass, cilantro, and lime juice. You don't need much yuzu kosho, just a little so it doesn't overwhelm a dish. The paste keeps well for months in the refrigerator.

BASIC RECIPES

AJÍ AMARILLO OR ROCOTO PASTE

If you find fresh ají amarillo or rocoto peppers or a bag of the frozen peppers (see page 22), consider making homemade paste as I usually do. (If you can only find whole jarred or canned peppers, I recommend buying the premade paste instead, which is very good quality and is what is called for in the recipes in this book. The brine the jarred and canned peppers are stored in diminishes their flavor.)

If making your own, keep in mind that the heat of homemade pastes varies depending on the peppers, but it is usually not as strong as the store-bought pastes. Frozen peppers can also lose some of their heat over time, and I add a little olive oil to my version for a more balanced flavor (the jarred versions are usually purely pureed peppers with a pinch of salt and citric acid as a preservative). Start with about one-third more homemade paste to the store-bought amounts listed in my recipes, then add more homemade paste to taste. So, if a recipe calls for 1 tablespoon (3 teaspoons) of store-bought paste, start with 1 tablespoon plus 1 teaspoon of fresh ají amarillo paste. With any produce, it's never an exact science, so let your tongue be the judge.

Blanching tames the heat just enough and makes the peppers easier to peel. It's a good idea to wear plastic gloves as

you clean the peppers. The heat can do a number on your skin if you forget you've handled the peppers and touch your face.

1 **To make Pepper Paste:** Slice about 1 pound (10 to 12 large) fresh or thawed frozen ají amarillo or rocoto peppers in half lengthwise. Remove the stems, lay the peppers flat on a work surface, and use a spoon to gently scrape out the seeds and most of the veins. Don't go overboard on scraping, or you won't have much flesh left. Fill a medium pot halfway with water, bring to a boil, and blanch the peppers for exactly 2 minutes. Strain, rinse the peppers under cold water for a minute or two, and let cool completely.

2 Peel the cooled peppers, discard the skins, and lay the peppers on a kitchen towel or paper towels to absorb some of the excess water (do not fully dry them). Put the peppers in a blender and puree until chunky. With the motor running, slowly drizzle in ¼ cup extra-virgin olive oil until the mixture turns into a smooth puree. If you don't have a professional-style blender, you may need to add another tablespoon or two of olive oil to get things going.

3 Spoon the paste into a glass jar and top it off with a good ½ inch of extra-virgin olive oil, cover, and refrigerate for up to 3 weeks (as you use the paste, top it off with more olive oil). Or freeze the paste in a flat, thin layer in a medium plastic food storage bag so you can break off small pieces as needed. **Makes about 1 cup.**

AJÍ PANCA AND MIRASOL PASTE

The jarred versions of dried pepper pastes like ají panca are typically very good quality, but if you do find the dried peppers at a good spice shop or Latin market, by all means, make your own paste. In the recipes in this book, I only use ají panca (not mirasol, the dried version of ají amarillo peppers), as it adds a unique smoky flavor to dishes. If you find ají mirasol, you can also turn them into a paste with this recipe. Compared to fresh ají amarillo peppers, the dried version has a more concentrated flavor that is similar to dried tomatoes versus fresh tomatoes. (A tablespoon or two of ají mirasol paste is great in meaty stews or bean dishes, or add a little more olive oil to make a sauce for meats, as you might a sun-dried tomato sauce.) Just don't substitute ají mirasol for ají panca paste in recipes in this book. The flavors are very different.

Unlike fresh pepper pastes like ají amarillo, pastes made from dried peppers tend to be around the same heat index or a little hotter than the store-bought versions, especially if you leave behind a few seeds or interior membranes. Use equal amounts of the homemade paste as the jarred in the recipes, or start with a little less if you are concerned about the heat.

1 **To make Pepper Paste:** Place 3 to 4 ounces dried, whole ají panca or mirasol peppers (18 to 24 medium peppers, if using ají panca) in a medium bowl. Add enough simmering hot water to cover the peppers, and place another bowl on top. (If needed, use a canned product to weigh down the bowl so the peppers are fully submerged.) Soak the peppers until softened, at least 6 hours or preferably overnight. Strain, and reserve the soaking water. Remove the stems from the peppers, open them up, and scrape out all of the seeds and the interior membranes to tame the heat. Rinse the peppers under running water to remove any lingering seeds.

2 Put the peppers in a blender along with ¼ cup of the reserved water and puree until chunky. If necessary, add another tablespoon of reserved water. With the motor running, slowly drizzle in ¼ cup extra-virgin olive oil until the mixture turns into a smooth puree. If you don't have a professional-style blender, you may need to turn off the blender and stir the mixture with a spoon a few times to get things going. If necessary, add another tablespoon or two of olive oil.

3 Spoon the paste into a glass jar and top it off with a good ½ inch of extra-virgin olive oil, cover, and refrigerate for up to 3 weeks (as you use the paste, top it off with more olive oil). You can also freeze the paste in a flat, thin layer in a medium plastic food storage bag so you can break off small pieces as needed. **Makes 1¼ to 1½ cups, depending on the number of peppers used.**

PUREED GARLIC & GINGER

Keep pureed garlic and ginger in the refrigerator, and spoon out a dollop when needed, or freeze the puree for even longer storage. (Store-bought jarred garlic pastes have a very flat, musty flavor, so they're not good substitutes.) If you only need a small amount, use the quick grated method below, but it's so easy to make a big batch and freeze the pastes. If you only need a little, or don't have enough cloves or ginger around to make a full batch, make the quick version. Keep in mind that in cooked recipes, the quick method is much more forgiving with ginger, since it doesn't tend to burn at high heat like garlic.

1 **To make Pureed Garlic or Ginger:** Combine about 1¼ cups peeled garlic cloves (4 to 5 heads) or 1 cup roughly chopped peeled fresh ginger in a blender with 3 tablespoons water. Puree the garlic or ginger until finely chopped. With the blender running, slowly drizzle in 3 tablespoons olive oil until you have a smooth, fluffy puree. Store the puree in the refrigerator for up to 1 week, or freeze the puree in a flat, thin layer in a medium plastic food storage bag so you can break off small pieces as needed. **Makes about 1 cup.**

2 **Quick Grated Garlic or Ginger:** With a Microplane zester, very finely grate 1 large or 2 small cloves garlic or about ½ inch peeled fresh ginger (be careful when your fingers get close to the zester). Mix in about ¼ teaspoon olive oil to make a paste. **Makes ½ to ¾ teaspoon, or however much you need.**

GARLIC CHIPS

Garlic chips are a simple way to make a crunchy, flavorful topping for vegetables, meat, or seafood dishes.

To make Garlic Chips: Thinly slice 6 to 8 large cloves of garlic. Fill a medium saucepan with 1 inch of olive oil, and heat over medium heat until warm but not bubbling. Add the garlic and cook, swirling the garlic chips around in the pan occasionally until they turn light golden brown, 8 to 10 minutes. Use a slotted spoon to remove any chips that turn brown before the others, and transfer them to a paper towel–lined plate. When

the rest of the garlic chips have turned light brown, drain them over a bowl to reserve the oil. Reuse the oil to fry another batch or to sauté chicken or vegetables. Store the garlic chips at room temperature, uncovered, for up to 8 hours. **Makes a small handful of garlic chips.**

MOCK YUZU JUICE

Fresh yuzu is difficult to find outside of Japan (see Resources, page 261, for sources), so I use frozen unsweetened and unsalted yuzu juice (check the label carefully). When a recipe calls for a small quantity of yuzu juice, only a tablespoon or two, you can substitute fresh lime juice. For sauces that rely on a large amount of yuzu juice, like ponzu (recipe follows), I use a ratio of roughly 60 percent fresh orange juice to 40 percent fresh lime juice, or about ⅓ cup orange juice to ¼ cup lime juice.

HOMEMADE PONZU

Homemade Japanese ponzu is nothing like the bottled, store-bought sauce, which, to me, tastes like a really bad fast-food sauce. In Japan, many home cooks make their own by infusing briny ocean flavors like kombu seaweed and bonito flakes (see Resources, page 261) into citrusy yuzu juice, soy sauce, and rice wine. Make it yourself, and you'll understand why. You stand by while the ingredients do all of the hard work (the longer you let the flavors infuse, the better—up to 1 month). The sauce keeps for several months in the fridge, so I don't want to hear any excuses.

1 **To make Ponzu:** Gently wipe a roughly 5-inch square of kombu seaweed with a damp kitchen towel to remove the white, salty residue. Place the kombu in a large food storage container or bowl and add 3 cups thawed frozen unsweetened yuzu juice (or substitute 1¾ cups fresh orange juice and 1¼ cups fresh lime juice), 1½ cups soy sauce (preferably a good-quality Japanese brand like Yamasa), ⅓ cup mirin, ⅓ cup sake, ½ cup bonito flakes, and 1 medium orange, sliced into 5 rings (discard both ends). Cover and refrigerate for at least 1 week or up to 1 month to allow the flavors to meld.

2 Strain the sauce through a fine-mesh strainer. Occasionally remove the bonito flakes that accumulate at the bottom of the strainer. Cover and refrigerate the ponzu for up to 4 to 5 months. **Makes about 4½ cups.**

OILS AND BUTTERS

I love the complex flavors of oils and butters infused with herbs, peppers, and, in my world, always some kind of Peruvian pepper. Depending on how you store them, they can keep for weeks or even months.

ROCOTO OIL

Infusing oil with spicy rocoto peppers tames their heat just enough, and the garlic, tomato paste, and other seasonings add complexity. I drizzle this oil on shrimp dumplings (page 59), but it would be good on top of most fish. Or, just use it like your favorite hot sauce.

To make Rocoto Oil: Heat ¼ cup olive oil in a small saucepan over medium heat for a solid minute, then add 2 tablespoons finely minced red onions and cook until the onions are translucent, about 2 minutes. Stir in 1 tablespoon rocoto paste (page 34), 1 tablespoon tomato paste, and ½ teaspoon garlic paste (page 37) or 1 minced garlic clove. Simmer for about 1 minute, add 1 bay leaf and ⅓ cup water, stir, and raise the heat to medium-high. Boil until the water has almost evaporated, about 5 minutes. Remove the pan from the heat and pour in another ½ cup olive oil and 1 teaspoon sesame oil. Transfer the oil to a small bowl, cover, and refrigerate for 24 hours. Strain the oil through a cheesecloth-lined strainer (preferable) or at least twice through a fine-mesh strainer. Do not push down on the solids. Cover and refrigerate the rocoto oil for 2 to 3 weeks. **Makes a generous ½ cup.**

AJÍ AMARILLO BUTTER

Everything from Conchas a la Parmesana (Parmesan-baked scallops, page 53) to the simplest steamed or grilled summer corncobs or baked potatoes loves this mildly spiced butter.

To make Ají Amarillo Butter: Place 8 ounces (1 cup) room temperature unsalted butter in the bowl of a stand mixer fitted with the paddle attachment and mix on medium-low speed until fluffy, about 2 minutes. Add 2 tablespoons ají amarillo paste (page 34) and whip for 2 minutes more, or until the pepper paste is fully incorporated into the butter. Wrap the butter in plastic wrap and refrigerate for up to 1 week, or freeze the butter in a flat, thin layer in a medium plastic food storage bag so you can break off small pieces as needed. **Makes 1 cup.**

MAYONNAISES AND AIOLIS

Peruvians love mayonnaise. *Really* love it. I usually get a few wide-eyed stares from the uninitiated when they watch me spoon mayo on just about everything—sandwiches, tiraditos, and so much more. I use these flavored mayos more like sauces, so they should be pretty bold, on the saltier and spicier side. Japanese mayonnaise (see Resources, page 261) tastes more like an aioli, so you don't get that distinct vegetable oil flavor that I really don't like in some mayonnaises. It's worth seeking out, but you could substitute your favorite unsweetened mayo. These have enough other flavors to cover up any off-flavor in the average store-bought mayonnaise.

All of these recipes make about 1 cup, but you can easily cut any in half, or increase the quantities for a crowd. The aiolis will keep, covered, in the refrigerator for up to 5 days.

AJÍ AMARILLO AIOLI

Mix together 1 tablespoon fresh lime juice, 2 to 3 teaspoons ají amarillo paste (to taste; page 34), and 1 cup mayonnaise, preferably Japanese.

HUACATAY AIOLI

Mix together 1 tablespoon frozen huacatay, or 2 packed tablespoons fresh minced huacatay, the zest and juice of 1 large lemon, 1 to 1½ teaspoons yuzu kosho (to taste; page 33), a generous pinch of kosher salt, and 1 cup mayonnaise, preferably Japanese.

MALT VINEGAR–AJÍ AMARILLO AIOLI

Mix together 3 tablespoons malt vinegar, 2 to 3 teaspoons ají amarillo paste (to taste; page 34), and 1 cup mayonnaise, preferably Japanese.

YUZU KOSHO AIOLI

Mix together the zest of 1 lime, a generous squeeze or two of fresh lime juice, 2 to 2½ teaspoons yuzu kosho paste (to taste; page 33), and 1 cup mayonnaise, preferably Japanese.

SRIRACHA AIOLI

Mix together 2½ to 3 tablespoons Sriracha (to taste) and 1 cup mayonnaise, preferably Japanese.

PICKLES

I grew up eating the bold-flavored radishes and other vegetables that my mom pickled in a spicy-sweet white vinegar and ají amarillo pepper brine. I loved them, but it wasn't until I worked in Asian restaurants abroad that I understood how a delicate, quick-pickled vegetable can turn a simple dish into something incredible. Use this quick-pickling braise to make crispy, Japanese-style pickled cucumbers, carrots, and radishes, or blanch baby squash, bell peppers (for a crunchier version, leave the peppers raw), or Fresno chiles to soften them up before adding them to the pickling liquid.

How you cut the vegetables also changes their texture. For a crispy sandwich or tiradito topping, finely dice cucumbers (or cut them into matchsticks) and let them marinate briefly, no more than a day. Leave thinly shaved radishes in the marinade for a couple of days, and you've got a good stand-in for store-bought pickled ginger. And little chunks of peeled, uncooked eggplant are one of my favorite vegetables to pickle. When you leave them in the brine for a few days, they soften up into tangy, pillowy bites. The brine makes about 2 cups, enough for 1 large or 2 smaller jars. How many pickles you wind up with varies depending on the type of vegetables and the size you cut them, but it's easy to quickly make another batch of brine if you need more.

1 To make the Brine: Heat a medium saucepan over high heat until hot. Add 3 tablespoons whole black peppercorns and shake the pan a few times until they smell toasty, about 45 seconds. Immediately pour in 2 cups unseasoned rice vinegar and 2 cups sugar. Bring the liquid to a boil and turn off the heat. Stir again to make sure the sugar has dissolved. Let cool completely before using. **Makes about 2¾ cups brine.**

2 To prepare the Vegetables: Slice 3 to 4 cups vegetables however you would like. Fresh cucumbers and carrots are nice finely chopped, sliced into matchsticks, or thinly sliced into rounds about ⅛ inch thick. Radishes and ginger work well very thinly sliced or shaved. I like to cut unpeeled eggplant into small pieces about 1 inch long (Japanese or Chinese eggplant are best, as they have fewer seeds, but globe eggplants also work). Baby squash and chile peppers can be sliced in half if they are large; bell peppers can be cut into chunks or finely diced. Blanch vegetables like baby squash, seeded sweet bell peppers, or Fresno or other chiles (or for a crunchier texture, leave the peppers or chiles raw, whichever you prefer) before brining them. Blanch the vegetables in simmering water until crisp-tender (just a few seconds for finely sliced vegetables or up to 60 seconds for larger chunks), and immediately dunk them in an ice bath.

3 To make the Quick Pickles: Pack the vegetables into a medium food storage container or several glass jars. Pour in enough brine to completely submerge the vegetables. Refrigerate at least overnight or for up to 3 days, depending on your preference. Fewer days makes them crunchier and lightly pickled; longer and they will be softer and more intensely flavored. (With eggplant, always wait until they have softened, 2 to 3 days.) Strain and save the brine (discard the peppercorns or return them to the brine for additional spiciness). Refrigerate the pickles, covered, for up to 1 week. You can reuse the brine one more time (within 3 to 4 days), if you'd like.

STOCKS

A basic stock shouldn't be complicated. Throw on a pot of water while you are cooking dinner and toss in complementary flavors using ingredients you already have in the fridge and pantry. Any time you cook whole fish or chicken, freeze the frames or carcasses and bones in the freezer so you are ready to go. I use chicken stock even for meat-based stews and braised meats. The guidelines below are for a 12-quart stockpot. If you don't have a pot that large, cut the quantities down slightly. **Makes 4 to 5 quarts, depending on the size of your pot and how long the stock simmers.**

Basic Aromatic Vegetables: 2 medium red onions, peeled and halved, or 2 to 3 cups red onion hearts (see page 45); a few stalks celery; a few carrots, peeled; and, if you have one, ½ large daikon radish, peeled and cut into chunks

Seasonings: Meaty 3- to 4-inch knob peeled and lightly smashed fresh ginger, 5 or 6 leafy sprigs of thyme, 2 bay leaves, a few whole black peppercorns, 1 tablespoon kosher salt (or more as needed)

FLAVORING INGREDIENTS:

For Fish Stock: 4 to 5 pounds well-cleaned fish bones from halibut, cod, flounder, or other lean, non-oily fish, with at least 1 large or 2 small heads and tails, if possible

For Chicken Stock: 4 to 5 pounds mixed chicken necks, backs, and other bones (a little meat on the bones adds flavor), or the quartered frames of 2 whole chickens

For Vegetable Stock: Include the daikon, if you can, and add another onion, carrot, and celery stalk with the basic aromatic vegetables

1 Toss all of the vegetables, basic seasonings, and bones, if making fish or chicken stock, into a large stockpot (around 12 quarts). Fill the pot with water to within a few inches of the top. Bring the water to a boil, then reduce the heat to maintain a vigorous simmer.

2 For chicken or vegetable stock, simmer the broth for a solid hour, then strain. Discard any bones and vegetables. Return the broth to a simmer and cook for 20 to 30 minutes longer, until reduced by about one-third, to concentrate the flavors. Let cool completely and season very lightly with salt (you can add more salt later, depending on what you are cooking). Refrigerate the stock for up to 5 days, or freeze it in small batches.

3 For fish stock, simmer the broth for 40 minutes, strain, and return the liquid to the pot. Return the broth to a simmer and cook for 20 to 30 minutes longer, until reduced by about one-third, to concentrate the flavors.

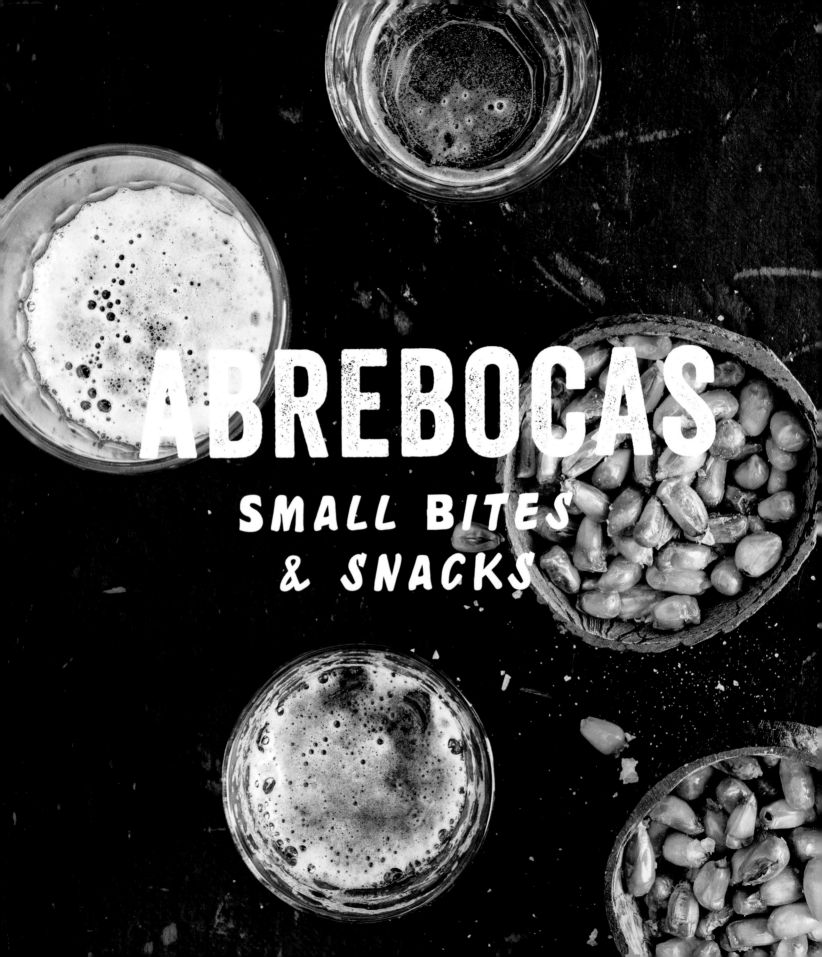

ABREBOCAS

SMALL BITES
& SNACKS

MANY OF THE RECIPES IN THIS CHAPTER ARE BASED ON THE SNACKS AND SUPPERS THAT I LOVED TO EAT GROWING UP, THE FOODS THAT MEAN *FAMILIA* AND FRIENDS TO ME.

At some of my restaurants, I have called the first section of my menu *abrebocas*, meaning small bites and cocktail nibbles. In some Spanish-speaking countries, *abrebocas* is slang for appetizers, but not so much in Peru. To me, the word is similar to the phrase *abre tú boca*, "open your mouth." When you grow up with twelve siblings packed around the dinner table, you quickly learn to sit down, stop talking, and focus on the task ahead: *Abre tú boca*, or you're going to miss out.

Here is a solid sampler of Peruvian dishes to get started with: quick snacks like cancha—toasted and seasoned dried corn kernels—that you can dig your fingers into all day, elegant-looking appetizers that you find in restaurants all over Peru, and the simple sandwiches that moms usually serve for a late breakfast or lunch (you might serve them for brunch), but that I eat any time. I usually serve these abrebocas in little portions, as small bites, but you can also serve most picnic-style or turn them into main courses for family suppers.

SALSA CRIOLLA

MAKES 1½ TO 2 CUPS

In Peru, *salsa* is a catchall word that refers to both sauces and relishlike condiments. The most common is salsa criolla, a true relish-like with red onions, spicy peppers, and lime juice. You see it everywhere, alongside everything from the lightest ceviches to sandwiches, grilled meats, and stews. Red onions are almost always the base, along with salt, a good squeeze of lime juice, and traditionally a tiny amount of finely chopped ají limo chiles, but the ingredients are up to the person doing the chopping.

Many of the dishes I make already have plenty of heat, so I usually don't add chiles. Instead, to brighten up the flavors I prefer tomatoes and cilantro. You can swap out different spicy peppers or completely change the texture of the salsa by chopping the red onions as roughly or finely as you'd like. For a really fine texture, shave the onions *a la pluma*, or like feathers (see sidebar, opposite). The salsa will be more delicate, so I use it for tiraditos and ceviches.

Salsa criolla is simple to make, but it is very important to serve the salsa the right away. Even after just ten minutes, the onions will "cook" in the acid from the citrus and soften into a mushy mess. You can chop the onions, tomatoes, and cilantro an hour before you plan to use them and keep them in the fridge, but don't mix in the lime juice and the other ingredients until right before you serve the salsa. To make the onions really crispy, dunk them in a bowl of ice water for a few minutes before you mix them with the other ingredients. Because it is used more like a relish, not a cooking sauce or dipping salsa, my salsa criolla is usually pretty salty. Salt the main dish pretty lightly but go heavier on the salt in the salsa than your tongue first thinks is a good idea.

½ large red onion

2 plum tomatoes, cored and seeded

About ⅓ medium bunch fresh cilantro, leaves and top two-thirds of the stems

3 to 4 tablespoons fresh lime juice

2 tablespoons extra-virgin olive oil

Generous ½ teaspoon kosher salt, or to taste

¼ teaspoon finely ground black pepper

Chop the onion and tomatoes into neat, ¼-inch squares, or as large or small as you'd like, and place them in a medium bowl. Roughly chop the cilantro and add it to the bowl with the onions and tomatoes. Add 3 tablespoons of the lime juice, the olive oil, salt, and pepper, and toss everything together with your fingers or a spoon. Taste, and add more lime juice and salt to taste. The salsa criolla should be tangy with a noticeable salty finish. Use the salsa right away.

Jalapeño Salsa Criolla

The few times I do add chiles to salsa criolla, I actually prefer jalapeños, which is very un-Peruvian of me. They have a stronger green chile flavor that works well with corn-based dishes. I use the spicy salsa on Tamalitos Verdes (page 64) or on open-faced sandwiches.

Chop the red onion into small, neat, ¼-inch squares. Omit the tomatoes. Roughly chop the cilantro and add it, as well as 3 stemmed, seeded, and chopped jalapeños (scrape the peppers well to remove the spicy internal membranes), or to taste. Decrease the lime juice to 2 tablespoons, and add 2 tablespoons of Banyuls vinegar or good-quality red wine vinegar. Makes about 1¼ cups.

CHOPPING ONIONS

There's a saying in Peru that the corazón, *heart, of the onion is what makes you cry.*

I can tell you from experience that the heart (the core of the onion) has the same compounds as the rest of the onion that cause your eyes to tear up. The core does have a more concentrated flavor and often isn't as sweet, so I usually remove them anyway and save them for stock.

What really will make you cry is a dull knife. A sharp knife doesn't break down as many of the onion's cell walls, so all of the juices stay inside the onion. If you aren't used to chopping a lot of onions at once, the secret is to chop them very slowly, not crazy fast like you see chefs do on television. Concentrate on your job and slice the onions so the pieces are all the same size. I also never use a mandoline to finely shred onions. It breaks down the cell walls even more, so you lose the crunchiness that makes salsa criolla and so many other dishes with fresh onion so good. If you chop the onions and hour or so ahead, dunk them in ice water for a minute or two, then shake them dry with your hands to wake them up and get the crunchiness back.

To chop or slice onions:

Trim both ends off 1 large red onion, peel off the skin, and halve the onion from the root to the stem end (never through the middle). Use your fingers or a knife to pop out the interior cores (usually all white, with very little purple on the edges) and save them for stock.

Place one half, cut side down, on a work surface with your hands curled on top so your knuckles are very close to either end. Slice the onions as thick or thin as you like (¼ inch thick is good for salsa criolla), but try to make the slices all the same thickness.

Use the onions immediately, or refrigerate them for up to 1 hour. If refrigerated, transfer the onions to a bowl of ice water to crisp up for a few minutes. Drain and shake the onions a few times over the sink or a bowl to remove the excess water.

To slice onions a la pluma, like feathers:

Follow the instructions above for halving the onion and removing the cores. Use a very sharp knife to slice the onion as thinly as you can. Move the knife blade Japanese-style through each onion half in one clean motion, from the handle end toward the top, like you are slicing fish to make tiraditos (see page 92). You should be able to almost see between the slices. When slicing onions a la pluma, be sure to very finely chop all of your other ingredients like tomatoes and cilantro, so they lightly cling to the shaved onions when you toss everything together. **Makes about 2 generous cups.**

ANDEAN POPCORN

MAKES 2½ CUPS POPPED

SERVES 6

My uncle Lucio on my mom's side of the family was from the mountains, a man of pure Incan blood. In addition to Spanish, he spoke Quechua, the traditional language, and looked like a living Ekeko good luck charm, from his *chiquito* stature right down to his *yankees*, traditional shoes made from old tires. *Mi tío* never wavered from tradition, even when it came to snacks, and would only pop his maíz chulpe (large-kernel corn) straight up. In the Andes, herders stash the dried and toasted kernels in their packs as fuel for treks up the mountainside, and restaurants all over Peru serve the crunchy corn (the inspiration for American-style corn nuts) before a meal or as the traditional side for ceviche. It was one of the first traditional dishes he taught me how to make.

Be careful when you open the lid of the pot to check on the corn as it pops. The kernels sometimes pop right out of the pot and fly around the kitchen. (They can get very hot; the cancha kernels do soften slightly, but the crunchy outer shells initially hold on to the frying oil heat.) Like popcorn, I like mine on the saltier side.

½ cup canola or other vegetable oil
1½ cups dried maíz cancha, also known as chulpe corn
1 generous tablespoon coarse sea salt, or to taste

1 In a large, deep saucepot or Dutch oven with a lid, heat the oil over high heat for 2 to 3 minutes, until very hot. Add the corn, give the kernels a quick stir, and cover the pot with the lid. Reduce the heat to medium-high and cook the cancha, shaking the pan every once in a while, for 3 to 4 minutes, until the corn begins to pop more vigorously and then noticeably slows. It should smell toasty.

2 Remove the pan from the heat and let cool for a minute or two (do not remove the lid). Partially open the lid away from you, like a shield, so the cancha doesn't pop into your face. Be very careful, as the oil is very hot and the kernels can pop out of the pan. Most of the kernels should be dark golden brown. If they are still yellow, cover the pot and return it to the stove over high heat for about 1 minute more.

3 Let the cancha cool in the pot, covered, for a few minutes, then very carefully remove the lid and drain. Transfer the hot cancha to a heatproof medium bowl, sprinkle with the salt, and use a spoon to evenly distribute the salt all over the cancha. Let the cancha cool for at least 20 minutes, discard any burnt pieces, and season with more salt to taste. Serve immediately, or let cool completely cool and store in a food storage container or resealable plastic bag at room temperature for up to 1 week.

SPICED CANCHA

Traditionally, cancha is seasoned only with salt. But for me, cancha is all about having fun, and like popcorn, the toasted kernels have that ability to take on almost any seasonings you toss their way. I sometimes add paprika and lime zest, with a sprinkle of cayenne for a more *picante* version, but play around with whatever spices you like. If you store the cancha after seasoning, some spices will settle to the bottom of the container or bag, so give it a good shake before serving to redistribute the seasonings.

To make spiced cancha: When you've moved the hot cancha to the bowl, stir in about ½ teaspoon sweet paprika and 1 teaspoon lime zest (or other seasonings) with the salt. When the cancha cools, season it with more salt to taste.

SPICY EGGPLANT PUREE

MAKES ABOUT 1 CUP

SERVES 4 TO 6 AS COCKTAIL STARTERS

Arabic spreads like chickpea hummus and eggplant baba ghanoush are pretty common sightings at London cafés and restaurants. When I first arrived in London, they seemed very exotic, more so because they were covered in really good olive oil. Canola oil is the workhorse oil in most Peruvian home kitchens, but when I first started cooking with olive oil, I was an instant convert. This recipe is my take on a spicy eggplant puree with fiery rocoto peppers. It's also an excuse to pour on more really good olive oil.

Eggplant is *una esponja*, a sponge. It soaks up all of the flavors you offer it, but still holds on to its own character—just what a good chef hopes to accomplish in his cooking. Rocoto peppers really wake up the flavors in eggplant, but ají amarillo paste also works well if that's what you have in the refrigerator.

2 medium Japanese or Chinese eggplants, or 1 small globe eggplant (1 pound), grilled or roasted and charred (see page 186)

1 teaspoon pureed garlic (page 37), or finely minced

1 tablespoon tahini

2 teaspoons rocoto paste, store-bought or homemade (page 34) plus more as needed

1 tablespoon fresh lime juice, plus more as needed

½ teaspoon kosher salt, plus more as needed

Really good extra-virgin olive oil, for drizzling

A few pinches of smoked paprika

3 or 4 fresh parsley leaves, chopped

Plenty of thinly sliced grilled or broiled crusty bread or crackers, for serving

1 Peel the cooked eggplants in a bowl of cold water, discard the skins, and lightly dry the flesh on a paper towel (you should have about 1 cup). Place the flesh in a blender with the garlic, tahini, rocoto paste, lime juice, and salt, and puree until smooth. If you don't have a high-powered blender, you may need to stir the mixture once or twice to get things going. Taste, and add more rocoto paste, lime juice, or salt, if you'd like.

2 Transfer the puree to a wide, shallow serving bowl and pour olive oil generously over the top. Don't be shy. The oil should cover the eggplant puree. Sprinkle the paprika and the chopped parsley over the puree and serve it with the grilled bread.

ARTICHOKES WITH PISCO-LIME BUTTER & HUACATAY AIOLI

SERVES
6

Franciscan monks from Spain were probably the first to bring *alcachofas*, artichokes, down south to Peru. Giant *criolla* artichokes, with triangular leaves and spiky tips, are the variety popular in Peru. You'll find them piled up in market bins, often with the hearts floating in a lime-water bath nearby to save you the trouble of trimming the artichokes. The more common green globe variety that you find in the United States are a big export business today. I've always loved alcachofas, but no one else in my family really ate them. When I went to the market to do the weekly shopping, I'd bring home a couple to boil and eat by myself with nothing more than a little garlic, ají amarillo paste, and a few squeezes of lime juice mixed together as a dipping sauce—so good.

The sauces served with artichokes are talked about so much, it's easy to forget the flavors a good braising liquid can bring to the table. Toss whatever citrus you have in your produce drawer into the pot, along with some root vegetables and a big knob of ginger. Grilling alcachofas is actually my favorite way to get the good, charred flavor that makes the artichoke flavors really pop, but if you don't have time to light the grill, you can sauté the artichokes in Pisco-Lime Butter (page 50) and then broil each for a few seconds.

3 citrus fruits (whatever you have on hand), preferably 1 lemon, lime, and orange

4 large artichokes, or about 2 pounds baby artichokes

1 (2- to 3-inch) knob fresh ginger, peeled and quartered

1 stalk celery, quartered

1 large carrot, quartered

1 bay leaf

1 tablespoon kosher salt

½ cup pisco or white wine (optional)

Pisco-Lime Butter (recipe follows)

About ½ cup huacatay aioli (page 38), or your favorite aioli or mayonnaise

1 lime, cut into wedges, for serving

1 Halve whatever citrus you are using and squeeze the juice directly into a large stockpot or Dutch oven. You don't need to fish out the seeds. Fill the pot about one-third full with water.

2 If using large artichokes, use kitchen scissors or a sharp knife to remove the spiky tips on each leaf. Cut off about 1 inch from the top of the artichoke and if the stem is long, trim it to about 1 inch and peel the stem. If using baby artichokes, peel off the tough outer green skin from the stems and cut about ¼ inch off the top. Drop the artichokes into the citrus water.

3 Toss the ginger, celery, carrot, bay leaf, and salt into the pot and add the pisco (if using). Add more water as needed to cover the artichokes by about 1 inch. Place a saucepan or a metal bowl with a can of tomatoes inside on top of the artichokes to keep them submerged. Bring the water to a low boil over medium-high heat and cook the artichokes until tender, 25 to 30 minutes for large artichokes and 12 to 15 minutes for baby artichokes. Use tongs to transfer the artichokes to a strainer and rinse them under cold water for a

RECIPE CONTINUES

good 30 seconds so they cool quickly. Halve the large artichokes through the stem; leave the baby artichokes whole. At this point, you can cover and refrigerate the artichokes for up to 1 day.

4 Prepare a regular or hibachi grill for direct, high-heat cooking. If using baby artichokes, thread them on a few skewers. When the grill is hot, place the large artichokes, cut side down, on the grill, or lay the skewered baby artichokes on the grill. Grill the artichokes until you get good char marks, about 2 minutes, then flip them and brush the tops of the artichokes with the pisco-lime butter. Grill for another minute or so until the artichokes are nicely browned on the bottom and brush them again with the butter. Flip, grill for another minute, or until the butter begins to turn nutty brown and caramelize, and brush the artichokes one more time with the butter. Transfer the artichokes to a plate.

5 To serve, arrange the artichoke halves, cut side down, on serving plates, or scatter the grilled baby artichokes on the plates. Serve plenty of the huacatay aioli alongside the artichokes for dunking the leaves, and don't forget the lime wedges. Put a small knife nearby so whoever is lucky enough to peel off the last leaves can cut the heart to share.

PISCO-LIME BUTTER

Makes about ½ cup

I love this citrusy garlic butter on almost any grilled fish, from whitefish to salmon. An ear of corn slathered with it is crazy hard to refuse.

4 tablespoons (½ stick) unsalted butter
2 tablespoons pisco
1 teaspoon pureed garlic (page 37)
2 tablespoons fresh lime juice
¼ teaspoon kosher salt, or to taste

1 In a small saucepan, heat the butter, pisco, and garlic paste over medium-high heat until the butter melts and the mixture just begins to simmer. Remove from the heat and stir in the lime juice and salt.

2 If not using immediately, you can pour the pisco-lime butter into a covered container and refrigerate for up to 3 days, if you'd like. Gently rewarm the butter on the stove over low heat, but be careful not to brown or burn it.

PARMESAN SCALLOPS WITH SPINACH & PERUVIAN BÉCHAMEL

SERVES **6** AS AN APPETIZER OR **2** OR **3** AS A MAIN DISH

I felt so grown-up the first time at my uncle Ruben's house when I learned how to make *conchas a la parmesana* when I was ten or eleven years old. For such a common, everyday dish (in Peru, at least), it's such an *elegante* presentation. The scallop shell doubles as a baking and serving dish. Years later, when I actually *was* grown up and working in a fancy hotel restaurant in London with equally elegant clientele, we had a few customers in from Milan in one night. They swore by the traditional Italian view that seafood and cheese should never be paired together. We got into a lively conversation (I pointed out that we have generations of Italians in Peru; we even use the word *ciao* to say good-bye instead of the Spanish word *adios*), and they eventually agreed to let me try to convince them otherwise. Instead of the more traditional mix of butter, ají amarillo, lime juice, and Parmesan, I made the scallops with my creamy Parmesan-béchamel sauce (see sidebar, page 55) as the base. They loved it and gave me big hugs and loud Italian kisses. I probably should have also thanked them. Parmesan arrived in Peru with Italian immigrants.

In Peru, the dish goes by the name *conchitas a la parmesana* because the scallops used are often smaller than those you find in the United States. I use massive scallops (what are called jumbo scallops in the States), so I couldn't call this dish "little" anything. If you manage to get your hands on scallops with the orange roe still attached, even better. It's the caviar of scallops.

If you have all of the components ready, this is a very quick dinner party dish, but it is really important to not overcook the scallops or they will become tough. Cook them until just medium-rare, so they almost melt when you cut into them. With the butter sauce and béchamel, this is a very rich dish, so plan on one per person as an appetizer. For a casual supper, bake two *conchas* per person, three if you are really hungry, and bake several together in larger au gratin dishes. If your fishmonger doesn't have scallop shells, look online for "scallop baking shells" from European importers, or use ramekins.

2½ tablespoons frozen unsweetened yuzu juice, thawed, or fresh lime juice

1 teaspoon ají amarillo paste, store-bought or homemade (page 34)

¾ teaspoon kosher salt

2 bunches baby or 1 bunch mature spinach, or 1 (10- to 12-ounce) bag baby spinach

6 jumbo sea scallops (about 2 ounces each), or more if smaller (about 12 ounces total), with their shells, if available

6 tablespoons ají amarillo butter (page 38), at room temperature

Peruvian Béchamel (page 55)

½ cup grated Parmesan (about 2 ounces)

1 Preheat the oven to 400°F and position a rack in the bottom third.

2 In a small dish, whisk together the yuzu juice, ají amarillo paste, and salt and set aside.

3 Fill a medium saucepan halfway with water and bring to a boil. If using bunched fresh spinach, remove any tough stems and wash the leaves well. If using prewashed bagged baby spinach, you don't need to stem the spinach. Add the spinach to the boiling water and stir briefly, then drain immediately. Rinse the spinach under cold water for about 15 seconds to cool it and firmly squeeze out any excess water. Spread out the leaves on a few paper towels to dry.

4 Rinse the scallops and their shells under cold running water to remove any grit and gently pat both dry with paper towels. Spread 1 tablespoon of the ají amarillo butter on the bottom of each scallop shell, or in six 8-ounce ramekins or small au gratin dishes. Divide the spinach among each shell or ramekin (a good

RECIPE CONTINUES

2 tablespoons in each), and nestle one scallop on top of each. (If you are serving the scallops as a main course, divide the butter, spinach, and scallops evenly among two or three wider au gratin dishes.)

5 Place the shells or dishes on a rimmed baking sheet and bake until the scallops just begin to turn white along the edges but are still translucent in the center, as few as 5 minutes if they are on the smaller end of "jumbo," or up to 8 minutes if larger. Remove from the oven and preheat the broiler to high.

6 Dived the béchamel among the scallops (1½ to 2 tablespoons each) and scatter the Parmesan on top. Broil the scallops until the cheese turns golden brown, 1 to 1½ minutes, depending on how close the scallops are to the broiler's flame (check the scallops regularly). After 2 minutes, even if the scallops still don't have much color, remove them from the broiler so they don't overcook. You can use a kitchen torch and quickly blast the béchamel and cheese in spots like you are making a crème brûlée crust, or serve the scallops as they are; they will still be good. Drizzle about 1 teaspoon of the yuzu–ají amarillo sauce on top of each scallop. Carefully transfer the hot scallop shells or dishes to serving plates and serve *inmediatamente*.

PERUVIAN BÉCHAMEL

Makes about ¾ cup

At home, I sometimes double or triple this béchamel sauce recipe so I have leftovers to make creamed spinach, or to spoon some on top of sautéed broccoli, cauliflower, or boiled potatoes for my kids. In honor of my Italian friends back in London, I may have to invent a seafood lasagna with plenty of Parmesan.

The sauce seasons both the spinach and scallops, so it should be on the saltier side. Adding a splash of lime juice after cooking really brightens all of the flavors. If the sauce separates as it cools, rewarm it over medium heat for a minute or two and stir until everything is reincorporated.

1 tablespoon olive oil
1 tablespoon unsalted butter
¼ cup roughly chopped shallots or red onions
¼ teaspoon ají amarillo paste (page 34)
½ teaspoon pureed garlic (page 37)
1 small bay leaf
¾ cup heavy cream
¼ cup grated Parmesan (about 1 ounce)
1 tablespoon all-purpose flour
1 teaspoon fresh lime juice
½ teaspoon kosher salt, or to taste

1 Heat a medium sauté pan over medium heat—not too hot. Add the olive oil and the butter. When the butter has melted, sprinkle the shallots into the pan and sauté them for 2 to 3 minutes, until translucent. With a wooden spoon, stir in the ají amarillo paste, followed by the pureed garlic and the bay leaf. Reduce the heat to medium-low and cook the sauce, stirring regularly, for 4 to 5 minutes, until the butter turns golden brown. If the butter begins to blacken, remove the pan from the heat for a minute or two, reduce the heat, then return the pan to the heat to continue cooking.

2 Stir in the cream, raise the heat to medium, and bring the cream to a low simmer. Stir in the Parmesan and the flour (don't worry if the flour clumps a little) and stir the sauce continuously for a good 2 minutes to cook out the raw flavor of the flour. The sauce should be pretty thick.

3 Remove the bay leaf and transfer the sauce to a blender. Add the lime juice and salt and puree until very smooth. Taste, and add a little more salt if needed. Use immediately, or let cool to room temperature and refrigerate in a covered container for up to 3 days. To serve, gently rewarm the sauce over low heat.

"PERUVIAN-STYLE" BÉCHAMEL

Chefs often have recipes that start as one thing and evolve into something else seemingly entirely on their own. This béchamel sauce is one of those recipes. While working on this book, my cowriter, Jenn, asked what made me combine several different cooking techniques to make my favorite béchamel; I hadn't even realized that's what I had done. For me, this was just what made sense to make a really flavorful béchamel.

In Peru, classic creamy sauces like *huancaína* sauce (page 168) are usually pretty simple, made by pureeing together all of the ingredients. Cooked sauces tend to start with an *aderezo*, ingredients that are slowly sautéed to give a sturdy flavor backbone to any dish. The idea is similar to a French mirepoix, only instead of white onions, carrots, and celery, an aderezo is often made from red onions, ají amarillo or panca paste, and garlic, but it varies. Sometimes hot sauces are pureed afterward in a blender to give them a creamy consistency, but not always.

On the opposite side of the creamy sauce world, there is a classic French béchamel. You cook up a roux of butter and flour, whisk in milk or cream, and simmer the sauce until it is thick and creamy. You can't add too many ingredients on the front end, or the sauce will get lumpy, which means the flavor tends to be rich with butter but not as complex.

Bringing the two together, to make my béchamel sauce, first, I make a really flavorful aderezo and sauté the ingredients slowly in butter to get that nice golden brown flavor. Next, I stir in the cream, bring it to a simmer, and add a little Parmesan and the flour (usually, to make a béchamel you add the flour to the butter before the cream). When you make the sauce this "backward" way, you get an incredible depth of flavor from the aderezo ingredients that you don't get with a classic roux. Since everything is pureed in the blender after the sauce thickens, as you would with a cold Peruvian cream sauce, it doesn't matter if you get a few lumps from adding the flour toward the end of cooking. And like any good Peruvian, I can't help but add a squeeze of lime juice at the end to brighten up the flavors. (Adding acid to a cream sauce is usually a surefire way to end up with a curdled sauce, but since you puree everything, it doesn't matter.) The result is a thick cream sauce with a more intense flavor.

FRIED OYSTERS, CALLAO-STYLE

SERVES
4 OR 5
AS AN
APPETIZER

When I moved to Los Angeles from London, I was so happy to be back on the Pacific Coast. I loved London, but the seafood in California was more like what I remembered from home, and the sunshine and T-shirt culture was much more my speed than rain and suits. And I was so happy to be on the same side of the globe as family and friends in Lima.

This recipe was one of the very first that I came up with when I got to L.A. The name is a riff on *chorritos a la chalaca*. *Chalaca* is a reference to Callao, Peru's main seaport just to the west of Lima, where mussels are steamed and served with a spicy rocoto pepper, red onion, and tomato salsa with plenty of lime juice. There are so many good fresh oysters in California, and I hadn't eaten a really good fried one in what seemed like forever, maybe never. Most are so thickly battered and fried that every last ounce of their delicate, briny flavor is gone. You might as well deep-fry spoonfuls of batter. But if you pan-fry the oysters on one side only, the fried side gets all crispy and golden brown, but the oysters stay medium-rare on the opposite side and they almost melt on your tongue. The trick is to flour the oysters very delicately, then slip them into oil that is hot enough to turn the batter golden brown, but not too hot, or the oysters will burn. It's pretty easy once you get the hang of it, but having an extra oyster or two around for experimentation doesn't hurt.

The Rocoto Leche de Tigre Salsa, really a combination of ceviche sauce and salsa, makes the oysters taste like they were just plucked from the sea, but if you don't have time to make it, you could make a quick Salsa Criolla (page 44). The oysters should not be gigantic, more medium in size (3 inches wide at most), or they won't cook evenly. And it probably goes without saying, but with any oysters, buy only the best quality fresh (never frozen) oysters from a reputable vendor. Save the Kumamotos for eating purely raw. They are too delicate to pan-fry and tend to fall apart.

13 or 14 medium oysters, shucked, shells reserved
About ½ cup all-purpose flour, as needed
2 teaspoons kosher salt, or to taste
Canola or other vegetable oil, for frying
Rocoto Leche de Tigre Salsa (recipe follows) or Salsa Criolla (page 44)

1 Rinse 12 oyster shell halves and pat them dry with a paper towel; arrange them on a serving platter and set aside.

2 In a medium bowl, whisk together the flour and salt. Hold one hand over the bowl with the flour mixture. Spoon about half the flour mixture into your palm and gently place one oyster in the middle of the flour. Lift up the oyster with the opposite hand and gently set the same (floured) side back down in the flour, like you are flouring something very fragile. If you jam the oyster into the flour, it will take on too much coating. Repeat the lifting process one more time and gently shake the excess flour off the bottom of the oyster. Place the oyster, floured side down, on a plate and flour the remaining oysters.

3 In a large, heavy-bottomed saucepan, heat about ¼ inch of oil over medium-high heat for 1 to 2 minutes, until hot but not smoking. Pick up one end of a "test" oyster with your thumb and index finger, as if you were holding a whole sardine by the tail, and hold the oyster with the floured side facing away from you. To keep the oil from splattering on you, gently lay the oyster into the pan, floured side down, in one swooping motion from the "sardine head" toward the tail. Fry the oyster until the bottom coating is golden brown, 1½ to 2 minutes. Use tongs to immediately flip the oyster and sear the opposite, uncoated side for a quick second or two—that's it. Transfer the oyster to a plate, floured side facing up.

4 Check the test oyster to make sure it is golden brown on the bottom but still very moist and juicy on the uncoated side. If not, adjust the heat as needed: If the flour fell off the oyster, the oil is not hot enough. If the oil is too hot, the oyster will begin to burn after 30 seconds. Cook the remaining oysters the same way. You can cook up to 6 oysters at a time, but they can overcook quickly, so I suggest you cook them in smaller batches. Transfer each oyster to a half shell with the floured side up.

5 Serve the oysters hot, as you fry them, with a little rocoto leche de tigre salsa spooned on top of each (about 2 teaspoons per oyster). Or serve them at room temperature once you finish frying all of the oysters. Add the salsa right before serving.

ROCOTO LECHE DE TIGRE SALSA

Makes a generous ½ cup

Keep fresh fish trimmings in the freezer so you can quickly mix up a small batch of Rocoto Leche de Tigre (as with any ceviche, make sure the fish is very good quality). Like any fresh salsa criolla, you can chop the ingredients up to an hour before serving, but don't mix them together until the very last minute.

¼ cup finely chopped red onions

2 tablespoons finely chopped plum tomatoes, cored and seeded

2 tablespoons finely chopped fresh cilantro leaves and tender top stems

2 tablespoons extra-virgin olive oil

About ½ cup Rocoto Leche de Tigre (page 78)

Mix together all of the ingredients in a small bowl. Use the rocoto leche de tigre salsa right away.

SHRIMP DUMPLINGS WITH SOY-LIME SAUCE & ROCOTO OIL

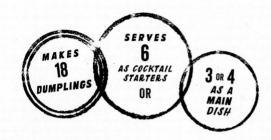

MAKES 18 DUMPLINGS

SERVES 6 AS COCKTAIL STARTERS OR 3 OR 4 AS A MAIN DISH

Peruvian food has many Asian influences, but it wasn't until I moved to London and worked at a really great sushi restaurant that I truly understood the fundamentals of Japanese cooking. Sushi chefs have incredibly fine-tuned palates. They're almost like sommeliers in that way.

My style of cooking definitely is not what you would call subtle. I like big, bold flavors that taste as loud as the streets of Lima sound. Still, the sushi chefs I worked under taught me how to show respect for every contrasting flavor and texture that goes into each dish. These dumplings, called *hakaw* in Peru after the Cantonese word for dumpling, are a good example. As you bite into them, the sweet, tender shrimp contrasts with the herbal crunch of fresh lemongrass, leeks, and cilantro, and then you get a spicy and salty kick from the yuzu kosho, a spicy Japanese yuzu-chile paste that you really don't see much in Peru.

These are best fried as you make them (to keep the filling from making the dumpling wrappers soggy), but if you dry off the shrimp carefully as I do, you can refrigerate the shaped dumplings for a good hour or so. Then pan-fry and steam them "to order" for appetizers or a light supper. And since everything is finely chopped, I wouldn't waste your jumbo shrimp dollars here. Large or medium shrimp work great.

SHRIMP FILLING

8 ounces peeled shrimp (14 to 16 medium), thawed if frozen

2 large egg whites

1 teaspoon pureed ginger (page 37) or finely zested fresh ginger

1½ teaspoons pureed garlic (page 37) or very finely minced garlic

1½ teaspoons yuzu kosho paste

2 teaspoons potato starch or cornstarch

¼ cup very finely chopped fresh cilantro leaves and tender top stems

⅓ cup very finely chopped leeks

1½ tablespoons very finely chopped shallots or red onion

2 tablespoons very finely chopped lemongrass (about 1 stalk)

18 wonton wrappers

Canola or other vegetable oil, for frying

Soy-Lime Dipping Sauce (recipe follows)

1 tablespoon rocoto oil (page 38; optional)

10 to 12 celery leaves or fresh cilantro leaves, torn in half or roughly chopped, for garnish

1 Devein and finely chop the shrimp, leaving a few small chunks of meat for texture. Place the chopped shrimp on paper towels to fully drain. (Blot the top of the shrimp with a paper towel to dry as much as possible.)

2 In a medium bowl, whisk together the egg whites, ginger, garlic, yuzu kosho, and potato starch until no lumps remain. Use your hands or a large spoon to fold in the chopped cilantro, leeks, shallots, lemongrass, and chopped shrimp until well combined.

3 Stack 2 or 3 wonton wrappers at a time on a work surface. Use a 3-inch round ring mold or biscuit cutter to cut the wrappers into circles almost the size of the wrapper. Arrange the circles side by side on the work surface and place a scant 1 tablespoon of the filling in the middle of each. Place a lightly moistened paper or kitchen towel nearby.

4 One at a time, fold each wrapper in half to form a tacolike shape to loosely enclose the filling (do not seal the dumpling wrapper at the top). Stand the base of the "taco" upright on your work surface and pinch together the bottom right and left corners of the wonton wrapper. Use your index finger and thumb on both hands to pull the top of the "taco" outward and pinch together the two opposite sides of the wrapper to make a rectangular, open-faced dumpling. The moisture from the filling should help seal the edges of the wrapper, but if needed, moisten your hands on the damp towel to help seal the wrapper. If some of the filling starts to bulge out of the center as you work, push it back down with your finger. Repeat the shaping process with the remaining dumplings. Arrange the dumplings in a single layer in a casserole dish lined with a paper towel. Fry the dumplings right away, or refrigerate for up to 30 minutes.

RECIPE CONTINUES

5 To cook the dumplings, have a kitchen towel or kitchen mitt at the ready. If any of the dumplings have opened slightly, pinch the corners back together. Pour a thin layer of oil, 2 to 3 tablespoons, into a large, wide saucepan (at least 2 inches deep) with a lid. (Nonstick is best, but any large pan will work.) Arrange half of the dumplings on top of the cold oil and place the pan over very high heat. Sear the bottom side of the dumplings until golden brown, 2½ to 3 minutes. Shake the pan every so often or gently push the dumplings around with a spoon so they don't stick and brown evenly. Reduce the heat to low, wrap one arm in a kitchen towel or put on a long oven mitt to cover your arm, and very carefully pour ¼ cup water down one side of the pan, avoiding the dumplings (be careful—the water will sizzle when it hits the oil and the steam will be very hot). Immediately cover the pan with the lid and steam the dumplings until the filling turns white, a sign that they are firm and cooked through, 45 seconds to 1 minute (do not overcook, or the dumplings will become gummy). Transfer the dumplings to a plate and tent them loosely with a piece of foil.

6 Drain the remaining oil, carefully wipe out the pan with paper towels, and repeat the frying process with the remaining dumplings. Arrange all of the cooked dumplings on a serving platter and drizzle a generous tablespoon of the soy-lime sauce on top of them. Drizzle the rocoto oil (if using) all over the plate and scatter the celery leaves on top. Serve *inmediatamente* with the remaining soy-lime dipping sauce on the side.

SOY-LIME DIPPING SAUCE

Makes about ¼ cup

2 tablespoons soy sauce, preferably a Japanese brand like Yamasa
1 tablespoon unsweetened rice vinegar
Juice of ½ lime (about 1 tablespoon), or to taste

Combine all of the ingredients in a small bowl. Taste, and add another squeeze of lime juice if you'd like. You can make the dipping sauce 2 to 3 hours before serving the dumplings. Keep the sauce at room temperature.

CASSAVA ROOT FRITTERS WITH SERRANO-LIME DIPPING SAUCE

MAKES 18 TO 20 SMALL FRITTERS

SERVES 6 TO 8 AS SNACKS OR COCKTAIL STARTERS

All over Peru, yuca, or cassava root, is cut into thick strips, fried, and served like steak fries alongside secos (stews), sandwiches, or on their own. When I'm hungry for a quick snack, *yucas fritas* do the job, but in my opinion, the starchy root vegetable is so much better when mixed with flour to make *yuquitas*, light cassava root fritters that are the equivalent of beignets. They always remind me of when I was little and my friends and I would go through two dozen yuquitas along with our *sopa rachi*, a thick Cantonese-style chicken soup (see sidebar, page 62). I think that's why I like to stuff the fritters with buttery Spanish Manchego cheese today. Not only are the fritters great on their own, but when you break one open, you get this long, fantastically gooey string of cheese, the sort of thing kids (and this adult) love.

I make my yuquitas pretty big, but the smaller version here is good for a party and doubles or triples easily for a crowd. The batter is very forgiving, so you can make it ahead and let it rise slowly overnight in the refrigerator. The fritters also keep well in the oven for half an hour or so after you fry them. Look for frozen cassava (often labeled yuca—see page 266) at well-stocked grocery stores or Latin markets. Use young Manchego or a similar nutty, full-flavored cheese that melts well, not the hard aged Manchego *viejo* that is more like Parmesan.

8 ounces frozen yuca or cassava root (about two 4-inch-long pieces)

1½ teaspoons active dry yeast

2 teaspoons sugar

¾ cup all-purpose flour

1 teaspoon kosher salt

About 1 tablespoon olive oil

Canola or other vegetable oil, for frying

18 to 20 (¾- to 1-inch) cubes young (not aged) Manchego or similar cheese (about 5 ounces)

Serrano-Lime Dipping Sauce (page 62)

1 Place the frozen yuca in a medium saucepan and cover it with about 2 inches of water. Bring the water to a low boil over medium-high heat and cook until the yuca is almost fall-apart tender, about 25 minutes. Scoop out about 1 cup of the cooking water and set it aside in a medium bowl. Drain the yuca and put it in a separate medium bowl. While still warm, mash the yuca with a potato masher or a large fork, discarding any large, fibrous strands as you work. Use your fingers to smash any larger pieces of the vegetable that remain. Mashing requires some muscle; add a tablespoon or two of the reserved cooking water to help, if needed. You should have about 1 cup mashed yuca.

2 Stir the yeast and the sugar into ¾ cup of the reserved cooking water (it should be lukewarm, not hot). Allow the yeast to hydrate for a minute or two, then mix in the flour and the salt. Using a large spoon or your hands, fold in the mashed yuca and the olive oil until well combined. The batter should be very moist, almost like a very thick pancake batter. If not, add another 2 to 3 tablespoons of the reserved cooking water. Transfer the batter to a clean bowl, cover with plastic wrap, and let rise at warm room temperature until more than doubled, 1 hour or longer, or refrigerate the dough overnight.

3 Preheat the oven to 250°F. Line a baking sheet with a few layers of paper towels. In a medium, deep saucepan, heat 2½ to 3 inches of oil over medium-high heat until it registers 350°F on a deep-fry thermometer, or fill a deep-fryer with the recommended amount of oil and set the temperature to 350°F. Test the oil's temperature: Drop a small nub of the batter into the hot oil. It should bubble fairly vigorously and rise to the top after a few seconds. If the oil smokes, reduce the heat. After about 2 minutes, the batter should turn light golden brown, the color of beer-battered fish, not dark hushpuppies (if the fritter

RECIPE CONTINUES

turns dark brown, reduce the heat slightly; if it's too light, increase the heat as needed).

4 When the oil is the right temperature, quickly shape the fritters one by one. Put a small bowl of cold water near your work surface, dip your hands in the water, and shake off the excess. Use your non-dominant hand as your flat work surface, holding your fingers side by side and your palm facing up. Scoop a generous 1 tablespoon of the batter with your other hand and plop the batter down on your outstretched fingers. Stretch out the batter into a 2-inch pancake and place a cube of the cheese in the middle. Roughly pinch and smooth the batter over the cheese to form a ball (it doesn't need to be perfect).

5 Drop the fritter into the oil, dip your hands in the bowl of water again, and quickly repeat the shaping process to make 3 or 4 more fritters. Do not to overcrowd the oil. Cook the fritters until very light golden brown, 2½ to 3 minutes. Use tongs to flip each fritter once or twice (they should be bobbing at the top of the oil, like apples) and evenly brown them on all sides. Use tongs, a spider, or the fry basket to transfer the fritters to the lined baking sheet to drain excess oil. If not serving immediately, put the fritters on a rimmed baking sheet lined with a wire rack and place them in the oven to keep warm for up to 30 minutes. Fry the remaining fritters the same way. When ready to serve, pile the fritters onto a big platter or on individual plates and serve the serrano-lime dipping sauce on the side.

SERRANO-LIME DIPPING SAUCE

Makes about ¾ cup

This may be my new favorite sauce. It's so good on grilled or baked white fish (add the sauce after cooking), and lately, I've been stirring it together with equal parts mayonnaise to make a sandwich spread or salad dressing for summer tomatoes and cucumbers. If you don't have a professional-style blender, be *paciente*. It may take a little while for the cilantro and peppers to puree, but they will get there. You can always help them along by stirring the mixture once or twice.

5 to 6 medium serrano chiles
1 small or ⅔ large bunch cilantro, leaves and top two-thirds of the stems, roughly chopped, or to taste
3 tablespoons fresh lime juice
¾ teaspoon kosher salt, or to taste
3 tablespoons extra-virgin olive oil

Stem, seed, devein, rinse, and roughly chop the peppers. Place them in a blender and add the cilantro, lime juice, and salt. Puree until smooth. With the blender running, slowly drizzle in the oil. Taste, and add another squeeze of lime juice or a pinch of salt if needed. The sauce should be tangy and noticeably salty on the back end. Use the serrano-lime dipping sauce right away, or refrigerate it in a covered container for up to 3 days; just before serving, add another squeeze of lime juice to brighten up the flavors.

SOPA RACHI & YUCAS FRITAS

When I was in elementary school, my dad had the best bribe for getting not only me, but several of my friends, out of bed. Our church was near Lima's Chinatown, a stretch of streets known as Calle Capón. The standing deal was that if we went to 6:00 a.m. mass, our reward would be breakfast at Restaurante Arakaki. The restaurant is very famous and has been around since 1940s. It's a tiny hole-in-the-wall place with plastic linoleum floors and usually only locals inside. They come for the best sopa rachi (pork belly soup), which is what we call Cantonese-style congee.

Congee is prepared differently all over Asia. The Peruvian version has become a very famous dish at Peruvian-Chinese restaurants. There, the rice is usually cooked down into a steaming, thick, milky porridge filled with shredded cooked chicken or giblets (intestine at Restaurante Arakaki) and topped with bean sprouts and scallions at the last minute, so they stay crunchy. At the table, you drizzle just enough soy sauce on top so you can see the color of the soup lightly change as you stir it in with a little lime juice, then you top everything with a spicy green chile salsa.

The soup always comes with a big platter of what the restaurant calls yucas fritas (cassava root fries) but are really yuquitas, the soft, beignetlike yuca fritters. You eat a little soup, break open a fritter, and eat it like bread, on the side, or use the fritter to sop up more of the soup. If you ever eat there, you will understand why on Sundays, I always woke up before even the sun wanted to get up.

HUEVOS AL VAPOR
(STEAMED EGGS)

I have Chinese blood by association—in mí familia—*the same as family.*

The father of my nine oldest brothers and sisters was Chinese-Peruvian (our mom married my father and had four more children, including me). The Chinese food influence was already ever present in Lima, but that family connection is partly why so many of my favorite comfort foods have Chinese roots—especially snacks.

My mom once woke up in the middle of the night and heard someone in the kitchen rustling around. I was too little to reach the counter, so she found me on a chair leaning over the stove. I love eggs, always have, and was frying one up. I slid the fried egg into a bowl with a little soy sauce and leftover rice to sop up all the juices, and went back to bed after I ate it. I had no idea my mom was watching me quietly from around the corner to make sure I was safe.

After that, I started spending a lot more time on kitchen chores with my mom. I'm not sure whether she was worried I might get up and start a fire (*probablemente*), or just had a sense that I would come to love cooking. Maybe a little of both. I still love a fried egg, but one of my favorite Chinese-influenced snacks, and one of the first *mi mamá* taught me to make, is still these simple steamed eggs.

The only trick is getting the ramekin or other baking dish out of the pot of simmering water. When I was little, I would get so excited that I would sometimes burn my hands when I reached in with just a towel (not a good idea). Use tongs, and hold them firmly shut around the ramekin so it doesn't slip, or even better, use the slip-proof clamp tongs for canning and preserving. If you wake up the whole house while you are rustling around and suddenly need more than one late-night snack, use a larger pot that will fit several ramekins and increase the cooking time by a few minutes.

To make a steamed egg:

Break one egg into a small, lightly oiled ramekin, fill one half of the eggshell with a little stock (fish, chicken, or whatever you have around), and pour the stock (about 1 tablespoon) into the ramekin. Add a pinch of salt and mix everything together with chopsticks or a fork so the egg yolk gets all excited and runny. Cover the egg-filled ramekin snugly with a piece of foil and arrange one corner of the foil along the top edge of the ramekin so it is easy to lift and peek in as the egg cooks. Put the ramekin into a small pot and fill the pot with enough water so it comes a good way up the sides of the ramekin. Bring the water to a low boil over medium-high heat, reduce the heat to low, and simmer until the egg has the texture of a very moist custard, or is cooked however you like. Check on the egg after 4 minutes, but it usually takes a good 5 to 6 minutes. The ramekin will dance around the pot to the beat of the simmering water as the egg steams. (While the egg steams, heat up a little leftover rice to eat alongside.) Top the egg custard with a few dashes of soy sauce and scoop it on top of the rice. Pour a drizzle of good-quality olive oil and sprinkle a few diced scallions or spicy peppers on top. **Makes 1 really good late-night snack.**

MINI GREEN TAMALES WITH WILD MUSHROOM– SECO SAUCE

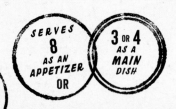

MAKES ABOUT **12** TAMALITOS

SERVES **8** AS AN APPETIZER OR **3** OR **4** AS A MAIN DISH

The tamales of northern Peru are very different from Mexican tamales. Instead of masa, Peruvian tamales are made with fresh choclo, a large-kernel sweet corn from the Andes. When cooked, they are moist and almost melt in your mouth. The tamales are served with seco (page 151), a green sauce that is used in dishes all over Peru. It usually is made from the tasty leftover juices from slow-cooking meats and chicken, but I also make a vegetarian version (page 206).

A little Peruvian home cook secret: If you are short on time, turn the choclo base into *pepián*, a homey, polentalike corn stew. Stop cooking the choclo while the filling is still super moist, and top it with the seco sauce. You can add mushrooms or a little roasted chicken, whatever you'd like, but I usually just spoon a little seco sauce on top. Pepián is so creamy and comforting, it is an excellent stand-in when you don't have the time to make the tamales.

About 20 corn husks

1 (16-ounce) bag frozen choclo (see page 28), thawed

4 tablespoons (½ stick) unsalted butter, or vegetable shortening if making vegan tamales

1 generous cup Seco Secreto (page 206)

Kosher salt

About 1 generous cup Wild Mushroom–Seco Sauce (recipe follows)

¾ to 1 cup Jalapeño Salsa Criolla (page 44), or your favorite salsa

1 Put the corn husks in a medium bowl, cover with warm water, and set aside to soak for about 10 minutes. Drain and set aside on paper towels to dry. To make tamale ties, tear off 18 to 20 shoestring-like strips about ¼ inch thick from 1 to 2 husks.

2 While the corn husks soak, in a food processor, process the choclo until finely ground, with the texture of a chunky puree, a good minute.

3 In a medium saucepan, melt the butter over medium-high heat for about 1 minute. Add the pureed choclo and sauté for a minute or two, stirring constantly, then add the seco sauce and 1½ cups of water. Bring the sauce and corn to a simmer, reduce the heat to low, and cook, stirring often, until reduced and thickened to even more of a porridgelike consistency, about 25 minutes, stirring occasionally. Reduce the heat if the corn begins to stick to the pan too much (the mixture is dry and will stick some). Season the choclo with salt to taste, remove from the heat, and set the corn mixture aside to cool for about 15 minutes.

4 To fill the tamales, lay 2 soaked husks on a work surface so the two wide ends overlap by 3 to 4 inches in the center, and the pointed edges face east and west to form a diamondlike shape. Mound about ¼ cup of the corn mixture in the center of the husks to form a rectangle about 3 inches long. Fold the top edge of the husks snugly over the filling and repeat with the bottom edge. Next, fold both sides of the husks inward to form a little package about 4 inches long and 2 inches wide. The filling should be snugly enclosed in the husks. Wrap one of the ties around the middle of the tamale and tie the ends firmly together to cinch the center like a belt (if the tie breaks, begin again with a new tie). Tie the tamale a second time around the center so it is securely sealed. Repeat with the remaining filling and husks. (At this point, the tamales can be covered and refrigerated for up to 1 day before steaming.)

5 Fill a steamer with water and bring the water to a simmer. (If you don't have a steamer, place a large metal colander over a deep pot so it rests on the handles and does not touch the bottom. Add just enough water so the bottom of the colander is not submerged, bring the water to a simmer, then reduce the heat to low.) Stand the tamales upright in the steamer or colander, cover, and steam for about 45 minutes. (Don't stack them, or the tamales will cook at different times from bottom to top.) If using a colander, check to make sure there is always enough water at the bottom of the pot, and add more as needed. Remove the steamer or pot from the heat and keep the tamales covered so they stay warm.

6 Serve the tamales with the wild mushroom–seco sauce and jalapeño salsa criolla alongside. Or, unwrap the tamales and plate them individually with the sauce and salsa spooned generously on top.

PEPIÁN *If you'd like to serve this as a corn stew, in step 3, remove the corn mixture from the heat when it still has a soupier texture, after about 15 minutes. Season with salt to taste. Serve with the wild mushroom–seco sauce and jalapeño salsa criolla on top.*

━━━

WILD MUSHROOM–SECO SAUCE
Makes about 1½ cups

This is a very forgiving sauce, so it's a good opportunity to play around with different varieties of mushrooms. It also reheats nicely, so you can make it ahead and serve it with tamales one night, a good steak the next. If you are making a vegan version, use olive oil instead of butter. Too much olive oil can make mushrooms taste oily, so use a little less.

3 tablespoons unsalted butter
1 tablespoon olive oil, or more as needed
16 ounces mixed Japanese or any wild mushrooms, cut into 1- to 2-inch chunks if large
1 teaspoon pureed garlic (page 37) or finely grated garlic
About 1 cup Seco Secreto (page 206)
Kosher salt

In a large sauté pan, heat the butter and the olive oil over medium-high heat until hot. (If you'd rather not use butter, use a generous 2 tablespoons oil instead.) Add the mushrooms and garlic and sauté, stirring often, until the mushrooms begin to brown and shrink, 8 to 10 minutes, depending on their size. Add the seco sauce, scrape up any browned bits from the bottom of the pan, and cook until the sauce has reduced slightly and the mushrooms are very tender, about 5 minutes more. Season the sauce with salt and use immediately, or remove from the heat and rewarm when the tamales are ready. Or, let the sauce cool completely, cover, and refrigerate it for up to 2 days before rewarming over medium heat, stirring often.

FRIED FISH WITH SWEET POTATO CHIPS & MALT VINEGAR AIOLI

In Peru, the batter for fried fish doesn't usually have beer, but after thirteen years in London, I get it. The carbonation in beer lightens the batter and helps it puff up when fried, and it adds a subtle yeastiness that I really like with the briny flavors in seafood. British pub food can sometimes be a little on the *tímido* side, so I serve the fish with a malt vinegar aioli spiced with ají amarillo peppers. I also like to cut the fish into much smaller pieces so they cook evenly, so they make really good appetizers.

Some of the white-fleshed fish typically used for frying can be pretty bland, but paiche has a bright, clean flavor with a firm, meaty texture that tastes like it was made for frying. If you can't find paiche, substitute another firm white fish like black cod. The cornstarch and egg white give these fish sticks a light texture like Japanese tempura, and, thanks to the paiche's firm texture, these stay piping hot longer than most fried fish. Gather your crew, open a few beers, and have a Peruvian-style fish fry served straight from the fryer.

1 (1½-pound) paiche or black cod fillet, or other firm white-fleshed fish

Canola or other vegetable oil, for frying

1⅓ cups all-purpose flour

1 cup potato starch or cornstarch

2 teaspoons baking powder

12 ounces (1½ cups) brown ale such as Newcastle, or other medium-bodied beer

1 large egg white

Kosher salt

A few tablespoons chopped fresh parsley, for serving

Camote Frito (recipe follows), or sure, a bag of sweet potato chips or any kind of french fries

1 cup malt vinegar–ají amarillo aioli (page 38)

1 Cut the fish fillet into pieces about 3 inches long and 1 inch wide and put them on a paper towel–lined plate. You should have about 16 pieces. Depending on the cut of the fillet, some of the pieces may be thicker than others. That's fine—the thinner pieces will just cook a little faster.

2 Line a baking sheet with two or three paper towels. In a medium, deep saucepan, heat 2½ to 3 inches of oil over medium-high heat until it registers 350°F on a deep-fry thermometer, or fill a deep fryer with the recommended amount of oil and set the temperature to 350°F.

3 In a medium bowl, whisk together 1 cup of the flour, the potato starch, and baking powder. Whisk in the beer until the mixture has the consistency of lumpy pancake batter, and set the batter aside, uncovered, to lightly ferment for about 30 minutes. Place the remaining ⅓ cup flour in a small bowl.

4 Whip the egg white to stiff peaks. If using a stand mixer, you may need to release the mixer bowl and raise it with your hands for the the whisk to reach the bottom (place your hands on the outside of the bowl and lift it up slightly). Fold the egg white into the beer batter until just incorporated; do not overmix.

5 Test the oil temperature: Drop a small nub of batter into the oil. The oil should bubble fairly vigorously and the nub should rise to the top. (If the oil smokes, reduce the heat.) Sprinkle the fish lightly on both sides with salt. Roll 3 or 4 pieces at a time very lightly in the flour (dust off any excess) then submerge the fish in the batter. Working one at a time, remove the fillets with your fingers or tongs, and immediately transfer to the hot oil. Repeat with the remaining fillets and fry the fish until the batter is very light golden brown (it will not be dark) and the fish is cooked through, 2 to 4 minutes, depending on the thickness of the pieces. The bubbles in the hot oil will noticeably decrease in size when the fish is almost ready. Flip the fish with tongs once during the frying process so it browns evenly on both sides.

6 Use tongs, a spider, or the fry basket to transfer the fillets to the paper towel–lined plate and sprinkle them lightly with salt. Transfer the fried fish to a serving plate, sprinkle it with the parsley, and pile some sweet potato chips and a bowl of the spicy malt vinegar aioli nearby. Keep battering and frying the remaining fish fillets, and eating and sharing them as you go.

CAMOTE FRITO (FRIED SWEET POTATOES)

Boiled sweet potatoes are a traditional accompaniment to many classic Peruvian dishes, including ceviches. Fried sweet potatoes are loved as much as, maybe more than, regular fried potatoes in Peru. They're served more as snacks, but I also like them as sides. You get that nice contrast of the super-crispy, golden brown outside with the tender, sweet middle. And unlike regular potatoes, which require double-frying to get a crispy crust, with sweet potatoes, the extra sugar helps the outside crisp up after one trip to the deep-fryer. Fry up thin, crispy potato chips to go with sandwiches or fish and chips, or thin matchstick-size pieces as more *elegante* garnishes for things like Paiche Lettuce Wraps (page 120).

1 **To make Fried Sweet Potatoes:** Slice both ends off 1 large, unpeeled sweet potato. For potato chips, cut the potato into very thin slices about the thickness of kettle-fried chips, around ⅛ inch thick (a mandoline works well). If you're making matchstick fries, stack a few of the potato chip slices, trim the edges to make a square, and cut them into thin matchsticks.

2 Preheat the oven to 250°F. Line a baking sheet with two or three paper towels. In a medium, deep saucepan, heat 2½ to 3 inches of oil over medium-high heat until it registers 350°F on a deep-fry thermometer, or fill a deep fryer with the recommended amount of oil and set the temperature to 350°F. Test the oil temperature: Drop a piece of potato into the oil. It should bubble fairly vigorously and rise to the top (if the oil smokes, reduce the heat).

3 Working in batches, fry the sweet potatoes without crowding the oil (one or two batches, depending on the size of your frying pot). For chips, fry the potatoes until they are crispy and golden brown and the oil bubbles begin to slow, 5 to 8 minutes. (The time varies depending on how thick they are cut; remove one with tongs to taste how crispy it is.) For the matchsticks, the fry time is usually 2 to 4 minutes, but let your eyes and mouth be the judge. Use tongs to turn the potatoes once or twice as they fry so they brown evenly on all sides.

4 Transfer the potatoes with tongs, a spider, or the fry basket to the paper towel–lined baking sheet in a single layer (so they do not steam). Immediately sprinkle with sea salt or kosher salt to taste before you start the next batch. **Makes about 30 potato chips or 3 handfuls of matchsticks per potato.**

PERUVIAN FRIED CHICKEN WITH ROCOTO AIOLI & SALSA CRIOLLA

MAKES **4** PICNIC SERVINGS.

MÁS IF EVERYONE IS UNDER 4 FEET TALL

My kids, by far the toughest restaurant critics, went through a phase when they refused to eat anything at my restaurants other than my fried chicken, an adaptation of the American dish (we batter and fry more seafood than poultry in Peru). It was the best compliment I've ever received. My Anticucho Sauce (page 112) has a very similar flavor to the more complicated chicken marinade I usually make, but takes just a few minutes to mix together. Sure, my kids are used to a little chile heat; if you like, cut back slightly on the amount of ají pepper pastes in the marinade. I encourage you to give the marinade a trial run first.

I usually use chicken breast in this recipe, but lately, I've been substituting skin-on chicken thighs for that really great, juicy flavor that you can only get from dark meat. When you cut chicken thighs into small pieces, they fry up quickly so the meat doesn't dry out and the skin gets nice and crispy. If you can't find boneless thighs with the skin, buy bone-in thighs and trim them yourself (save the bones for stock). Or sure, use boneless chicken breast. The chicken really is best if you marinate it overnight, but you could marinate the chicken for just a few hours.

About 2 pounds boneless chicken thighs, or 2½ pounds bone-in thighs with skin (or use chicken breast strips)

About 1 cup Anticucho Sauce (page 112)

Canola oil, for frying

1 cup all-purpose flour

1 cup potato starch or cornstarch

2 teaspoons kosher salt, or to taste

2 teaspoons freshly ground black pepper

½ cup rocoto aioli (page 38), or your favorite aioli or mayonnaise

¾ to 1 cup Salsa Criolla (page 44)

1 Trim any big pieces of fat off the chicken thighs, but leave some smaller bits of fat attached. If using bone-in thighs, carefully trim the meat off the bone and leave the skin attached to the meat. Cut each thigh into two or three strips about 1½ inches wide, put them in a medium bowl or food storage container, and pour the anticucho marinade on top. Toss the chicken pieces around in the marinade then let them settle so that every piece is just about covered; if the pieces are not almost covered, use a slightly wider bowl or container so they lie flat. Cover and refrigerate the chicken for at least 3 to 4 hours or, better still, overnight.

2 Remove the chicken from the refrigerator at least 30 minutes before frying. Preheat the oven to 250°F and line a baking sheet with two or three paper towels. In a medium, deep saucepan, heat a good 2 inches of oil over medium-high heat until it registers 350°F on a deep-fry thermometer, or fill a deep fryer with the recommended amount of oil and set the temperature to 350°F.

3 Whisk together the flour, potato starch, salt, and pepper in a medium bowl and set aside. Remove three or four pieces of chicken from the marinade and toss them in the flour mixture to lightly coat all sides.

4 Test the oil temperature: Moisten a small bit of flour with a little marinade and drop the nub of batter into the oil. It should bubble fairly vigorously and rise to the top (if the oil smokes, reduce the heat). Fry the chicken until the crust is golden brown and the meat is still very juicy but no longer pink inside, about 5 minutes, sometimes a minute or two longer for thicker pieces, less if using boneless breast. Check a piece by cutting it in half. Use tongs, a spider, or the fry basket to carefully transfer the chicken to the paper towel–lined baking sheet, and place the baking sheet in the oven to keep the chicken warm (you can hold the chicken in the oven for up to 30 minutes). Bread and fry the remaining chicken pieces.

5 Serve the chicken hot with the rocoto aioli and salsa criolla. If you are taking the chicken on a picnic, let it cool completely, then arrange it in a single layer in a paper towel–lined casserole dish or food storage container. Cover and serve the chicken at room temperature. After 2 to 3 hours, you will need to refrigerate the chicharron de pollo. It will keep for up to 1 day, but the chilled chicken crust will no longer be as crispy.

FRIED PORK SANDWICH WITH SALSA CRIOLLA

SERVES 10 TO 12 OR MORE, IF YOU CAN KEEP THE PORK NIBBLERS OUT OF THE KITCHEN

At least in my family, when your whole family shows up on Sunday, you make *pan con chicharrón*. It seems there's never enough of these fried pork belly sandwiches to go around. Somehow, twenty-five people turns into sixty brothers, sisters, cousins, aunts, uncles, nieces, and nephews. When I'm back in Lima, it's usually up to me to figure out how to feed everyone—entirely my fault, as I'm also usually the one who called everyone to announce I was in town. One thing I learned from my mom was how to stretch whatever is on the stove by turning it into a component of something else instead of the main course. A giant, juicy sandwich like pan con chicharrón is always in the running.

The components are simple: braised and fried pork belly, chunks of fried sweet potato, and tangy salsa criolla all stuffed inside a giant hoagielike roll with plenty of mayo. We are lucky that pork belly is an everyday meat in Peru, a very humble cut with crazy flavor. In the United States, the belly can get pricey, so I also make the sandwich with *costillas*, pork ribs (use the small, meaty baby back ribs, not giant spare ribs). When you are making sandwiches, the meat from two or three racks goes a long way toward feeding a small crowd on a budget.

The pork is usually slowly braised in water for several hours until the liquid almost evaporates and the meat gets super tender; then you slice the pork and quick-fry it until crisp. I like to simmer the pork in a big-flavored stock, so it infuses flavor into the meat, and then fry the pork in olive oil instead of its own fat so you get an almost confitlike flavor. Plus, you're left with a rich pork stock that you can strain and use for dumpling soup, or just stir in cooked noodles or rice and handful of chopped scallions. So good.

The most important thing with such tender meat is to leave the braised pork alone in the pot to cool once it's cooked, and then refrigerate it for several hours or overnight. I mean it. *¡No tocar!*—do not touch! If you try to fry the warm meat right away, the tender pieces will completely fall apart. Refrigeration helps keep the incredibly tender meat from falling apart as you fry it. Strain the leftover frying oil and use it for frying potatoes or another pot of chicharrón.

I can go on forever when it comes to pan con chicharrón, but one last thing: Since you can braise the pork a day or two ahead, all you have to do when everyone shows up is fry the meat and let them pile up their own sandwich. If you're making ribs, they're also good on their own, still on the bone with the mayo as a dipping sauce and salsa criolla on the side. I like a bolder huancaína sauce (page 168) or mayo made from the same serrano-lime dipping sauce I serve with Yuquitas (page 62), but regular mayo is also very good.

BRAISED PORK

1 (5-pound) skin-on center-cut pork belly, or 5 to 6 pounds (2 nice-size racks) baby back pork ribs

2 carrots, cut into a few chunks

2 celery stalks, cut into a few chunks

1 large red onion, quartered

1 (2-inch) nub fresh ginger, unpeeled, cut into 3 or 4 pieces

6 large cloves garlic, lightly smashed

2 teaspoons whole black peppercorns

2 star anise

½ cinnamon stick

2 bay leaves

About 8 cups (64 ounces) homemade chicken stock (page 40) or low-sodium store-bought broth

TO ASSEMBLE

Extra-virgin olive oil, for frying

3 medium yams or sweet potatoes

12 to 15 sandwich-size torta rolls, lightly broiled or grilled, or 2 to 3 large ciabatta loaves, sliced and lightly broiled or grilled

1 cup Salsa a la Huancaína (page 168), or ½ cup Serrano-Lime Dipping Sauce (page 62) blended with ½ cup mayonnaise, or 1 cup plain mayonnaise, preferably Japanese

A good 3 to 4 cups Salsa Criolla (page 44)

1 Place the pork belly in a very large Dutch oven or tall stockpot. You may need to slice the slab in half and stack the

RECIPE CONTINUES

pieces so they fit. If using ribs, cut them into four sections each (don't peel off the silver skin) and stack them in the pot. Tuck a few of the larger vegetables beneath the pork, and pile the rest of the vegetables and spices on top of the pork. Cover the pork and vegetables with the chicken stock; add water, if needed, to cover the pork completely. Bring the stock to a high boil, then reduce the heat to medium-low. Cook the pork at a low boil, uncovered, until super tender when pierced with a knife, a good 3 hours. During the first hour, occasionally skim off the foam that accumulates on top of the stock. Check the pot every half hour or so, and add water if needed so the pork is always completely submerged (always bring the stock back to a low boil).

2 After about 3 hours, turn off the heat and remove the pot from the stove. Allow the pork to cool, untouched, for at least an hour; 2 hours is even better. Gently lift the pork out of the pot with both hands underneath the meat (so it doesn't break in half), or a giant spoon or spatula; use two spoons or spatulas if the slab of pork belly is large. Put the pork into a 9 x 13-inch baking dish, or whatever you can fit the pieces in without stacking the meat. Strain the pork broth, discarding the vegetables, and reserve the broth for soup or rice. Let the meat cool completely, untouched. Cover and refrigerate the pork for at least 6 hours, or better still, overnight. You can refrigerate the pork for up to 2 days at this point. Let it come to room temperature before using.

3 If using pork belly, slice the meat against the grain into ½-inch-thick pieces (if the pork belly is very large, you can cut the pieces in half to better fit the bread). If using ribs, slice the slabs into individual ribs but leave the meat on the bones.

4 Line a baking sheet with two or three paper towels. In a medium saucepan, heat a good 2 inches of oil over medium-high heat. (You can use canola oil, if you don't have enough olive oil, or use a deep-fryer, if you'd rather.) When the oil is good and hot, fry a few slices of the pork belly or ribs at a time until golden brown on all sides, 2 to 3 minutes. Flip the pieces a few times during cooking so they brown evenly. Transfer the meat to the paper towel–lined baking sheet, and repeat the frying process with the remaining pork belly or ribs.

5 Fry up the yams as directed on page 67 (count on 2 or 3 slices per sandwich) and put out your bread and the huancaína sauce so everyone can assemble their sandwiches. Toss the salsa criolla together at the last minute, and serve it along with the pork with the other condiments for the sandwiches. If you have any leftovers, let the meat cool completely, cover, and refrigerate for up to 3 days. (If serving leftovers, remake fresh salsa criolla; the onions will have become soggy.)

SPICY TUNA SANDWICH WITH CUCUMBER-JALAPEÑO RELISH & YUZU KOSHO AIOLI

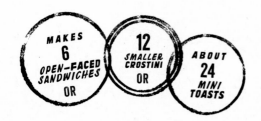

MAKES 6 OPEN-FACED SANDWICHES OR 12 SMALLER CROSTINI OR ABOUT 24 MINI TOASTS

I'm guessing that we all grow up with certain "house rules." In mine, not eating breakfast was the equivalent of a cardinal sin. One morning, my mom showed up outside my elementary school classroom door with a tightly wrapped sandwich in her hand. I took one look at my mom's face and regretted not eating breakfast. She pulled me outside and stood there until I finished every bite, with my friends loving every minute of the side show. I never skipped breakfast again.

Peruvians eat a lot of sandwiches for breakfast and brunch. With my mom, it was either Pan con Chicharrón (page 70) or *pan con tuna*, the Peruvian version of a tuna sandwich. I still love a good pan con tuna. It is usually made with canned tuna, but I've upgraded over the years to sushi-grade fish. I also like to play around with different condiments like yuzu kosho aioli and a Sriracha version, and I serve the sandwiches open-faced so I have more options for parties, picnics, or even just a weeknight dinner. I've made these sandwiches into all kinds of things, from giant hoagies with two-foot long baguettes for *fútbol* matches to elegant crostini on one-bite toasts for cocktail parties. They are also a good use of leftover trimmings and scrapings from sushi-grade tuna (see sidebar, page 75). Trim your fish when you get home, and you've got an excuse to make this sandwich for lunch.

1 cup finely diced and scraped trimmings from sushi-quality tuna (see sidebar, page 75) (about 8 ounces)

About ¼ cup Sriracha aioli (page 38), or to taste

3 (½-inch-thick) slices from a large, fat sourdough country loaf, cut in half, or 12 (¼-inch-thick) slices sourdough baguette (about 2 inches long), or 24 melba toasts or other small crackers

Extra-virgin olive oil

1 to 2 ripe large Hass avocados

Juice of ½ lime or ¼ lemon

Kosher salt

Cucumber-Jalapeño Relish (recipe follows)

¼ to ½ cup yuzu kosho aioli (page 38), or more Sriracha aioli

1 In a medium bowl, mix together the tuna and the Sriracha aioli. Cover and refrigerate while you make the other sandwich components, or for up to 4 hours.

2 If making sandwiches or crostini, brush the bread lightly with olive oil and lightly grill or broil both sides until crispy. In a medium bowl, mash together the avocados, lime juice, and a nice pinch of salt.

3 To assemble the sandwiches or crostini, generously spread the smashed avocados on each slice of bread, like a mayonnaise. I like a thick, ½-inch layer of avocado, but use however much you'd like. Divide the spicy tuna among the bread and top with the cucumber-jalapeño relish. Dollop or drizzle the yuzu kosho aioli on the top, and you're ready to go.

4 If you are making mini cocktail toasts, spoon 2 teaspoons of the spicy tuna on each toast, followed by a dollop of cucumber-jalapeño relish. Put the yuzu kosho aioli in a squeeze bottle, if you have one, and squeeze a little on top. Or, use a ½-teaspoon measuring spoon to dollop the aioli on top of the relish, or to taste.

RECIPE CONTINUES

CUCUMBER-JALAPEÑO RELISH

Makes about 1 cup

Every home cook piles his or her own condiments on pan con tuna, but the toppings are usually pretty simple, maybe Salsa Criolla (page 44) or just onions mixed with ají amarillo or rocoto pepper paste and mayonnaise. The jalapeños in this relish are my tribute to an American tuna sandwich, as you see the peppers so much here. I also really like all of the flavors together, with the light crunch of cucumbers against the more intense red onions, a little cilantro, and the jalapeños for a little heat.

Japanese and Persian cucumbers have fewer seeds and thinner skins than the chubby garden variety at many grocery stores, so you don't have to bother with peeling or seeding them. If you use a thick-skinned variety with a lot of seeds, peel and seed them before chopping.

½ cup finely chopped Japanese or Persian cucumbers
½ cup finely chopped red onion
About ⅓ bunch finely chopped fresh cilantro, leaves and top two-thirds of the stems
½ to 1 medium jalapeño, seeded and finely chopped
3 tablespoons extra-virgin olive oil
¼ teaspoon finely ground black pepper
¼ teaspoon kosher salt, or to taste

Toss together all of the ingredients in a medium bowl, adding more or less jalapeño to taste. Taste, and add more salt as needed. Serve the relish right away.

ATÚN (TUNA)

My mom could turn every last piece of any meat, fish, or poultry we were lucky enough to have on the table into something good to eat. I think it is even more *importante* with fish like tuna to use as much as you can.

Tuna is an amazing fish, incredibly engineered and as efficient as a race car, with a delicate, buttery flavor and texture that almost melts on your tongue. Bluefin is the equivalent of the Incan gold of the species and the most prized for sushi. The best-quality fish can fetch hundreds of thousands of dollars, especially in Japan. All that incredible flavor comes at another high price: Environmental experts say bluefin will likely disappear in our lifetime.

There are other top-quality tuna options for sushi-style dishes. Bigeye in particular has an excellent flavor, both cooked and raw. It is the tuna I use most often. There are still some overfishing issues, but you can more easily find sustainable options. The Monterey Bay Aquarium's Seafood Watch is a good resource. Even still, we need to show our respect for the whole animal.

Once, I walked in on one of my sous chefs cleaning a large, beautiful whole tuna. She had all of the scraps off to one side, destined for the trash bin (tuna meat is so dark, the head, tail, and skeleton don't make very clean-tasting fish stock). This was a super-fresh fish—even the blood was still glistening. I gathered up the bloodiest parts of the skeleton, rinsed them in a colander to wash away all of the impurities, and slowly cooked down the blood with soy sauce, rocoto peppers, ginger, and sugar to make a soft, gummy candy (a preparation that I learned at a Japanese restaurant in London). My chefs loved it, and the "blood" candy was a good lesson that there are *no excusas* for letting anything go to waste. With good-quality ingredients, there is always something tasty that you can make. Worst-case scenario, at least you tried to make something new with an ingredient that would have gone in the trash anyway.

Trimming tuna: For tiraditos or any other sushi-style dishes, you want the best, nonmarbled cuts of the fish. The meat should look uniformly bright red, with very little white sinew. Sometimes, even a good steak from the fish market has a few sinewy sections that look more like a marbled beef steak. Cut those pieces off the fish and save all of the scraps. If you are trimming a skin-on fillet, scrape off the bits of flesh still clinging to the skin with the blade of a sharp knife, and save the tasty scrapings for pan con tuna or as a causa topping (see pages 73 and 101).

Gather up all of your trimmings and scrapings, and chop them again. For a superfine texture, like when making tiny one-bite cocktail toasts, I press the fish through a food mill or ricer. As you fold the tuna trimmings into mayonnaise or whatever other ingredients you are using, the tuna almost melts into the dressing.

CEVICHES, TIRADITOS Y CAUSAS

PERUVIAN SUSHI BAR

THE BEST SEAFOOD IS NOT COMPLICATED. INTERESTING, YES, BUT NOT FUSSY.

Peruvians have long appreciated that idea. Ceviche is probably the most famous dish in Peru, the place where the lime juice–based raw fish dish was born. Tiraditos are a lot like Japanese sashimi or Italian carpaccio, only the raw fish is typically lightly seared and served with different sauces. Like ceviche, they are a good example of locals making use of the top-quality ingredients that were right in front of them (for more on that folklore, see page 79).

Traditional causas (chilled potato casseroles topped with chicken salad or similar everyday toppings) aren't usually included in the same sentence as ceviches and tiraditos, but I tend to think of them on the same plane. Like tiraditos and ceviches, there were so many cultural influences over the years in each causa variation—Incan, Spanish, Japanese, and more. It's one of the things I love about Peruvian food. You can almost taste the different cultures all *mixto*, mixed, together in whatever you are eating.

The recipes in this chapter are my version of those ceviches, tiraditos, and causas, often with more of a Japanese influence than you usually find in Peru. Many are seafood based, as to be expected with tiraditos and ceviches, but these days, I also appreciate a vegetable tiradito (and always, a classic chicken causa). Sometimes, the simplest dishes are the most fun palettes for experimenting with unexpected flavors.

LECHE DE TIGRE
TIGER'S MILK

MAKES ABOUT 1 CUP

Other than very fresh, top-quality fish, *leche de tigre* is the most important component in any ceviche. People say the name comes from the sauce's purported aphrodisiac qualities. It has a powerful, lime juice "bite" that some say is so good, it is hard to stop drinking the "tiger's milk." There is another story that I will keep to myself.

Any extra tiger's milk is often served in a glass alongside the seafood. You drink it down quickly, like a shot of hard alcohol to clean your palate after the meal (ceviche is typically ordered together with a big helping of battered and fried mixed fish). In the old days, you would just pick up the bowl to drink the juice after you finished, like sipping milk from a cereal bowl. I'm guessing ceviche shop owners got tired of kids like me spilling their leche de tigre all over the floor, but for me, those last messy sips are still one of the best parts of ceviche.

The ingredients vary by region and by ceviche chef, but lime juice is always the base. Regardless, to make a good leche de tigre, the ingredients need to be very cold. Once you have pureed the base ingredients, you have to pour the lime juice into the blender very slowly, with the motor running to emulsify the sauce, the same way you add olive oil to make mayonnaise. Use the best-looking pieces of fish for the ceviche, and save any trimmings or end pieces for the leche de tigre. Don't make the sauce more than an hour or two before you plan to use it. The lime juice will "cook" the pureed fish in the sauce, so the sauce will lose its bright, fresh flavor and taste like it has been baked (one of my biggest pet peeves with bad ceviche). This is also why all of your ingredients need to be cold before you make the sauce. If you do make the leche de tigre an hour or two ahead, be sure to keep it refrigerated.

The variations that follow are my takes on the different types of the sauce that you'll find in Peru to go with different seafood dishes (or, in some regions of the country, they simply use different peppers). In California, my regulars asked me to come up with a vegetarian version of ceviche—no small challenge with a raw fish–based dish. But I must admit, even as a die-hard (fish) ceviche fan, I really love the Blackened Eggplant Ceviche (page 87) that came out of that experiment.

2 tablespoons roughly chopped firm white-fleshed fish, such as corvina, paiche, striped bass, yellowtail, or halibut

1 large or 2 small cloves garlic, quartered

1 (½-inch) piece fresh ginger, peeled and roughly chopped

¼ large stalk celery (tender top end), thinly sliced, plus a few leaves, if you have them

2 tablespoons roughly chopped red onion hearts (see page 45) or red onions

¾ cup fresh lime juice (from about 6 limes)

1½ tablespoons kosher salt

About 5 small ice cubes

In a blender, combine the fish, garlic, ginger, celery, onion, and a few tablespoons of the lime juice and puree until the ingredients are well combined. With the blender running, add the salt, then very slowly pour in the remaining lime juice so the sauce emulsifies. With the blender still running, add the ice cubes a few at a time until the sauce is smooth and frothy. Use immediately, or refrigerate the leche de tigre for up to 1 hour, or 2 hours if you really must.

VARIACIONES:

Rocoto Leche de Tigre
Add 1 to 1½ tablespoons rocoto paste, to taste, when pureeing the fish and vegetables.

Ají Amarillo Leche de Tigre
Add 1 to 1½ tablespoons ají amarillo paste, to taste, when pureeing the fish and vegetables.

Leche de Tigre Vegetariano
Omit the fish and add 1 tablespoons rocoto paste, 1 tablespoon tamari, and 1½ teaspoons sesame oil when pureeing the vegetables.

THE FOLKLORE OF CEVICHE, TIRADITOS & CAUSAS

If you ask a local about traditional Peruvian dishes, be ready to listen to a story or two, especially when it comes to tiraditos, ceviches, and causas.

Ceviche

Ceviche is the most well-known dish, and the one with the most difficult roots to trace. At its most basic, raw fish is served in a lime juice–based sauce called leche de tigre. Two types of corn—crispy, popped Cancha (page 46) and tender boiled choclo corn (page 28)—are usually served alongside, with crunchy, red onion–based Salsa Criolla (page 44) on top.

Today, the word is sometimes spelled *seviche*, but more commonly along the coast, you see ceviche or *cebiche* painted on a sign out front of a little seaside café. In Peru, locals say the version with a "b" evolved from English speakers who would ask for the "sea-beach" dish served on the beach that they'd heard was so good. There is also a Quechua (which the Incas spoke, as do many locals today) word for a dish called *siwichi*, but the name probably comes from somewhere else.

Some historians trace modern ceviche to the fish preparations of the Incas even earlier, to the Moche, the dominant civilization in northern Peru from the early second to around the eighth century. They supposedly preserved raw fish with fermented juices and ate it with local ají peppers, which isn't all that different from partially "cooking" raw fish in lime juice (modern ceviches also use various ají peppers for spice). The dish developed into today's version when the Spanish colonists brought those limes, along with other now local ingredients, to South America in the fifteenth and sixteenth centuries.

There is also a practical story behind modern ceviches. Before refrigerators, fishermen delivered their predawn catch to restaurants during the first few hours of daylight. To keep the fish from spoiling in the heat, restaurants had to serve the fish by midday, so the *cevicherias* were only open for lunch. Today, even with modern-era refrigeration, many still only keep daylight hours. In Lima, you'll also see the *carretillas*, pushcarts, that ceviche vendors use to make a quick batch on the spot. I actually prefer to eat ceviche at night, for a light and refreshing supper.

Tiraditos

The folklore around tiraditos centers around local *pescadores*, fishermen. When they came in from their early morning fishing runs, they would supposedly slice off thin strips of fish as they cleaned their catch for snacks. They tossed the raw fish strips onto the hot rocks along the coastline for a few seconds to barely sear the fish and ate the fish right there, with a squeeze of lime juice.

My guess is the dish likely evolved in home kitchens. Still, I've always liked the fisherman story, and the word *tiradito* refers to the Spanish verb *tirar*, or "to throw," so who knows, maybe there is some truth there.

Causas

Causas are chilled, layered potato casseroles with a thick spread of smashed avocados, then often chicken or tuna salad, or whatever leftovers are around, on top. In the most traditional versions, you can count on some sort of decorative topping—pot luck casserole art.

The history varies depending on whom you ask, but *kausay*, the Quechua word for "existence" or "sustenance of life," goes back to pre-Columbian times. The word may not have even directly referred to causas, but to me, they show an enduring appreciation of potatoes.

In a lot of ways, causas today serve the same social and crowd-feeding function as potato salads in the American South, only the Peruvian version is more of a complete dish. I can't say that I am still drawn to many of those old-school flavors, but I will always have a soft spot for the leftover chicken and canned tuna versions. You may even spot a few riding shotgun in Lima on *mototaxis* (converted motorcycles with bench seats in back for passengers) dressed up in their Sunday potato-garnish finest and headed to a family gathering.

CLASSIC CEVICHE "CREOLE" WITH ROCOTO TIGER'S MILK

SERVES
4
AS A
MAIN
DISH

Ceviche criollo, Creole-style ceviche, is one of the most classic styles of ceviche. It is a variation on the *ceviche de carretillas* that street vendors quickly mix up to order in their little pushcarts with rocoto paste instead of the fresh peppers (rocoto peppers are a very spicy pepper typically used in traditional ceviches). You could call it (really good) fast-food ceviche, though ceviche is already pretty quick to make. *Criollo* is a reference to Creoles, locals of Spanish descent, who were considered higher ranking in the old Peruvian class system than those of purely local blood. It also refers to the melting pot of foods that evolved in Peru after the Spanish came with not just Spanish influences, but African, Chinese, Japanese, Italian, and so many more.

As with the other ceviches, use whatever firm, non-oily white-fleshed fish looks good at the market, and be sure to get a little extra to make your Rocoto Leche de Tigre (page 78). The amount of rocoto pepper paste in this recipe is pretty light. If you like your ceviches extra-spicy, go for it and stir in a little more of the pepper paste.

½ medium red onion, heart removed (use it to make Leche de Tigre, page 78)
1 pound firm white-fleshed fish such as corvina, striped bass, yellowtail, paiche, or halibut, cut into generous 1½-inch cubes (about 2 cups) and well chilled
About 1 cup Rocoto Leche de Tigre (page 78), well chilled
Kosher salt
Pureed garlic (page 37), as desired
About 1½ cups choclo (see page 28)
2 handfuls (about ½ cup) Cancha (page 46; optional)
¼ bunch fresh cilantro, roughly chopped, or a small handful of roughly chopped celery leaves or whole micro greens

1 Slice the onion "a la pluma" (see page 45) and set aside. In a medium bowl, combine the fish and rocoto leche de tigre. Use your fingers to gently toss the fish in the sauce until well coated, add the onion, and toss again. Be careful not to break up the pieces of fish. Taste the ceviche and adjust the seasonings by tossing the seafood with more salt and a little pureed garlic, if you like. Make it your own.

2 Spoon the ceviche into the center of each of four wide, shallow serving bowls. Divide the choclo and cancha (if using) among the plates, setting the choclo to one side of the ceviche and the crunchy cancha on the opposite side. Sprinkle the cilantro on top. Serve *inmediatamente*.

SELECTING FISH FOR CEVICHE

In Peru, ceviche is made from fish like corvina and *lenguado*, sole, or whatever came in from the fishermen that day. You can find corvina at some seafood markets in the United States but you can use any firm, white-fleshed fish. Striped bass, yellowtail, paiche, and halibut are all good. But not every fish can or should be made into ceviche. As a general rule, look for the same type and quality of fish you might use to make sashimi, as it's essentially being eaten raw (although the acid in the limes very lightly "cooks" or texturally changes the fish). Don't use oily fish like black cod or Chilean sea bass, which are too firm to serve raw and have a much better texture when cooked. The same goes for tiraditos. The exception are fish with darker meat like salmon and tuna, which both make good sushi and also good tiraditos. The fish flesh is oily, but in a buttery way, and both almost melt in your mouth when served raw.

MIXED SEAFOOD CEVICHE WITH AJÍ AMARILLO TIGER'S MILK

SERVES 4 AS A MAIN DISH

Ceviche mixto is the most traditional Peruvian ceviche, made with whatever mixed fish was caught that day. Use this recipe more as a guide and choose whatever is the best-looking seafood you find at the market, but stay away from oily fish (see sidebar, opposite). Keep a bag of choclo, the Peruvian corn served with ceviche, in the freezer and plenty of limes on hand, and you can have an incredible lunch on the table in a few minutes.

I like to very quickly blanch scallops and squid before using them in ceviche so you get a contrasting texture with the raw fish (squid, like octopus, should always be partially cooked before being eaten). A fast dip in boiling water is all they need. Shrimp you need to cook a little longer. Cancha, the crunchy Andean popped corn kernels, and camote, boiled sweet potato, are the traditional garnishes for ceviche. (I don't always include sweet potato, but if you boil some for another dish, chill and slice the leftover and tuck a few pieces alongside the fish.) In Peru, you also always find choclo, the giant white corn kernels, alongside. Together, they round out all the other flavors and textures dancing around in the ceviche, but it would be a shame to skip making ceviche just because you don't have them around. The seafood will still be delicious on its own.

Whole calamari with the tentacles give the ceviche a great texture contrast, but you can use the rings. Cilantro is the traditional garnish for ceviche, but lately I've been loving the baby leaves from stalks of celery or micro greens. The more delicate flavors are really nice with the fish.

Kosher salt

4 jumbo sea scallops, or 10 to 12 smaller bay scallops

3 ounces whole squid bodies and tentacles, bodies cut into ¼-inch rings and tentacles cut into 2 or 3 pieces if large, or about ½ cup sliced squid rings

4 extra-large or 8 medium-large shrimp, peeled and deveined but tails intact, butterflied if large (see page 123)

½ medium red onion, heart removed (use it to make Leche de Tigre, page 78)

1 pound firm white-fleshed fish such as corvina, striped bass, yellowtail, paiche, or halibut, cut into generous 1½-inch cubes (about 2 cups) and well chilled

About 1 cup Ají Amarillo Leche de Tigre (page 78), well chilled

Pureed garlic (page 37), as desired

About 1½ cups choclo (see page 28; optional)

A few handfuls of Cancha (page 46; optional)

¼ bunch fresh cilantro, roughly chopped, a small handful of roughly chopped celery leaves, or a small handful of micro greens

1 Fill a large bowl with ice and water (use plenty of ice). Fill a medium saucepan halfway with water, add about 1 teaspoon salt, and bring the water to a boil.

2 Put the scallops in a strainer with a handle, lower the strainer into the water, and immediately remove the strainer from the water. Transfer the scallops to the prepared ice bath. Return the water to a boil and quickly blanch the squid in the same way. Return the water to a boil one more time, drop the shrimp directly into the water, and cook until the flesh barely begins to turn white all over, at least 30 seconds or up to 1 minute, depending on how big they are. Drain the shrimp and immediately add them to the ice bath. Let the seafood chill in the ice bath for a few minutes, then transfer them to paper towels to lightly dry. Use the blanched seafood immediately, or transfer to a covered container and refrigerate for up to 1 hour.

3 To make the ceviche, slice the onion "a la pluma" (see page 45) and set aside. In a medium bowl, combine the raw fish, blanched scallops, squid, and shrimp, and the ají amarillo leche de tigre. Use your fingers to gently toss the seafood in the sauce until well coated, add the onion, and toss again. Be careful not to break up the pieces of fish. Taste the ceviche and adjust the seasonings by tossing the seafood with salt and a little pureed garlic, if you like. Make it your own.

4 Spoon the ceviche into the center of each of four wide, shallow serving bowls. If using, spoon the choclo and cancha on one side of each bowl, and scatter the cilantro on top. Serve *inmediatamente*.

CEVICHE WITH CRISPY FRIED CALAMARI & AJÍ AMARILLO TIGER'S MILK

SERVES
4
AS A
MAIN
DISH

If you go to a cevicheria (sometimes spelled *cebicheria*) in Peru, you'll see the locals ordering *jalea mixta*, a platter of fried mixed seafood, with their ceviche. You take a bite of one and then a bite of the other. The tangy, raw seafood and the hot, crunchy, fried seafood are perfect together. This ceviche is my version of both of those dishes in one.

Ask for whole baby squid tentacles or the tentacles from bigger squid at your seafood market. When fried, the tentacles curl up and become extra crispy on the outside and tender on the inside. If you can't find them, the presliced rings from the squid bodies also work. The potato starch in the batter keeps them on the lighter side, so don't expect these squid to get as dark as some fried seafood.

Canola or other vegetable oil, for frying
½ cup all-purpose flour
½ cup potato starch or cornstarch
¾ teaspoon kosher salt, or more as needed
¾ teaspoon freshly ground black pepper
1 large egg
1 tablespoon milk or water
6 ounces squid tentacles, cut into 2 or 3 pieces if large, or whole calamari bodies, cut into ¼-inch rings, or a mix of both (about 1 cup)
½ medium red onion, heart removed (use it to make Leche de Tigre, page 78)
1 pound firm white-fleshed fish such as corvina, striped bass, yellowtail, paiche, or halibut, cut into generous 1½-inch cubes (about 2 cups) and well chilled
About 1 cup Ají Amarillo Leche de Tigre (page 78), well chilled
Pureed garlic (page 37), as desired
¼ bunch fresh cilantro, roughly chopped, a small handful of roughly chopped celery leaves, or a small handful of micro greens

1 In a medium, deep saucepan, heat 2½ to 3 inches of oil over medium-high heat until it registers 350°F on a deep-fry thermometer, or fill a deep fryer with the recommended amount of oil and set the temperature to 350°F.

2 Mix together the flour, potato starch, salt, and pepper in a large bowl. (Use a bowl large enough so the calamari doesn't stick together when you bread it.) Crack the egg into a small bowl and whisk it with the milk. Toss the calamari first in the egg mixture, shake off the excess, and then in the flour mixture. Leave the calamari in the bowl with the flour.

3 Use a frying thermometer, or sprinkle a little flour in the oil to test the temperature. The flour should bubble nicely (if the oil smokes or the bubbles foam up, reduce the heat). When the oil is hot, toss the calamari around in the flour mixture one more time so all the sides are well coated. Use your fingers to separate the calamari tentacles and rings into individual pieces. Fry the calamari in two or three batches, depending on the size of your pot, until the crust is light golden brown and the bubbles in the frying pot slow down and become noticeably smaller, 2½ to 3 minutes. Transfer the fried calamari to a paper towel–lined plate and season with salt. If there is a lot of extra batter in the pot after your first batch, use a skimmer to fish some of it out between batches.

4 While the calamari is frying, slice the onion "a la pluma" (see page 45) and set aside. Combine the fish and leche de tigre in a medium bowl. Use your fingers to gently toss the fish in the sauce until well coated, then add the onion and toss again. Be careful not to break up the pieces of fish. Taste the ceviche and adjust the seasonings, if needed, by tossing the fish with more salt and a little pureed garlic, depending on what you like. Make it your own.

5 Spoon the fish mixture and leche de tigre sauce into the center of each of four wide, shallow serving bowls and sprinkle the cilantro on top. Put the calamari in a medium bowl to pass at the table. Serve *inmediatamente*.

SHOPPING FOR MARISCOS (SEAFOOD)

During summer vacations when I was a kid, I always looked forward to visiting Ana Maria, one of my older sisters who lived in Chimbote, a port city north of Lima that is still one of Peru's largest fishing centers.

It's a beautiful place with boats bobbing in the marina and the Andes jutting up in the background like on a postcard. The beach was 4 to 5 kilometers (around 3 miles) from my sister's house, but it wasn't hard to convince a friend to walk all the way down there with me to find lunch. We'd reach our hands into the sea to pluck off the tiny clams clinging to the rocks. We washed off any grit right there in the seawater and piled up the clams, dozens of them, in a bucket for the trip home. The ocean had already done all of the hard work, so the clams only needed a few squeezes of lime juice, ají amarillo peppers, and salt. We'd eat them straight out of the bucket—instant ceviche. (And we'd pile on the hot peppers just to see who could take the heat.) To me, that's what eating the freshest raw seafood is all about.

Today, it's not always as easy to source the best-quality seafood. But the more time you spend around it, you begin to notice the subtle differences in good- versus fantastic-tasting seafood. In my experience, the best-tasting fish and shellfish were treated with the *respeto*, respect, they deserved during life and in death. That respect needs to go all the way up the chain of command, from those who (hopefully) harvested the seafood sustainably, on to the fishmonger, and finally to us.

Unfortunately, choosing seafood that is *fantástico* isn't always as easy as asking your fishmonger for the freshest catch of the day. Here are a few tips.

Find a fishmonger you trust.

It's easy to be drawn in to the beautiful seafood in the cases, but observe the fish purveyors. A good fishmonger, like a good chef, is one who is proud to be a teacher. Look for someone who is inspired by your questions, not just interested in making a sale. How do they handle the seafood? Fish is not a firm and tough protein like beef. If handled roughly, it can fall apart. A good fishmonger will place, not slap, a whole fish on the counter to be cleaned and filleted. Back home, store the fish properly to keep the flavor and texture at its peak (see page 86).

Seafood should look vibrant and healthy, and should not have a strong "fishy" smell.

A common misconception is that anything hours out of the sea will taste incredible. It will be "fresh," yes, but even fish caught the same day you buy it may not taste as good as one that is three days out of the sea. Fish and shellfish should have a color that says, "I was healthy, and hopefully, happy, when I was alive." Beyond how the fish was handled after it was killed, the conditions of its tank (if farm-raised) or the oceans or rivers it grew up in (whether they were polluted or relatively clean) are key. Even fish and shellfish that are white or pale in color, like paiche, cod, and scallops, should look bright and vibrant. If you are buying a whole fish, touch the skin. It should be firm, not give too much, with a bright color to both the skin and eyes.

Frozen seafood is not necessarily lesser quality than fresh.

Some of the best-quality seafood is flash-frozen shortly after being fished or harvested, especially shrimp, scallops, and fish that isn't local. They often taste "fresher" than never-frozen fish and shellfish that have sat in a fishmonger's case for days, and you can thaw the seafood whenever you need it. (Granted, with today's fish packaging regulations, it can be difficult to know which frozen seafood is the best quality, but try different brands to see which you trust.) Shellfish like mussels and crustaceans like lobsters and crabs are an exception. In general, they should still be alive when you buy them.

How to Store Fish and Shellfish

FRESH FISH

If your fishmonger did not already fillet the fish, clean the fish soon after you get home. Oxygen causes the fish's flesh to break down more quickly, so I like to wrap fillets in plastic to keep out the oxygen. If the fish is of good quality and kept in the refrigerator, it should stay fresh tasting for two days, maybe longer.

To store fish fillets: Place individual fish fillets or large chunks of fish meat on a very lightly dampened piece of paper towel and wrap it snugly in a piece of plastic wrap. Fold the plastic around the fish a few times, like making a cocoon, so the fish is securely enclosed.

FRESH SHELLFISH

Unlike fish, live mollusks like mussels, clams, and oysters, and crabs and lobsters need oxygen to breathe. They should never be submerged in water, stored in a sealed container, or covered with plastic wrap. To extend the shelf life of crustaceans like lobsters, I sometimes blanch them a day or two before I need them. (Remove the meat from the shells and discard the shells.) You can refrigerate the lobster meat for up to two days.

To store shellfish: Refrigerate live shellfish in a bowl or a large, shallow baking dish loosely covered with a moist paper towel. Use them as soon as possible, preferably the same day. Be sure to discard any mussels or clams that do not open after they have been cooked.

FROZEN SEAFOOD

The best way to thaw frozen seafood is in a salted ice bath for six to eight hours in the refrigerator, or overnight, if you have the time. Add enough salt to the water so you can taste the salt but the water isn't as salty as the ocean, especially with tuna and other dark fish. (The salt helps bring out the vibrant color of the fish, which tends to fade.) You can also thaw fish or shellfish more quickly in an ice bath at room temperature. As the seafood thaws, change the water two or three times so it is always clean. You don't want the fish or shellfish to pick up any off flavors from the liquid the flesh releases as it thaws—and we all enjoy a clean bath.

BLACKENED EGGPLANT CEVICHE WITH VEGETARIAN TIGER'S MILK

SERVES
4
AS AN APPETIZER OR SIDE

If I told my friends in Peru that I served a vegetarian (actually, vegan) ceviche at my restaurants in Los Angeles, they would laugh. There isn't such a thing as ceviche without fish, but life is a little different in California. And I have to say, this is one of my favorite dishes. Eggplant gets insanely smoky when you char it until the skin is black as the night and the flesh is so tender it almost melts. The texture is similar to raw fish, and eggplant happens to pair really well with the tamari, lime juice, and other bold ingredients in the vegetarian leche de tigre. I love the flavor contrast with the spicy rocoto peppers and tangy lime juice in the vegetarian leche de tigre, and the "pop" of crispy quinoa on top for a different texture. You could serve the "ceviche" as an appetizer or a side dish, or for a dinner party—unlike fish ceviches, you can plate this a little in advance without worrying that it will spoil.

2 medium Japanese or Chinese eggplants or 1 American (globe) eggplant (1 pound), grilled or roasted and charred (see page 186)

About 1 cup Vegetarian Leche de Tigre (page 78), well chilled

Coarsely ground sea salt

2 scallions, white and green parts, thinly sliced on an angle

Good-quality extra-virgin olive oil, for drizzling

A few teaspoons crispy quinoa (see sidebar, page 201; optional)

Grilled or toasted crusty sliced bread or crostini, for serving

1 If using Japanese or Chinese eggplant, cut the eggplant into 3 meaty sections so you have several large chunks. Chop larger globe eggplants into generous 1½-inch cubes.

2 Spoon a generous ¼ cup of the leche de tigre into four wide, shallow serving bowls. Arrange the eggplant slices in the center of each bowl or pile up the cubed eggplant in a pyramid shape. Taste and season with a little salt if needed. Scatter the scallions over the eggplant, drizzle each serving generously with the olive oil, and sprinkle the crispy quinoa on top (if using). Serve the bread alongside the eggplant to sop up the extra leche de tigre sauce.

CLASSIC YELLOWTAIL SASHIMI-STYLE WITH AJÍ AMARILLO–LIME SAUCE

MAKES
8
SLICES

SERVES
2
AS AN
APPETIZER
OR

4
AS COCKTAIL
STARTERS

A little heat brings all of the flavors to the surface in whatever you are cooking. With tiraditos, either quickly blast the fish slices with a cooking torch, or heat the back of a spoon over a gas burner and move it quickly over the top of the slices to barely cook the outer edges of the fish. Using a cooking torch really is easier, and you don't have the trouble of the spoon sometimes sticking to the fish. The center of each fish slice should be rare, with a sushilike texture.

8 (¼-inch-thick) slices firm white-fleshed fish such as corvina, striped bass, yellowtail, paiche, or halibut, from a center-cut fillet (see page 80)
½ teaspoon pureed garlic (page 37)
½ teaspoon pureed ginger (page 37)
2 teaspoons sesame oil
2 teaspoons extra-virgin olive oil
About ½ cup Ají Amarillo–Lime Sauce (recipe follows), well chilled
2 teaspoons soy sauce
A few teaspoons wasabi tobiko or finely diced fresh cilantro stems (see sidebar)

1 Neatly arrange the fish slices side by side on one large or four small plates with about ½ inch of space between each. If you are using a large, round serving platter, you can arrange the fish in a circle, like the rays of the sun, or use a long, rectangular plate and arrange the fish down the middle.

2 In a small ramekin, use your index finger or the back of a small spoon to mix together the garlic and ginger purees. Make a single swipe on the top side of each slice of fish with your finger, dipping it lightly back in the paste every time.

3 Swirl together the sesame and olive oils in a small ramekin and drizzle about ½ teaspoon on top of each slice of fish. If using a cooking torch, quickly sear each slice of fish for no more than 2 to 3 seconds each with the torch. The fish should barely begin to turn white on the top. Or, heat a large, stainless-steel spoon directly over the flame of a gas burner until scalding hot.

(Choose an older spoon that you aren't attached to, in case it bends or chars.) Quickly move the back of the hot spoon over the surface of a slice of fish, moving the spoon continuously so it doesn't stick to the fish. Reheat the spoon and repeat with the remaining slices of fish.

4 Drizzle the ají amarillo–lime sauce on top of the fish, using about a scant tablespoon per slice, followed by the soy sauce. Sprinkle the wasabi tobiko on top. Serve *inmediatamente*.

AJÍ AMARILLO–LIME SAUCE

Makes about 1 cup, enough for 2 large tiradito plates

This sauce is the base for both the yellowtail and paiche tiraditos on page 91. Make one batch and try them both.

⅓ cup ají amarillo paste (page 34), or as needed
⅓ cup fresh lime juice
⅓ cup extra-virgin olive oil

Whisk together all the ingredients. Cover and refrigerate for up to 2 days.

"POOR MAN'S CAVIAR"

In Japan, "poor man's caviar" refers to tobiko, or flying fish eggs. In my kitchen, finely diced cilantro stems share the same honor. Both are inexpensive ways to give a dish a contrasting "pop" of texture. The natural, light orange tobiko eggs are my favorite, but use the green, wasabi-infused eggs when you want a spicy blast.

Finely chopped cilantro has a very different flavor than fish eggs, but brings a similar "pop" of texture to so many dishes. The key is to chop the stems as finely as you can.

PAICHE SASHIMI-STYLE WITH AJÍ AMARILLO–TAMARI SAUCE & SERRANO CHILES

MAKES **8** SLICES

SERVES **2** AS AN APPETIZER OR **4** AS COCKTAIL STARTERS

Paiche is a lot like the river in which it lives. Describing the prehistoric fish or the Amazon to those who have never seen either is not easy, but both are amazing. Paiche was on the endangered list not so long ago, considered doomed and near extinction. Today, the fish is back, thriving in its old neighborhood—the Amazon jungle—thanks to sustainable farming (see page 93), and is an important part of modern Peruvian cuisine.

In this dish, I really like the way crisp vegetables contrast with the texture of the tender fish. Soaking the cabbage and red onion in cold water makes them extra crispy. For the crispiest vegetables, you need to change the water several times. Slice them as thin as you can, so they are almost shredded. The bolder flavors in tamari are best with this tiradito, but substitute soy sauce if that's all you have in the pantry.

About ⅓ cup very finely sliced green cabbage

About ⅓ cup "a la pluma" red onion (see page 45)

8 (¼-inch-thick) slices firm white-fleshed fish such as corvina, striped bass, yellowtail, paiche, or halibut, from a center-cut fillet (see page 80)

2 teaspoons sesame oil

2 teaspoons extra-virgin olive oil

1 tablespoon finely minced fresh cilantro leaves and tender top stems

About ½ cup Ají Amarillo–Lime Sauce (page 88), well chilled

2 teaspoons tamari, or 2½ teaspoons soy sauce, plus more for serving

½ small serrano chile, cut crosswise into 8 thin coins

1 Cut the finely sliced cabbage and red onion into bite-size pieces. Submerge the vegetables in a small bowl of very cold water for 15 minutes. Add ice if the water is not very cold, and change the water at least once. Neatly arrange the fish slices side by side on one large or four small plates with about ½ inch of space between each. If you are using a large, round serving platter, you can arrange the fish in a circle, like the rays of the sun, or use a long, rectangular plate and arrange the fish down the middle.

2 Swirl together the sesame and olive oils in a small ramekin and drizzle about ½ teaspoon on top of each slice of fish. If using a cooking torch, quickly sear each slice of fish for no more than 2 to 3 seconds. The fish should barely begin to turn white on top. Alternatively, heat a large stainless-steel spoon directly over the flame of a gas burner until scalding hot. Quickly move the back of the hot spoon over the surface of a slice of fish, moving the spoon continuously so it doesn't stick to the fish. Reheat the spoon over the gas flame and repeat with the remaining slices of fish.

3 Drain the cabbage and red onion and dry them off lightly with a paper towel. Return the vegetables to the bowl and toss them with the cilantro. In a small bowl, mix together the ají amarillo–lime sauce and tamari and drizzle the sauce on top of the fish, using about 1 tablespoon per slice. Neatly arrange 1 generous teaspoon of the cabbage–red onion salad in the middle of each slice of fish and top each mini salad with 1 serrano slice. Pile the remaining salad in the middle of the plate if you are using a round platter, or alongside the sliced fish if you are using rectangular platters. Drizzle a few drops of tamari all over the plate. Serve *inmediatamente*.

HOW TO SLICE RAW FISH SASHIMI-STYLE

It wasn't until I learned to properly cut fish sashimi-style that I appreciated how the simplest-looking tasks often require the most skill and focus.

Japanese sushi chefs use their kitchen knife almost like a blade or sword to make one clean, long slice that glides across the fish or meat. (Western-style butchering uses more of a chopping or sawing motion.)

If you are a fish-slicing novice, firm fish like yellowtail are a good place to start. Once you get the hang of the slicing motion, you'll be more confident to try it with more delicate fish. Remember, your most important tool is your knife. A Japanese sushi knife isn't long because it looks pretty, but because you need to use the whole blade when you slice through the fish. You can use any large knife; just be sure the blade is very sharp.

One 3- to 4-ounce fillet of fish (depending on the type and portion of the fish), cut into a rectangle about 3 inches long by 2 inches wide, will yield about 8 slices (2 appetizers or 4 smaller cocktail servings). You can serve tiraditos as starters, as I do at my restaurants, or as part of a light lunch or supper. Save any fish trimmings for Causas (page 101), or, if you are using tuna, Pan con Tuna (page 73).

1 Run a very sharp knife against the grain of the flesh from end to end to remove the skin, if needed.

2 Press two fingers firmly against one end of the fish fillet. Place the handle end of your knife blade at an angle with the other hand. Move the knife blade in one clean motion, from the handle end to the tip of the blade, to make a slice a generous ¼ inch thick.

3 If necessary, lightly pound thicker or uneven end cuts of fish between sheets of plastic wrap with the back of a spoon to make all the slices about the same size and thickness.

PAICHE

Paiche ("pye-chay") is truly a living fósil, *fossil.*

In the wild, the giant river fish dates to the Jurassic Period and can weigh up to several hundred pounds and reach 7 to 8 feet in length. Beyond being giant (and, I think, very beautiful), paiche is unusual in that it can also breathe air through lunglike tissue, which helps the fish survive during droughts. Those shallow muddy waters of the Amazon and the fish's large, lumbering size are also why it was considered unsalvageable from extinction as recently as twenty years ago. The fish became almost too easy for locals to hunt as their main protein source (you will still see paiche meat in various dried, shelf-stable forms at outdoor markets throughout the Amazon), and deforestation has unfortunately also destroyed the fish's habitat.

But like the American buffalo, sustainable farming has helped to save the paiche. Amazone, a paiche farm nestled in the small city of Yurimaguas (a few winding, mountain jungle hours outside of Tarapoto), farm-raises the ancient fish in several dozen river-adjacent pools on their property. Because the fish have lungs, the water does not need to be changed often, making it more conservation friendly (the paiche there are also only grown to around 25 pounds). The white-fleshed meat is incredibly versatile, with a subtle flavor and flesh that holds together well when cooked yet is also very tender, and has very few bones, which is handy for the chef. Like poultry, paiche has both lighter and darker meat, which makes it fun for playing around in the kitchen (both types of meat are interchangeable in recipes). It works well in everything from fried dishes (see page 66) to lightly seared preparations (see page 120) or baked, and even as ceviche—not bad for a fish that's been hanging out in the jungle for so long.

SWEET-AND-SOUR SALMON SASHIMI-STYLE WITH ORANGE-MISO SAUCE

MAKES 8 SLICES

SERVES 2 AS AN APPETIZER

OR

4 AS COCKTAIL STARTERS

I love the contrasting flavors and textures in this tiradito: sweet and sour, crunchy and soft. If you use a large, round plate and arrange the salmon in a circle, the slices look like the rays of the sun. The ponzu sauce really needs to be homemade (page 37). The jarred stuff sucks all the life out of fresh seafood. It is usually way overseasoned and heavy.

About ⅓ cup Rocoto Leche de Tigre (page 78), well chilled

1 tablespoon plus 1 teaspoon homemade ponzu (page 37)

8 (¼-inch-thick) slices salmon, from a center-cut fillet (see page 80)

2 generous tablespoons Blood Orange–Miso Sauce (recipe follows)

A few teaspoons very finely minced fresh chives or cilantro stems (see sidebar, page 88), for garnish

A few teaspoons crispy quinoa (see sidebar, page 201), for garnish (optional)

Good-quality extra-virgin olive oil

1 Mix together the leche de tigre and ponzu in a small dish and spoon the sauce on the bottom of one large or four small plates. Neatly arrange the fish slices on top of the sauce with about ½ inch of space between each slice. If you are using a large, round serving platter, you can arrange the fish in a circle, like the rays of the sun, or use a long, rectangular plate and arrange the fish down the middle.

2 Place 1 scant teaspoon of the blood orange–miso sauce in the center of each slice of fish. Lightly sprinkle the chives decoratively along one edge of the fish slices and sprinkle the quinoa (if using) on the opposite edge of each slice (or use more chives). Drizzle the olive oil lightly over the sauce and fish, and serve *inmediatamente*.

BLOOD ORANGE–MISO SAUCE

Makes a generous ¼ cup, enough for 2 large tiradito plates

You know a fruit with the same color as the bright red blood of a healthy, fresh-caught fish is going to be really good in a tiradito sauce. (If you can't find blood oranges, use regular oranges. It will still be very good.) This sauce doubles or triples well; just cook it a few minutes longer until it reduces by about half. Saikyo miso (see page 265) is worth seeking out for its subtle, balanced flavor, but more widely available shiromiso is a good substitute.

1 tablespoon ají amarillo paste (page 34)

1 tablespoon saikyo or shiro (white) miso

2 tablespoons sake

1 tablespoon fresh lime juice

3 tablespoons fresh blood orange juice

2 tablespoons mirin

Stir together the ají amarillo paste, miso, sake, and lime juice in a small saucepan. Add the orange juice and mirin and bring to a low boil over medium-high heat. Boil until the sauce has reduced by almost half, about 5 minutes. Remove from the heat, let cool completely, and refrigerate the blood orange–miso sauce for up to 3 days.

SEARED TUNA WITH SPICY PONZU SAUCE & APPLE-CUCUMBER RELISH

MAKES **8** SLICES

SERVES **2** AS AN APPETIZER OR

4 AS COCKTAIL STARTERS

I grew up eating mostly stir-fries and Chinese-style rice dishes, but I wasn't really exposed to the Japanese side of Peruvian cooking until I was a teenager. One day after school, a friend's mom, who was Japanese-Peruvian, made *pulpo* (octopus) tiraditos, a very traditional tiradito, with a spicy soy sauce as a snack for her houseful of rowdy boys. I went crazy for the sauce. When I asked her for the recipe, *mis amigos* thought it was so funny. ("Ricardo, you cook?") My friend's mom sent me to the Mercado de Surquillo, a very famous and huge old market in Lima, to buy something called "wasabi." I'd never heard of the Japanese horseradish with the strange name. I loved it, and still use wasabi in sauces whenever I can, like with this tuna.

In this recipe, the bold taste of wasabi in the spicy ponzu sauce works really well with the bigger flavors in tuna and the tangy sweetness of the green apple (my twist on cucumber relish). Lightly pan-searing a thick block of tuna before you slice it does the same work as using a cooking torch to sear the individual slices with hot oil in my other traditional tiradito recipes. You want good color and flavor on the outside of the tuna, but the inside should be rare, with a deep red color. If you don't have garlic chips it's not a deal-breaker, but they are really good.

1½ teaspoons honey

1½ tablespoons fresh lime juice

2 tablespoons finely diced unpeeled green apple

1 generous tablespoon finely diced unpeeled Persian or Japanese cucumber or peeled English cucumber

1 (4- to 5-ounce) center-cut piece tuna, trimmed into a rectangle about 4 inches long by 2 inches wide and 1½ inches thick

Kosher salt and freshly ground black pepper

A good drizzle of olive oil

About ¼ cup Spicy Ponzu Sauce (recipe follows)

8 garlic chips (page 37; optional)

Good-quality extra-virgin olive oil

1 If the honey has solidified, warm it in the microwave for a few seconds or on the stovetop. In a small bowl, stir together the honey and lime juice, then toss the apple and cucumber in the dressing. Refrigerate the apple-cucumber relish while you make the tiraditos.

2 Season the block of tuna generously on all sides with salt and pepper, as you would a beef steak. Fill a medium bowl with ice and water (use plenty of ice). Heat the oil in a medium skillet over high heat until very hot, about 2 minutes. Sear the tuna on one side until the flesh just begins to color, about 5 seconds if the oil is the right temperature. If it doesn't color quickly, remove the tuna from the pan and let the pan heat a little longer. Flip the tuna and repeat the searing process on the remaining three sides (do not sear the ends). Immediately transfer the fish to the ice bath. Let cool for no more than 1 minute, then lightly pat it dry on all sides with a paper towel. Place the tuna on a cutting board and slice it against the grain into 8 pieces (see page 92).

3 Spoon the spicy ponzu sauce on the bottom of one large or four small plates. Neatly arrange the fish slices on top of the sauce with about ½ inch of space between each slice. If you are using a large, round serving platter, you can arrange the fish in a circle, like the rays of the sun, or use a long, rectangular plate and arrange the fish down the middle.

4 Place 1 generous teaspoon of the apple-cucumber relish in the center of each slice of fish and, if desired, nestle 1 garlic chip on top of the relish. Drizzle the olive oil lightly over the fish slices and serve *inmediatamente*.

SPICY PONZU SAUCE

Makes about ½ cup, enough for 2 large tiradito plates

Homemade ponzu makes all the difference in the flavor of any sauce. It keeps for months in the fridge, and only gets better as it ages.

½ teaspoon ají amarillo paste (page 34)
¼ teaspoon wasabi paste
2 tablespoons homemade ponzu (page 37)
5 tablespoons Ají Amarillo Leche de Tigre (page 78)
About 1 tablespoon tamari or soy sauce
½ teaspoon sesame oil
1 teaspoon extra-virgin olive oil

Stir together the ají amarillo paste, wasabi paste, and ponzu in a small bowl until well combined. Add the leche de tigre, tamari, sesame oil, and olive oil and stir again. Cover and refrigerate the spicy ponzu sauce for up to 4 hours.

BRAISED OCTOPUS WITH ACEITUNA BOTIJA SAUCE & OLIVE TAPENADE

This recipe is my updated version of the classic octopus tiradito *pulpo al olivo*, or octopus with creamy Botija olive sauce. The first time I cooked octopus, I'd talked my way into running a catering gig in Lima for a couple hundred people. I overheard a guy asking if anyone knew a caterer for a convention he had coming up. I told him that sure, I had done catering gigs before, which was a complete lie, but I was a confident sixteen-year-old—or maybe *estúpido* is the better word.

I rounded up a couple of my friends, and we headed down to the docks where we bought the most *gigante* live octopus we could find. It had beady black eyes and looked like it would be more than happy, given the chance, to strangle all of us with its tentacles. The fisherman handed the pulpo over in a plastic sack, and we hailed a taxi and tossed it in the trunk. We were almost home when we heard the sirens of a police car. When our cabdriver pulled over, we all looked at each other. Which of us was the idiot who did something wrong? It turned out that the octopus was a little Houdini. It had escaped from the bag, and its tentacles were dangling out of the trunk. We shoved the octopus back into the bag, closed it *tightly* this time, and when we got home, fired up a huge pot of water and got that octopus into the pot *rápidamente*. I don't remember what I made with that octopus, only that the catering event was a success. Today, this is the octopus dish I would make to really impress the pulpo uninitiated at an event. Since you can boil and slice the octopus up to a day ahead, it's also very easy to assemble at the last minute.

¼ cup homemade ponzu (page 37)

1 tablespoon extra-virgin olive oil

8 (¼-inch-thick) slices octopus tentacle (3 to 4 ounces), blanched (see sidebar, page 100)

3 to 4 tablespoons Aceituna Botija Sauce (page 181)

About ¼ cup Botija Olive Tapenade (recipe follows)

1 small heirloom tomato, sliced into small wedges

4 or 5 thin slices Persian or Japanese cucumber, quartered

Small handful of arugula

1 Mix together the ponzu and olive oil in a small dish and spoon the sauce on the bottom of one large or four small plates. Neatly arrange the octopus slices on top of the sauce with about ½ inch of space between each slice. If you are using a large, round serving platter, you can arrange the octopus in a circle, like the rays of the sun, or use a long, rectangular plate and arrange the octopus down the middle.

2 Drizzle the aceituna Botija sauce on the octopus slices and place a small dollop (about 1 teaspoon) of the Botija olive tapenade in the center. Mound the tomatoes, cucumbers, and arugula in the center of the platter along with any remaining tapenade, or alongside each individual plate. Serve *inmediatamente*.

BOTIJA OLIVE TAPENADE

Makes about ½ cup, enough for 2 large tiradito plates

3 tablespoons extra-virgin olive oil

1 teaspoon fresh lime juice

1 teaspoon soy sauce

Generous pinch of salt and freshly ground black pepper

2 tablespoon finely chopped Peruvian Botija olives or Kalamata olives

2 tablespoons finely chopped freshly roasted or jarred red bell peppers

2 tablespoons minced shallots

Stir together the olive oil, lime juice, soy sauce, and salt and black pepper in a small bowl. Add the olives, roasted peppers, and shallots and toss all of the ingredients to combine. Use right away, or cover and refrigerate for up to 4 hours.

PREPARING PULPO
(OCTOPUS)

Octopus is somewhat of a foreign sea beast to some people. When cooked the right way, the octopus skin will be firm and a little chewy with tender meat inside, but it's a little trickier to cook than most seafood. The tentacles, which are muscles, will contract and turn rubbery if you cook them too quickly, so don't ever let the water boil vigorously.

You can also use a pressure cooker, which I tried for the first time while competing on a television cook-off show (we all learn new things when we are under kitchen pressure—literally). Ten minutes in a pressure cooker, followed by a 20 minute rest in the cooking water (with the pressure cooker still locked), and I had some of the best octopus I'd ever eaten. Fortunately, the judges liked it, too. I also always use the simple tenderizing techniques I learned from Japanese sushi chefs when I was in London. Most of the octopus you find today is sold frozen, usually only the tentacles, which are all you need. You can boil and slice the octopus up to a day before you plan to serve it.

To prepare octopus: Preheat the oven to 350°F. If using frozen tentacles, thaw them completely. Cut the tentacles into two or three sections if they are large. Fill a medium saucepan halfway with water, bring the water to a boil, then reduce the heat to maintain a simmer and add the octopus and 1 tablespoon salt. Simmer the octopus (don't let the water boil) until tender, 30 to 45 minutes, depending on the thickness of the tentacles. To test, prick the octopus with a knife. The skin will be firm, but when you cut through it, the middle of the tentacle should be much softer. Don't overcook the octopus or it will become rubbery. Drain, transfer the octopus to a baking sheet, and put it in the oven for 5 minutes to dry out completely. Remove the octopus from the oven and let cool completely.

Slice the tentacles at an angle, as when slicing other raw fish, only very subtly move your knife back and forth like the waves of the ocean as you slice. This will help tenderize the meat. To tenderize each slice further, make small, crosshatch slashes with a sharp knife on both sides of each piece. Don't go very deep—you just want to lightly score the surface of the flesh.

CHILLED POTATO CAKES

MAKES
ABOUT
6
CUPS

Peruvians have been cooking with native potatoes for thousands of years, so you might say we have our own mashed potato rules. Creamy, not light and fluffy, is the goal with causas, the potato base for Peruvian-style chilled casseroles. The key to causas is kneading the potatoes like pasta dough after you mash them up with ají amarillo paste, lime juice, and oil. Canola oil is what most people use, but I really prefer the flavor of olive oil. With help from the oil, the potatoes get a really incredible, almost silky texture. The potato "dough" holds its shape well when spread into a casserole dish or cut up into mini "sushi-style" causas, as I call them.

My mom smashed her *papas amarillas*, the yellow-fleshed potatoes used to make causas in Peru (here, I use red-skinned or any other waxy potatoes), the old-fashioned way, with a fork, so they were a little chunkier. I like to rice the potatoes to get the smoothest causas, but either way works. You need to mash the potatoes while they are still hot so they break down consistently. When they are barely cool enough to handle, really get in there and use the palms of your hands to work the potatoes for a few minutes. Be *paciente*—after a few minutes, the potato "dough" will become very smooth.

I go heavier on the salt in my causa bases to balance out the toppings, which I serve a little less seasoned, but do what you like. If spiciness is a problem, cut back on the ají amarillo paste. I used to add half as much pepper paste when my kids were little, but I don't think I'll be doing that much longer. Both have quickly become fiery little Peruvians.

3½ pounds red potatoes, scrubbed and peeled

3 tablespoons fresh lime juice

3 tablespoons ají amarillo paste, store-bought or homemade (page 34), or to taste

¾ cup extra-virgin olive oil, plus more for the pan

1 tablespoon kosher salt, or to taste

1 Halve the potatoes if they are small, or roughly chop larger potatoes into 1½-inch chunks. Place the potatoes in a large pot, cover them with water by a solid inch, and bring the water to a low boil over high heat. Boil the potatoes until very tender when pierced with a knife, 20 to 25 minutes, depending on the size of the potatoes. Drain the potatoes.

2 While the potatoes are still very warm, press them through a ricer or food mill into a large bowl, or put them in a large bowl and mash them with a potato masher or the back of a large fork until few lumps remain. Mix in the lime juice and ají amarillo paste, and use the palms of your hands to knead the potatoes for a minute or two. Turn the potatoes out onto a work surface, as I do, if you prefer or the bowl isn't large enough.

3 Make a well in the center of the potatoes, pour the olive oil in the center, and sprinkle the salt on top. Keep kneading the potatoes with the palms of your hands, like pasta dough, for about 5 minutes, or until the potatoes become almost silky. Taste and add a little more ají amarillo paste or salt, if you'd like. The potatoes should be nicely salted. Follow the instructions on page 103 for chilling and shaping the potatoes.

RECIPE CONTINUES

VARIACIÓNES

You can add flavor and color to your causa base. If you have a high-powered blender, the vegetables will puree to almost the consistency of paint. If not, they will be chunkier, but you'll still get good color.

Verde (Green)

Cut the quantity of potatoes down to 3 pounds. Blanch 2 bunches stemmed baby spinach, or one 10- to 12-ounce bag baby spinach, and squeeze it dry (see page 53, scallops a la parmesana). Puree the spinach in a blender with ¼ cup of the olive oil until very smooth. (If you don't have a high-powered blender, add a few additional tablespoons of olive oil if needed and stir a few times to get things moving.) In step 3, knead the remaining ½ cup olive oil into the potato base. When the potatoes are silky, knead the spinach puree into the potatoes for another minute or two until well combined and season with salt. Instead of fresh spinach, you can substitute ⅔ cup frozen spinach, thawed, cooked, and squeezed dry.

Rojo (Red)

Cut the quantity of potatoes down to 3 pounds. Roast 1 pound (about 4 medium) red beets, then peel and roughly chop them (see page 176). Puree the beets in a blender with ¼ cup of the olive oil until very smooth. (If you don't have a high-powered blender, add a few additional tablespoons of olive oil if needed, and stir a few times to get things moving.) In step 3, knead the remaining ½ cup olive oil into the potato base. When the potatoes are silky, knead the beet puree into the potatoes for another minute or two until well combined and season with salt. The color will vary depending on the potatoes. For a more intense reddish-purple color, add a few tablespoons of *chicha morada* (page 224), but only a little, or the punch will flavor the potatoes (my kids don't see this as a problem).

SHAPING CAUSAS

*I wouldn't be Peruvian if I didn't love causas, the Peruvian equivalent of
a chilled potato casserole with various toppings.*

Traditionally, even individual causas are usually pretty big, lasagna-size servings. You eat one, and you are full. Some of the toppings can also get pretty basic. I wanted fresher, lighter, and more unexpected flavors, so I came up with these small, bite-size causas that are more in line with sushi so people can taste several. As the chef, you can play around with different toppings. Use cookie cutters to make large molded causas or smaller bite-size shapes. (My daughter can cut out little pink potato hearts and stars with the beet causa base for what seems like all afternoon.) If you're short on time, there's always the old-school option: a Peruvian casserole. Once, I took a classic, casserole-style causa to a fancy chef's picnic, and everyone wanted to know about the "elegant" dish. My mom would have gotten a kick out of that.

You can top a casserole-style causa the day before you plan to serve it; just cover it well and keep it in the refrigerator (don't add vegetables that don't refrigerate well, like tomatoes, until just before serving). If you are making smaller, individual causas, it's best to top them within an hour or two of serving so the potato base doesn't dry out.

To make classic causas:

Lightly rub the bottom and sides of a 9 x 13-inch casserole dish with olive oil. With your hands, press the potatoes evenly into the dish and smooth the top with your hands or an offset spatula (with a casserole, it doesn't need to be perfectly smooth). Add whatever toppings you'd like, cover, and refrigerate for at least 6 hours or overnight. If you are using toppings like avocados that discolor or fresh seafood fillings, wait to add the toppings until serving the causa. Cut the casserole into generous squares and use a spatula to remove each causa (the first one can be tricky to remove—consider it a snack). **Serves 8 to 10 as a light main dish.**

To make sushi-style causas:

Lightly rub the bottom and sides of a large rimmed baking sheet with olive oil. With your hands, press the potatoes into the pan, starting at one edge, so you have a 10 x 12 inch rectangle about ¾ inch thick. The potatoes shouldn't reach all the way to the opposite side. Use an offset spatula to make a straight edge on the "open" end of the potatoes, then smooth the top as much as possible so they look nice when you add the toppings. Cover the baking sheet and refrigerate the causa base for at least 6 hours or up to 2 days. Slice the potatoes into 2 x 1-inch rectangles, or whatever size you'd like. To make panko-crusted causas (which need to be small to fry properly), cut the causas into 2 x 1-inch rectangles or use small cookie cutters to cut different-size rectangles and cutouts in each pan. To remove the causa base, start at the end of the rectangle that is not touching the edges of the pan and use an offset spatula to transfer the rectangles to a serving plate or work surface. Top each causa as you like. **The yield varies, but count on around 5 dozen 2 x 1-inch sushi-style causas or 3 to 4 dozen cut-out causas.**

To make larger molded causas:

Cover and refrigerate the causa base in a bowl for at least 6 hours or up to 2 days. Rub the inside of a ring mold very lightly with olive oil and place it on a serving plate. I use a 3-inch ring mold for a main-dish serving and smaller ring molds for appetizers. Use your fingers to press the causa base into the bottom of the mold so the potatoes come ¾ to 1 inch up the sides of the mold. Press down and smooth the top of the potatoes with your fingers or the back of a small spoon, spread the toppings all the way to the edges of the mold, and smooth them out nicely. Remove the ring mold. Swipe the inside with a few drops of olive oil before making more causas. **Serves about 18 as a light main course or side dish (using 3-inch ring molds), or more if you are making smaller causas.**

CAUSA SUSHI

The only trick to making good causas is you need to get in there and really knead the potatoes.

1 Mash the drained, cooked potatoes by hand or press them through a ricer. Mix in the other ingredients.

2 Leave the potato base in the bowl or turn it out onto a work surface, add the ají amarillo paste and lime juice, and knead the potatoes with the base of your hand for several minutes. Drizzle the olive oil on top and knead the potatoes for 2 to 3 minutes more, until smooth. (If you are making beet or spinach causas, add the puree and continue to knead until well incorporated.)

3 If making sushi-style or cut-out causas, spread the potato base on a rimmed baking sheet. If making molded causas, place the potato base in a bowl. Cover and refrigerate overnight.

4 Cut or mold the causas however you would like and add your toppings.

CAUSA OF LIMA

SERVES 8 TO 10 AS A MAIN DISH

There was almost always a *causa Limeña*, the specialty of Lima, on the table at our family gatherings, complete with my mom's retro black olive, hard-boiled egg, and cilantro design on top. Leftover chicken is the traditional topping, but I use crab when I want to make something special. If you'd like a thicker layer of the toppings, mold the base into a smaller casserole pan, or use only some of the shaped causas. *Mamá, te echo de menos.*

1 pound fresh lump crabmeat (about 2 generous cups), picked over, or shredded cooked chicken

⅓ to ½ cup mayonnaise, preferably Japanese

2 large ripe avocados, peeled (3 or 4 avocados, if you are making a casserole-style causa)

1 or 2 limes

Kosher salt

About 1 recipe causa base (page 101), pressed into a casserole pan and chilled, or shaped however you like (see page 103)

1 pint cherry or other small tomatoes, halved or quartered if large

Finely chopped fresh cilantro leaves, for garnish

1 In a medium bowl, gently toss together the crab with just enough mayonnaise to lightly moisten the meat. Try not to break up the large lumps of crab. In another bowl, use a fork to roughly mash the avocados. Squeeze in the juice of 1 lime and season with a pinch of salt, mix well, and add more lime juice to taste.

2 If you are making a casserole, spread the mashed avocado mixture over the potato base and scatter the crab salad on top. You can cover and chill the casserole overnight at this point, if you'd like. If you are making sushi-style or molded causas, divide the mashed avocado mixture and crab salad among them before serving.

3 To serve, scatter the tomatoes on top of the crab salad and gently press down on the tomatoes so they lightly adhere to the filling. Sprinkle the cilantro over the top, cut the causas if needed (for the casserole), and serve.

CAUSA LIMEÑA
(CAUSA OF LIMA)

When Peru went to war with Chile in the late 1800s, Lima was completely cut off from supply routes. Potatoes, limes, and ají amarillo peppers were supposedly the only foods available, so people mashed them up together "*por la causa*," or "for the cause," and refused to surrender. Or so the story goes about the causa Limeña, which is traditionally made with layers of the ají amarillo–spiced potato base, mashed avocado, chicken or tuna salad, another layer of potato, and olives and hard-boiled egg on top.

That might be stretching the truth a little. The word *causa* likely comes from *kausay*, the pre-Columbian, Quechuan word for "existence" or "sustenance of life" (the ancient potato dish likely morphed into more of a casserole topped with other ingredients after the Spanish arrived). But I'm siding with my hometown's "cause."

WESTERN-STYLE CATERPILLAR CAUSA ROLL WITH CRAB, CUCUMBER, & AVOCADO

MAKES 2 (6-INCH) ROLLS

SERVES 3 OR 4 AS PART OF A SUSHI PLATTER

The caterpillar roll was created by a Los Angeles sushi chef several years back, supposedly using the only ingredients he had in the kitchen. I'm not going to pretend that making a sushi roll look like a caterpillar and stuffing it with imitation crab is traditional or even counts as sushi, but I've always appreciated anyone who can invent something new from whatever is in front of them. This is my Peruvian causa version, with a potato base and fresh crabmeat.

I roll the causa like sushi, but if you don't have a sushi mat, you can make one from two kitchen staples: paper towels and plastic wrap (see sidebar).

8 ounces lump crabmeat (about 1 generous cup), preferably fresh, cleaned and picked over

1½ tablespoons very finely minced shallots

1 tablespoon fresh lime juice

Generous pinch of kosher salt

1 small Persian cucumber or ½ a Japanese cucumber

1 large, ripe but firm avocado (firm enough that the slices hold their shape)

About 1 cup causa base (page 101), well chilled

1 Lightly toss together the crab, shallots, lime juice, and salt in a small bowl. Refrigerate the filling while you prepare the rest of the causa, or for up to 4 to 5 hours.

2 Cut the ends off the cucumber and halve lengthwise. Lay one half of the cucumber on a work surface, cut side down, and cut it into 8 to 10 long, thin strips lengthwise. Save the second half for snacking.

3 Cut off both ends of the avocado. Halve it lengthwise, remove the pit, and carefully peel off the skin. Be careful not to bruise the flesh. Lay the halves, cut side down, on a work surface and cut each half crosswise into very thin (⅛-inch-

wide) slices. Lay two 8-inch-long pieces of plastic wrap on your work surface. Use the blade of a chef's knife to pick up one row of sliced avocado and place it on one sheet of plastic wrap. Gently press down on the avocado slices with your fingers so they fan out about 6 inches in a straight line, like the arms of a Japanese folding-paper fan. Fold the plastic wrap over the avocado. Do the same with the second avocado half.

4 Place a large piece of plastic wrap over your sushi mat so it hangs over the mat's edges by 3 to 4 inches on all sides. Toward the bottom of the sushi mat, spread ½ cup of the causa base into a rectangle about 6 inches long and 4 inches wide. Spread half of the crab filling (a generous ½ cup) about 1 inch from the bottom of the causa rectangle and shape the filling into a 2-inch-wide strip across the length of the causa (stop just before you hit the edges). Lay 4 or 5 strips of cucumber along the top side of the filling.

5 Starting at the bottom, use the sushi mat to roll up the sushi snugly like a cigar. When you get to the top of the roll, squeeze the roll together gently but firmly (you don't want to break the sushi roll). Unroll the mat, pick up one fanned avocado, and place it, plastic wrap side facing down, in the palm of your hand. Flip the plastic wrap upside down on top of the causa roll so the avocado slices cover the top of the roll. Use the mat or your hands to firmly "hug" the avocados onto the roll so they adhere. Slice the roll into 5 or 6 pieces. Make a second roll with the remaining ingredients, and serve both rolls *inmediatamente*.

DIY SUSHI MAT

If you don't have a sushi mat, you can rig up one at home with paper towels and plastic wrap. One of my sous chefs, who had spent a lot of time in sushi restaurants, taught me this clever technique.

To make a sushi mat: Lay out a very big sheet of plastic wrap, about 2½ feet long, on a work surface. Neatly stack six paper towels (full, not half-size, sheets) one on top of another. Place the stacked towels a few inches from the bottom left corner of the plastic wrap. Fold the bottom of the plastic wrap up over the towels to partially cover them, then fold the left edge of the plastic wrap inward to cover the left edge of the paper towels. Put your right hand in the center of the towels and, with your left hand holding the plastic-covered left edge, flip them over onto the plastic wrap so they are completely covered. Keep flipping the towels forward, working down the line of plastic wrap, until you run out of plastic wrap. Run your hands across the plastic-wrapped towels to press out any air, and securely fold in the top and side edges.

CRISPY CAUSAS

This panko-crusted causa base was the result of playing around in the kitchen. I loved how the super-crunchy fried panko contrasted with the causa toppings, and since frying makes the potatoes warm, the base works well with entirely different toppings. Sushi-style seafood, yes, but also leftover shredded meat and sauce from any of the beef, lamb, pork, or duck estofados (stews, page 151), or whatever leftover pot roast–style dish you have in the refrigerator.

To keep the potatoes from falling apart as they fry, make sure the causa base is well chilled, and slice the potato base into 1-inch squares or slightly larger pieces. For a quick version, instead of using cut-out causas, tear off little balls of the causa base, flatten them slightly, roll them in the breading, and fry up the tiny causa cakes. The fried causa bases really are best hot, so serve them right away. Keep them in the back of your mind whenever you make the causa base. Like leftover mashed potatoes, you can fry them up for a quick dinner later in the week.

Canola or other vegetable oil, for frying
¼ cup all-purpose flour
1 egg, lightly beaten
½ cup panko bread crumbs
12 bite-size (1-inch-square) causas, cut from a chilled causa base (page 101)

1 Line a baking sheet with two or three paper towels. In a medium, deep saucepan, heat 1½ to 2 inches of oil over medium-high heat until it registers 350°F on a deep-fry thermometer, or fill a deep fryer with the recommended amount of oil and set the temperature to 350°F. Use a frying thermometer or test the oil temperature, or just toss in a little panko; it should bubble fairly vigorously (if the oil smokes, reduce the heat).

2 Place the flour, beaten egg, and panko in three separate small bowls. Use one hand to dip a causa square first in flour, use the other hand to dip the causa into the egg, then use the "floured" hand to roll the square all over in the panko (a handy way to keep only one hand wet and covered in egg). Repeat with the remaining causa squares.

3 When the oil is hot, deep-fry the causa bases in two or three batches until the panko is golden brown, about 2 minutes. Gently flip the causas with tongs halfway through so they brown evenly on all sides. Use a slotted spoon to transfer the causas to the paper towel–lined baking sheet, being careful not to break the pieces. Top the causas and serve them warm, with room temperature or warm toppings.

MAKES 12 CRISPY CAUSA BASES

CAUSA TOPPINGS

Causa toppings should be fun, a place where you experiment. Mix and match these layers or make up your own recipes. All of these make one 3-inch molded causa or 3 or 4 mini sushi-style or cut-out causas, depending on their size.

First layer: About ⅓ cup chilled causa base (page 101), any variation (regular, beet, or spinach), to make one 3-inch molded causa, or 3 or 4 sushi-style or mini cut-out causas, depending on their size.

Causa de Pollo con Paltas (Chicken Causa with Avocados)

If you don't have leftover chicken, poach a few whole chicken breasts and season the broth intensely, as if you are making stock (see page 40). Strain the stock and serve it as a consommé shot with the causa, or make a simple pasta, rice, or noodle soup, and you've got an impressive lunch or light dinner.

Second layer: Mash together ½ large avocado with a squeeze of fresh lime juice and a pinch of salt. Stir in ¼ cup finely diced cucumber.

Third layer: Mix together 2 to 3 tablespoons Japanese mayonnaise and ½ teaspoon ají amarillo paste (page 34), or any flavored aioli (page 38). Fold in about ⅓ cup shredded chicken breast and season with salt and black pepper.

Garnish: Crispy Quinoa (page 201) or finely diced cilantro stems (see page 88)

Causa con Atún Picante (Spicy Tuna Causa with Cucumber)

My mom used canned tuna, which you can substitute, to make a tuna sandwich–style causa. But once you have sushi-grade tuna salad, it's hard to go back.

Second layer: 3 or 4 very thin slices cucumber

Third layer: Mix together a generous ¼ cup finely diced or scraped trimmings from sushi-grade tuna and 1 to 1½ tablespoons Sriracha aioli (page 38).

Garnish: Crispy Quinoa (page 201) or finely diced cilantro stems or tobiko (see page 88)

Causa de Conchas (Scallop Causa with Yuzu Kosho Aioli)

I serve these scallops sushi-style, but quickly blanch them if you'd rather (see page 81), or substitute blanched shrimp.

Second layer: 3 or 4 very thin slices cucumber

Third layer: Mix a generous ¼ cup finely diced scallops (about 2 ounces) with 1 tablespoon yuzu kosho aioli (page 38).

Fourth layer: Finely diced cucumber and a small dollop of yuzu kosho aioli

Garnish: Finely minced cilantro stems (see page 88)

Causa de Tres Colores (Multicolored Vegetable Causa)

Multicolored bases usually get the attention of the kids in the room. They also make very sophisticated-looking causas for parties.

Second layer: 3 or 4 very thin slices cucumber

Third layer: Mash together ½ large avocado with a squeeze of fresh lime juice and a pinch of salt. Stir in ¼ cup finely diced cucumber.

Fourth layer: A chubby slice of burrata cheese or fresh mozzarella

Garnish: Chopped cherry tomatoes and red onions with a drizzle of olive oil

caterpillar roll

spinach causa base with chicken salad and tomatoes

beet causa base with avocado, chicken salad, and crispy quinoa

spicy tuna causa

ANTICUCHOS

GRILLED VEGETABLES, FISH & MEAT

ANTICUCHOS ARE ANOTHER GOOD EXAMPLE OF PERU'S DIFFERENT CULTURES COLLIDING UNEXPECTEDLY—AND SO DELICIOUSLY—ON A PLATE.

This type of dish traces its roots to the Incan Empire, not only the ingredients, like the pepper pastes used in the sauce, but to similar styles of fire-roasted dishes. The word comes from the Quechua word *antikuchu* but originally referred to a very different style of porridgelike dishes. When the Spanish arrived in the late fifteenth and early sixteenth centuries, they supposedly encountered Peruvians selling anticucholike grilled foods on the streets, but the flavors in anticuchos as we know them today really didn't develop until much later.

As the Spanish settled in Peru, garlic and other new seasonings used in the basting glaze were integrated into our pantry ingredients. African slaves cooked up the *delicioso* organ meats discarded by the Spanish over open fires (traditional anticuchos are made from the heart, lungs, liver, and other organs of meats and poultry). And finally, in the late nineteenth and early twentieth centuries, immigrants from southern China brought, among other ingredients, soy sauce, the backbone of anticucho sauce.

My versions of anticuchos are a little more upscale than the traditional version, and I often serve them as small bites on their own, without the potatoes and other sides you usually get in Lima. At home, you can grill larger, supper-size portions or, as is more my style, enough for a block party.

FUNDACIÓN:

SALSA DE ANTICUCHO
ANTICUCHO SAUCE

MAKES ABOUT 1 CUP

All grilled-food street vendors have their own recipe for the basting glaze used for their anticuchos. You can charm them all you want as they sop up the glaze with a corn husk brush, but you're probably never going to get that sauce recipe. Anticucho recipes are held tight.

I've played around with my version a few times since I sold anticuchos on the street back in the day. I now know that the flavors get even better after a few days. I like to throw in a splash of beer for extra flavor, but if you're not a drinker, you can leave it out. In traditional anticucho sauces, the bright, spicy heat of ají amarillo peppers plays off the smokiness of the ají panca peppers. I love the sweeter, red bell pepper version on grilled chicken livers (page 118), tuna (page 125), or any mild-flavored white-fleshed fish. It's similar to a Spanish romesco sauce.

The sauce freezes well (if making the variation with bell peppers, add them once the sauce thaws). While you're at it, make a double batch, and you're ready to grill anytime.

⅓ cup ají panca paste (page 36)

3 tablespoons ají amarillo paste (page 34)

2 tablespoons red wine vinegar

1 tablespoon plus 1 teaspoon malt vinegar

1 tablespoon soy sauce, preferably a good-quality Japanese brand, or 2½ teaspoons tamari

2 tablespoons of your favorite dark or medium-bodied beer (optional)

3 tablespoons extra-virgin olive oil

3 tablespoons dried oregano leaves, preferably Mexican

2½ teaspoons ground cumin

2 teaspoons kosher salt

Whisk together all of the ingredients in a medium bowl. Cover and refrigerate the anticucho sauce overnight before using or for up to 1 week. Or freeze the anticucho sauce, in batches or spread out flat in a large food storage bag so you can break off little chunks as you need it.

VARIACIÓN:

Roasted Red Bell Pepper Anticucho Sauce

Omit the ají panca paste and add 1 tablespoon pureed garlic (page 37) and 1½ teaspoons finely ground black pepper. In a blender, puree 1½ large roasted red bell peppers into a paste (or use ⅓ cup jarred roasted peppers, drained). If the blender isn't cooperating, add a little anticucho sauce to help puree the peppers. Whisk the pepper paste into the anticucho sauce. **Makes about 1 generous cup.**

LA PARILLA (THE GRILL)

In Peru, parrillas, grills, are topped with a flat sheet of metal with dozens of small, cut-out holes. The semisolid surface helps the grill heat up quickly and stay very hot, like an iron skillet, but the holes let in smoke and all of that good flavor.

At my restaurants, I use grills with grates like you find here, but the grate is very close to the heat source, more like a hibachi grill. You can use any type of grill to cook the recipes in this chapter, but make sure it is very hot so whatever you are cooking gets a nice char very quickly. Direct-heat grilling is typically better for most Peruvian dishes.

Cook with the heat (the grill), not the direct flames of the fire.

It is so important to allow time for the grill to heat to the right temperature. A dark sear on the surface of whatever you are grilling is what gives you good flavor. To test the temperature, hold your hand 10 to 12 inches away from the grate and slowly count to six. The grill should be hot enough that you need to move your hand away from the grate. If you are cooking in a pan, allow extra time for it to heat up.

Dry sear when you can.

I like to put most beef, lamb, and other meats on a grill "dry," meaning neither the food nor the grill have been brushed with oil. Dry proteins in particular get a nice, dark char and absorb sauces and basting glazes better after cooking has begun. Blot any meats that you are dry cooking very lightly with paper towels before putting them on the grill. The dry grilling and "pull-up" technique I like to use works really well even for home grilling, but if you have trouble with the food sticking, moisten a towel with a neutral oil like canola and rub it lightly over the hot grill grate.

For thin, delicate foods, use my "pull-up" technique to prevent sticking.

Immediately after putting small, delicate fish fillets or thinly sliced meats and poultry on the grill, use tongs to gently but quickly lift them up several times in a row to keep them from sticking. After a few lifts, the outside of the protein should be partially cooked and firm enough that it won't stick to the grill or fall apart. (In order to do this, you need to add foods to the grate one at a time.) The opposite is true when you are grilling larger pieces of meat, poultry, or fish. You want to get a good, long sear on the bottom side of a burger or steak before that first flip.

Baste at the end of cooking.

My basting sauces tend to have a little sugar or other sweetener in them, which help get a nice, golden brown char but can also burn, so wait until the last few minutes of the grilling time to baste. Or cook smaller, bite-size portions so the food cooks very quickly and doesn't need to stay on the grill very long, like with my Paiche Lettuce Wraps (page 120).

SPICY GRILLED SWEET POTATO WITH SERRANO-HONEY GLAZE

SERVES
5 OR 6
AS A SIDE

I'm always surprised that so many people think of camotes, sweet potatoes, as something you only eat in the fall and winter. Sweet potatoes aren't heavy on their own—only when you weigh them down with a lot of ingredients like butter. In Peru, boiled sweet potatoes are one of the traditional sides for ceviche, which is about as light as you can get.

During the summer, I love to grill sweet potatoes. Because they are on the grill only briefly, you need to blanch them first so they cook all the way through. You can blanch them ahead, but the potatoes need to be firm enough so they don't fall apart on the grill. At home, I usually slice the potatoes into rounds and call it a day, but if you are having a party, you can cut the slices into fancy geometric shapes. Sometimes, when the potatoes are hot off the grill, I'll sprinkle a little sugar over them and use a cooking torch to brûlée the top for that extra little caramelized crunch.

1½ pounds sweet potatoes (about 3 medium), scrubbed and peeled
1 small cinnamon stick
2 whole star anise
Serrano-Honey Basting Glaze (recipe follows)
Sea salt (optional)
Thinly sliced serrano chiles (optional)

1 Cut the sweet potatoes crosswise into ¾-inch-thick slices; if the pieces are large, cut each slice in half. Or, carve them into bite-size circles or cubes. Put the sweet potatoes, cinnamon, and star anise in a medium saucepan with enough water to cover and bring the water to a boil. Reduce the heat to maintain a simmer and cook until the potatoes are tender but still firm when pierced with a knife, 5 to 10 minutes, depending on the size of the potatoes. When done, drain and rinse them under cold running water or dunk them in an ice bath to help the potatoes cool completely. Use right away or cover and refrigerate overnight. If the potatoes are cold, let them come to room temperature before grilling.

2 Prepare a regular or hibachi grill for direct, high-heat cooking. Blot off any water on the sweet potatoes and thread them onto skewers, 3 or 4 slices on each skewer, so they lay flat (side by side, not upright).

3 Brush one side of the potatoes generously with the serrano-honey basting glaze. Grill the potatoes in batches, sauced side down, until caramelized on the bottom, about 2 minutes if your grill is really hot. Mop the tops with the basting glaze, flip, and grill the opposite side until caramelized, a few minutes more. Brush the tops of the potatoes one more time with the glaze, let them cook another few seconds, and transfer the skewers to a plate.

4 Taste and drizzle a little more of the basting glaze on top of the potatoes, if you'd like, and sprinkle them with the sea salt and the sliced serranos (if using). Serve the potatoes on the skewers, or put them in a serving bowl and put the remaining serrano-honey sauce on the side for dunking.

SERRANO-HONEY BASTING GLAZE

Makes about ½ cup

Use this basting glaze on vegetables that already have a little
sweetness, like kabocha or other pumpkinlike squashes,
or mop it all over peeled ears of fresh summer corn before
cooking. You need to add the glaze toward the end of grilling—
the last 5 minutes or so—so the honey doesn't burn. The
serrano chiles need to hang out in the sauce for at least a day
and up to several days before you use them—the longer the
chiles sit in the sauce, the more kick it will have.

⅓ cup plus 1 tablespoon mirin
⅓ cup honey
1 to 2 tablespoons thinly sliced serrano chiles

In a medium saucepan, bring the mirin to a low boil and cook
until it has reduced by almost half, a good 5 minutes. Turn
off the heat, whisk in the honey, and let cool completely. Put
the sauce in a storage container with the peppers, cover, and
refrigerate overnight. For a spicier kick, leave the peppers in the
sauce for up to 3 days. When the sauce is as spicy as you'd like,
strain out the peppers and store the sauce in the fridge for up to
3 days more.

CAULIFLOWER STEAKS WITH YUZU KOSHO—AJÍ SAUCE

SERVES
4 OR 5
AS A SIDE

My love for yuzu kosho is straight out of my London days. I was lucky enough to work with some of the city's best sushi chefs and learned to appreciate more Japanese ingredients than those I had tasted growing up. I love the intense flavors of the spicy-salty paste, which is made from chile peppers and the peel of citrusy yuzu fruit. It was just asking to be made into an Italian-style "pesto" basting sauce with local ingredients like ají amarillo paste, Chinese influences like lemongrass, and cilantro and limes, which the Spanish brought to Peru—almost every corner of the world there.

If the cauliflower falls apart into florets as you slice the heads into steaks, *no importa*. Toss the florets into a grill basket and grill them anyway, or use them in a salad or *tortilla de arroz* (page 221). Make mini steaks out of the colorful baby cauliflower you can sometimes find at farmers' markets, or cut them in half into chubby little bites. Before grilling, blanch the cauliflower steaks until they are barely tender-crisp, then finish them on the grill to give them a nice smoky, caramelized char.

1 large head cauliflower, or several heads baby cauliflower
1 tablespoon kosher salt
6 to 8 tablespoons Peruvian Pesto (recipe follows)
2 limes

1 Cut off the root end of the cauliflower, stand the cauliflower head upright, and cut it lengthwise into meaty slices about 1 inch thick. Fill a large pot halfway with water, bring it to a boil, then add the cauliflower steaks and salt. Reduce the heat and simmer the cauliflower until just tender-crisp when pierced with a knife. The cooking time varies depending on the size of the steaks, but start checking after 2 to 3 minutes. Drain the cauliflower and let cool completely under cold running water or dunk in an ice bath. Use the cauliflower immediately, or cover and refrigerate overnight. If the cauliflower steaks are cold, let

them come to room temperature before grilling.

2 Prepare a grill or hibachi for direct, high-heat cooking. Blot off any water on the cauliflower, then brush one side with about half the pesto. Halve the limes, then cut each half into quarters.

3 Grill the cauliflower steaks in batches, pesto side down, until charred on the bottom, about 2 minutes if your grill is really hot. Lightly brush the tops with more pesto, flip, and grill the opposite side of the cauliflower until charred, a few minutes more. Break off a small piece of one steak to taste (or if you grilled any small florets that fell apart, pop one of those in your mouth) and brush the cauliflower again with pesto, if you'd like more spiciness. Transfer the cauliflower to a plate, squeeze the juice of about half a lime all over the top, and serve the remaining quartered limes alongside the cauliflower.

PERUVIAN PESTO (YUZU KOSHO—AJÍ MARINADE)

Makes about ½ cup

Ají amarillo and yuzu kosho, the Japanese citrusy pepper paste, give this all-purpose "pesto" two very different pepper flavors. The ají amarillo is on the sweeter side of hot, while the yuzu kosho is more of a salty heat because of the other ingredients in the pepper paste. The pesto has a bold flavor, so you don't need a lot, but it really intensifies the grilled flavor of mild seafood like shrimp and white-fleshed fish, or vegetables like cauliflower. At my restaurants, I use frozen unsalted yuzu juice, but I use lime juice when I'm on the road traveling to events, as I do here. Both are very good.

2 tablespoons yuzu kosho paste
2 teaspoons pureed ginger (page 37) or finely grated ginger
1 tablespoon pureed garlic (page 37)
1 tablespoon ají amarillo paste (page 34)
2 tablespoons very finely chopped lemongrass
2 tablespoons finely chopped fresh cilantro
2 tablespoons fresh lime juice
¼ cup extra-virgin olive oil

Combine all of the ingredients in a small jar or food storage container, seal, and shake well to combine. Refrigerate the pesto for up to 1 week.

GRILLED CHICKEN LIVER TERIYAKI

SERVES 8 TO 10 AS AN APPETIZER OR 3 AS A MAIN DISH

Chicken liver is probably my favorite part of a chicken, and I've tasted everything there is to taste on a chicken. It's so richly flavored, with a melt-in-your-mouth texture. When I was growing up (and not all that long ago in the United States), if you went to the market to buy poultry, a chicken was hung upside down and killed right there in front of you—so you knew it was fresh. Maybe that would shock some people in today's grocery store world, but unlike so much commercial chicken processing today, it's really very humane. And nothing went to waste—my mom used every single part of the animal that had given its life to feed her family, down to the fresh blood that the butcher handed over in a jar. Making at least three meals for our big family felt very respectful of that one chicken's life.

The first night, she might make *arroz con pollo* (chicken with green rice); the next night, with the chicken blood, she'd cook up a pot of *sangrecitas*, a stewlike pudding with garlic and spices thickened with potato starch. It is crazy good, and my mom always said also good for you (it's full of iron). At some point, a pot of *menudencia*, my favorite chicken gizzard stew, was usually bubbling on the stove. (I would volunteer to help serve the stew so I could fish around in the pot and make sure I got the best part—the liver.) So far, I haven't gotten very far with sangrecitas or menudencia at my restaurants, but chicken livers seem to be fair game in the United States.

As with all gizzards, buy your livers from a trusted source. That doesn't mean necessarily a fancy butcher, but simply a good grocer that you trust. I usually grill meats "dry" (see page 113) but with liver, you need a little oil to keep the meat from sticking. The marinade keeps the livers very moist, so baste them regularly. Combining Japanese teriyaki sauce and anticucho sauce isn't traditional, but the flavors are so good together, I like to think of it as my tribute to Chino-Peruvian cooking.

On days when you're not making chicken livers, the anticucho-teriyaki basting glaze would also be so good on any teriyaki-style grilled chicken or vegetables.

1 pound chicken livers, trimmed, rinsed, and patted dry
Canola or other vegetable oil, for brushing
About ¼ cup Teriyaki Sauce (recipe follows)
About ¼ cup plus 1 tablespoon Roasted Red Bell Pepper Anticucho Sauce (page 112)

1 Prepare a regular or hibachi grill for direct, high-heat cooking and place a fish grate on the grill. Weave the chicken livers like ribbon candy onto the end of 8 to 10 skewers. They should be tightly bunched around the skewer. (Threading them snugly helps keep the centers of the livers medium to medium-rare and the meat moist and tender; if using other parts of a chicken, like thigh or breast meat, leave a little space between each piece so they cook fully.) Brush all sides of the livers lightly with the oil. Mix together the teriyaki sauce and roasted red pepper anticucho sauce in a small bowl to make a basting glaze. Set aside about 3 generous tablespoons of the basting glaze in a separate small dish to use as a finishing sauce.

2 When the grill is very hot, place one skewer on the hot fish grate and immediately lift it and place it back on the grill three times in quick succession (this is the "pull-up" technique—see page 113). With that first skewer, if you have trouble with the livers sticking, brush a little oil lightly on the grill and let the grate heat back up. Add another skewer and repeat the lifting technique (add the skewers in batches, until you get the hang of it). Grill until the bottom side is well seared and the flesh turns brown about halfway up the sides, about 1 minute if your grill is really hot. Flip the livers, lift them quickly up and down again a few times on the opposite side, and grill them for 30 seconds, or until they just get nice color on the bottom.

3 Baste the livers generously with the teriyaki-anticucho glaze, flip, and brush the top sides with more glaze. Grill until the livers caramelize on the bottom, usually only 30 seconds more. At this point, keep basting the tops of the livers continuously as they cook. They should still be nice and pink in the center. Brush the livers generously with the glaze again, flip them one more time, and immediately transfer the livers to a serving plate, leaving them on the skewers for serving.

4 Drizzle the reserved teriyaki-anticucho glaze on top of the livers and around the serving plate.

TERIYAKI SAUCE

Makes about 1½ cups

Most of the store-bought teriyaki sauces you find in the United States are a mess of salt, sugar, and additives that taste terrible. Homemade teriyaki sauce has a rich, caramelized flavor, is easy to make, and keeps in the fridge for weeks. I use it on anything that needs a blast of salty-sweet flavor, like classic sautéed chicken or beef teriyaki, or on green beans with bonito flakes (page 191).

1 cup mirin
⅓ cup dry sake
½ cup soy sauce, preferably a good-quality Japanese brand, or ⅓ cup plus 1½ tablespoons tamari
⅓ cup sugar

1 In a medium high-sided saucepan, combine the mirin and sake and bring to a vigorous boil over medium-high heat, then let the liquid boil for 2 to 3 minutes to cook off the alcohol. (If a blue flame ever surges up, it's just the alcohol cooking off. Turn off the heat, carefully cover the pot, and the high flames should go away so you can resume cooking.)

2 Turn off the heat, stir in the soy sauce and sugar, and return the heat to medium. Simmer, stirring regularly, until the sauce turns a rich caramel color, thickens slightly, and smells nice and toasty, 4 to 5 minutes. Transfer the sauce to a small bowl to cool for 10 minutes before using (it will thicken more as it cools). Cover and refrigerate the teriyaki sauce for up to 3 weeks. Rewarm the sauce over low heat before using.

GRILLED PAICHE LETTUCE WRAPS WITH HONEY-MISO GLAZE

SERVES **10** TO **12** AS AN APPETIZER OR **3** AS A MAIN DISH

Yurimaguas is a small port city 600 miles northeast of Lima in the Amazon, and the only place where paiche, a now-flourishing Jurassic-era fish, is cultivated (see page 93). The first time I went to the sustainable farm just outside the city, I picked up a live one and held it in my arms for a few seconds. The farm guys who raise the paiche laughed and called it "still a baby," but that thing wiggled and slapped my chest so hard with its broad, orange-speckled tail that I still have a paiche tattoo.

I love that such a giant, strong fish can be so delicate on the inside; the meat almost melts in your mouth. When I first put these paiche lettuce wraps on my restaurant menu, I wasn't sure people would order a dish made with fish that they'd never heard of. I could hardly keep enough on the grill.

If you have the anticucho sauce in your freezer or can make it (and the honey-miso sauce) a few days ahead, this is an easy, and impressive, appetizer. Paiche can stand as long as overnight, even twenty-four hours, in a strong, vinegary marinade without its firm texture being affected, so it really picks up the flavors in the marinade. Just be sure to cut down the marinating time if you substitute a more delicate white-fleshed fish like black cod (salmon is also good). For a quick main course, serve the grilled fish fillets on their own with the cucumbers on top. I still like to cut the fillets into smallish pieces so they cook more quickly and the honey in the marinade doesn't burn.

About ¼ cup Honey-Miso Glaze (page 190)

About ¼ cup Anticucho Sauce (page 112)

1 (1-pound) paiche fillet, or substitute black cod, salmon, or another oily-fleshed fish

10 to 12 whole baby butter lettuce leaves

About ¼ cup sliced or diced pickled cucumber (see page 39), or fresh cucumber, preferably Japanese or Persian

Small handful of fried yams, cut into matchsticks (see page 67; optional)

1 Whisk together the honey-miso sauce and anticucho sauce in a small bowl. Slice the fish into 10 to 12 small pieces—each piece should fit inside a butter lettuce leaf. (If you aren't making lettuce cups, slice the fish into 6 fillets to make 3 main-course servings.)

2 Pour a little of the honey-anticucho marinade in a small baking dish, arrange the fish on top, and pour the rest of the marinade over the fish. Cover and refrigerate for 2 to 3 hours; if you are using paiche, you can leave the fish in the marinade overnight or up to 24 hours.

3 Prepare a regular or hibachi grill for direct, high-heat cooking and place a fish grate on top. When the grill is very hot, use tongs to transfer the paiche pieces one at a time to the fish grate (reserve the honey-anticucho marinade) and immediately lift each piece and place it back on the grill three times (this is the "pull-up" technique—see page 113). Add another piece of fish and repeat the lifting technique. (Add the fish in batches until you get the hang of it. If you are using larger fillets, let the fish rest on the grate without lifting it.) Grill until the bottom sides are well seared and the flesh turns whitish to about halfway up the sides, a good 2 minutes for small pieces or 5 minutes for larger ones if your grill is really hot. Flip the paiche, and if the pieces are small, lift them up and down again a few times on the opposite side (leave larger pieces alone). Grill for another minute, or a few minutes more if the pieces are larger, or until they just get a nice color on the bottom.

4 Baste each piece of fish with the reserved marinade, flip, and brush the top sides generously with more of the marinade. Grill until the fillets are medium, or firm to the touch in the center, usually only 2 to 3 minutes for small pieces or up to 6 minutes for larger, thicker fillets. Brush the fish generously with the marinade again, flip them one more time, and immediately transfer the fish to a clean plate.

5 To make the lettuce wraps, place each piece of fish in a butter lettuce "cup" and spoon any pan juices over the fish. Top each fillet with the cucumber and arrange a few fried yams on top, if using. Or, for a quick main course, you can put the fish fillets on a serving platter, along with the pan juices, and arrange the cucumbers on top.

GRILLED BUTTERFLIED SHRIMP WITH YUZU KOSHO–AJÍ SAUCE

SERVES 10 TO 12 AS AN APPETIZER OR 3 OR 4 AS A MAIN DISH

The Japanese sushi chefs I worked for in London taught me how to butterfly shrimp, a very simple technique with big results. Butterflying isn't just about making the shrimp look really good. When the shrimp lay flat on the grill, they cook more evenly and quickly, and you don't end up with a rubbery tail end and a raw shrimp belly.

If you find whole, giant shrimp with the heads still attached, they look incredible all lined up on a platter for a party. If you only have smaller shrimp, skip the butterflying and just skewer and grill the shrimp whole. I keep a little yuzu kosho pesto in my refrigerator at home that I use to grill this shrimp and mild vegetables like cauliflower (page 117). It also makes a good, quick weeknight supper with my kids.

2 pounds (20 to 24 extra-large) unpeeled shrimp with heads
About ¼ cup Peruvian Pesto (page 117)
2 or 3 quartered limes, for serving

1 Prepare a regular or hibachi grill for direct, high-heat cooking and place a fish grate on the grill.

2 Butterfly the shrimp: Working one at a time, lay each shrimp flat on a work surface with the legs underneath the body. Pierce the middle of the shell with the tip of a sharp knife and slice through the top shell and flesh toward the head (leave the bottom shell intact), then slice all the way through the head so you can open the top half of the shrimp like a book (see photo 1). Move the knife back to the middle of the shrimp and repeat the slicing process, only this time slicing through the shell and flesh down toward the tail, but leave the tail intact (see photo 2). Devein the shrimp, and at the head end, slice horizontally across the meat to disconnect the shrimp flesh (it should still be attached at the tail; see photo 3). Peel back the flesh and brush the exposed shell lightly with the pesto (see photo 4). Lay the flesh back on top of the shell and brush the top side of the flesh lightly with the pesto (see photo 5).

3 When the grill is very hot, lay the shrimp, shell side down, on the hot grill (grill the shrimp in batches if necessary) and brush the exposed flesh one more time with the pesto (see photo 6). Grill until the flesh turns whitish-pink along the edges but a gray line of uncooked flesh still runs down the center, usually about 2 minutes, depending on the shrimp's size. Flip the shrimp with tongs and grill for a count of five—I like to literally count out loud: "1, 2, 3, 4, 5."

4 Transfer the shrimp to a serving plate and serve immediately, with the lime wedges alongside.

GRILLED SCALLOPS WITH AJÍ AMARILLO AIOLI & WASABI PEAS

SERVES 10 TO 12 AS AN APPETIZER OR 4 AS A MAIN DISH

Scallops might be the perfect seafood for grilling. They're so meaty and satisfying, they hold together well when cooked, and the naturally sweet flavor is even better balanced by a quick char and simple sauce. Just be sure not to overcook them, so they stay tender and juicy, and with no natural fat, the scallops need a drizzle of oil to keep them from sticking. I like to lightly smash a few dried wasabi peas or some Cancha (page 46) to sprinkle on top, but you can use scallions or anything that gives a crunchy contrast to the tender flesh. If you are serving the scallops for a party, ask your fishmonger for the beautiful shells like with Conchas a la Parmesana (page 53). Wash out the shells by hand so you can reuse them.

1 tablespoon olive oil

2 teaspoons pureed garlic (page 37)

1 teaspoon kosher salt, or to taste

½ teaspoon freshly ground black pepper

10 to 12 jumbo sea scallops (about 1¼ pounds)

About ½ cup ají amarillo aioli (page 38)

6 to 8 wasabi peas or Cancha (page 46), lightly crushed, or 1 scallion, finely chopped, or a few fresh chives, finely chopped (optional)

1 Prepare a regular or hibachi grill for direct, high-heat cooking and place a fish grate on top. Use your fingers to mix together the olive oil, garlic, salt, and pepper in a medium bowl. Pat the scallops dry with paper towels and toss them in the seasoned oil. Thread the scallops onto four skewers (2 or 3 scallops per skewer) with plenty of space between each scallop.

2 When the grill is very hot, place the skewers on the hot fish grate one at a time and immediately lift each skewer and place it back on the grill three times in quick succession (this is the "pull-up" technique—see page 113). Add another skewer and repeat the lifting technique (add the skewers in batches until you get the hang of it). Grill until the bottom side is well seared and the flesh turns white to about halfway up the sides, a good 2 to 3 minutes for large scallops, a little less if they are smaller. Flip each skewer, lift them up and down quickly again a few times on the opposite side, and grill until the scallops are medium-rare, or still opaque in the center (cut one open to test, if needed), usually 2 minutes more if your grill is really hot, but it depends on the size of the scallops. Let your tongue be the judge. Immediately transfer the scallops to a clean plate.

3 Remove the scallops from the skewers, arrange on a platter, and top each with a generous teaspoon or two of the ají amarillo aioli. Serve hot, with any remaining aioli alongside. (For an impressive presentation, you can blast the aioli for a few seconds with a cooking torch until the top is caramelized in spots like crème brûlée.) For a quick main course, you can leave the scallops on the skewers, plate them individually, and put a generous dollop of the aioli alongside on each plate or in a separate bowl for dunking. Sprinkle the wasabi peas or other garnish on top, if desired.

GRILLED TUNA STEAKS WITH ROASTED RED PEPPER ANTICUCHO SAUCE

SERVES
6
AS A
**MAIN
DISH**

In the summer, whenever I visited one of my sisters in Chimbote, a fishing port city north of Lima, and needed a little pocket money, my teenage friends and I would go down to the docks. We would wait for the fishermen to pull in with their big nets so we could help them unload. This was back when the fishermen would literally throw out huge trawling nets, come back to the docks, and reel them in. They would sort through everything they caught right there on the docks and throw back whatever fish were too small (and any other sea animals). Local sea lions, known as *lobos marinos*, or "sea wolves," were in on the game and would sometimes lumber onto the docks or swim up nearby in the water and "break" the net by pushing it down with their fins to steal a few fish of their own. We tried to be more polite than they were (and were earning our keep by helping to sort fish), so afterward, the fishermen would let us pick out a fish or two to take home. We'd head back to my house to clean and cut the fish into little chunks to fry up as snacks for whoever was hungry. I still like to cut fish into smaller pieces, especially thicker cuts like tuna, because they cook more evenly. Big pieces of fish tend to overcook around the edges before the center is ready.

Tuna has such a delicate texture that it's better when cooked until only rare (medium-rare, if you must) so the flesh is still tender and very juicy. If you use swordfish, grill the steaks several minutes longer (the very firm flesh must be cooked thoroughly so it becomes tender). Make a whole batch of red pepper anticucho sauce and use the leftovers to grill cauliflower later in the week. You can also use the same technique with blackened eggplant (page 87).

3 large meaty tuna or swordfish steaks (2 to 2½ pounds each), about 1 inch thick

About ½ generous cup Roasted Red Bell Pepper Anticucho Sauce (page 112)

Steamed quinoa or rice, for serving (optional)

1 Cut each tuna steak into 2 or 3 medium-size pieces and put the fish in a medium bowl. With tuna, I usually have the whole fish and can cut the steaks into tidy rectangles that look nice on the plate, but trim the steaks however you can. Try to cut them as evenly as possible, so they cook uniformly. Set aside 3 tablespoons of the red pepper anticucho sauce in a small dish for serving. Coat all sides of the fish with the remaining anticucho sauce and let the fish marinate for 10 to 15 minutes.

2 Meanwhile, prepare a regular or hibachi grill for direct, high-heat cooking and place a fish grate on top. When the grill is very hot, place the tuna steaks on the fish grate (reserving the marinade in the bowl) and grill until the bottom side is well seared and the flesh colors to about halfway up the sides, 4 to 5 minutes if your grill is really hot. (Unlike for many of my grilling recipes, as they cook, do not lift the fish steaks; let them rest on the grate.) When seared, flip the fish steaks (use a spatula to gently loosen the fish if it sticks to the grill) and baste each with the marinade. Keep basting the fish every minute or two. Grill the tuna until rare, or still bright red in the center, usually only about 2 minutes more. (If using swordfish, grill until medium to medium-well or fairly firm to the touch, a solid 5 minutes or longer, depending on the thickness of the steaks.) Brush the fish generously with the marinade again, flip them one more time, and immediately transfer to a clean serving plate.

3 Drizzle the reserved red pepper anticucho sauce on top of the steaks and around the plate. Serve with quinoa or rice, if desired.

GRILLED PERUVIAN-STYLE ROTISSERIE CHICKEN

SERVES
5 OR 6
AS A MAIN DISH

I guess it's a compliment that imitators of Peru's famous rotisserie chicken are everywhere these days. Problem is, unless you happen to have a rotisserie grill, it can be difficult to mimic the slowly rotating spit that gives the chicken that almost black, fantastically charred crust that seals in the natural juices so the chicken doesn't dry out. Those oversize chickens sold at most supermarkets don't help, as the meat closest to the grill usually dries out before the chicken is cooked all the way through. These are the kinds of cooking challenges I get really excited about.

First, for best results, forget the idea of preparing and presenting a whole chicken like they do in the restaurants and split the chickens in half so they cook evenly. Easy enough—the hardest part is making sure the meat doesn't dry out. To keep it moist, I let the chicken halves sit in a spicy ají panca paste–soy sauce marinade for a good while, and then poach them slowly in plastic bags to mimic the French method of sous-vide cooking. The meat stays moist, and you lock in all of those marinade flavors. Once the chicken is cooked, a quick sear on the grill gives the skin that char that makes rotisserie chicken so tasty.

The recipe may look long, but the technique is more time-consuming than complicated (and most of that time is for marinating the chicken or poaching it, when you can be less attentive). For a party, you can marinate and poach the chickens ahead and toss them on the grill when everyone shows up with the beer and whatever else you're serving. These are also really good picnic chickens.

2 small chickens, preferably 3½ pounds each but up to 5 pounds if that's all you can find
Pollo a la Brasa Marinade (recipe follows)
Canola or other vegetable oil, for grilling

1 Remove the giblets and neck from the chickens and trim any excess fat around the neck cavity. Use kitchen shears or a sharp knife to cut each chicken in half alongside both sides of the backbone (save the backbone and neck for stock), flip the chicken over, and cut down the center of the breast to separate the chicken halves. Put the chickens in a large bowl and rub the marinade all over them, and place each chicken half in the middle of a large sheet of plastic wrap (a good foot long). Drizzle any marinade still in the bowl over the chicken halves, and wrap each up securely in the plastic wrap so the marinade doesn't leak out. Place two chicken halves in a large, resealable food storage bag (a good-quality bag is key, or it will break when simmered). Press as much air out of the bag as possible, seal, and do the same with the remaining two chicken halves. Refrigerate both bags for 12 hours or overnight.

2 When ready to cook, open each bagged chicken, press out any air, and seal the bags again securely. In each bag, arrange the two chicken halves so they lay flat next to each other. Build a 1-inch-tall pedestal for the chickens along the bottom of a large Dutch oven or stockpot with 3 or 4 round or other-shaped metal cookie cutters. (If you have two large Dutch ovens or wide-bottomed pots, make a stand in each so you can cook both bags of chicken at once; otherwise cook one bag at a time.) Place one bag on top of the cutters so the chickens lay as flat as possible and fill the pot with enough water to cover the bag. Place a smaller, heavy saucepan on top of the chicken to weigh it down and top the saucepan with a can of food, if needed, to submerge the chicken fully. (The water may be very close to the top of the pot, which is fine.) Bring the water to a low simmer, reduce the heat to low, and very slowly poach the chicken over low heat until the flesh is no longer pink between the legs and thighs, about 1 hour and 15 minutes for 3½-pound chickens, or 1 hour and 30 to 40 minutes if they are more than 4 pounds. The heat should be as low as possible so the chickens cook very slowly. If the water ever begins to simmer again, turn off the heat for 5 minutes.

RECIPE CONTINUES

3 With tongs, transfer the bagged chicken to a large bowl, let cool for 15 minutes, then open the bag to release the steam (be careful—it is very hot). It's fine if some of the marinade leaked out into the bags. Transfer the chicken to a bowl, pour the marinade over the top, and discard the bags and plastic wrap. If making the chicken ahead, let cool to room temperature, cover, and refrigerate in the marinade overnight. Let the chickens rest for at least 1 hour at room temperature before grilling.

4 Prepare a regular or hibachi grill for direct, high-heat cooking and lightly oil the grate with vegetable oil. When the grill is very hot, place the chicken halves on the grill, breast side down (reserve the marinade in the bowl). Sear each chicken half until the skin is blackened all over, usually a solid 5 minutes. Cook the chicken a little longer, if necessary; you want a nice dark color. Brush the chicken with the marinade, flip, and brush the skin (now facing up) with marinade. If the juices do not run clear when the thigh is pierced, grill the chicken several minutes longer, flipping and basting regularly, until they do.

5 Transfer the chickens to a serving plate and serve them right away, or let cool to room temperature before serving.

POLLO A LA BRASA MARINADE

Makes about 1¼ cups

If you don't want to cook whole chickens rotisserie-style as on page 126, you can use this sauce to simply marinate chicken thighs or breasts without cooking them sous-vide-style first. The marinade would also be very good with pork chops or tenderloin. Marinate the uncooked poultry or meat overnight before you toss it on the grill.

2 tablespoons ají panca paste (page 36)
¼ cup pureed garlic (page 37)
1½ tablespoons finely chopped fresh rosemary
1½ teaspoons ground cumin
1 teaspoon freshly ground black pepper
¼ cup soy sauce, preferably Yamasa
¼ cup red wine vinegar
½ cup extra-virgin olive oil

Whisk together the ají panca paste, garlic, rosemary, cumin, and pepper in a medium bowl, then add the soy sauce, vinegar, and olive oil. Use right away, or cover and refrigerate the marinade for up to 5 days.

PERUVIAN-STYLE BURGER WITH AJÍ AMARILLO YOGURT & PICKLED CUCUMBERS

MAKES
8
BURGERS

Hermanos, how we love them. One of my older brothers would sometimes stuff some cash in my pockets when he was hungry and send me out to a burger place in our neighborhood where some teenage gangs used to hang out. It wasn't something you worried about; it was just life in Lima at the time. You didn't want to lock yourself inside all day—burgers (and daily life) were calling.

For these neighborhood bullies, seeing a ten-year-old kid like me, so excited on his way to get fast food (it wasn't all that different back then as today), was like winning the lottery. They knew I must have had cash in my pockets, and would chase after me and steal my money or whatever I had just bought. To outsmart them, I started going only at night, when it was difficult for them to see me. I'd take a different path home every time, running like a mouse in a maze when they spotted me. To me, it was a fun game. I was so proud whenever I managed to outsmart them.

Back then, your family had to be the cops. When another one of my brothers found out what was going on, he showed up and told my harassers what would happen if they kept messing with his little brother. If you've ever had older brothers, you know how it works—they challenge you (a nice way of saying kick your rear) but also protect you. That was the last I heard from those guys.

As for this recipe, in the mountains of Peru, locals cook with alpaca, which I thought would make a great burger. Alpaca tastes similar to lamb, only not as gamey. It's worth looking for, but if you can't find alpaca, a mix of lamb and beef is also great. I don't recommend serving these burgers rare. The meat is more tightly packed than American-style burgers, so they take a little longer to cook—this is one time when cooking meat, for me at least, medium or medium-well is best. The yogurt sauce is really delicious with this meat mixture, but top the burgers with whatever you'd like.

BURGERS

2 pounds mixed ground lamb and ground beef, or 2 pounds ground alpaca

¼ cup leftover bacon drippings or rendered pork belly fat, melted but not hot

3 tablespoons Anticucho Sauce (page 112)

2 teaspoons kosher salt, plus more to taste

TO ASSEMBLE

2 ripe avocados

1 lime

8 good-quality hamburger buns, lightly toasted

Ají Amarillo–Cumin Yogurt Sauce (recipe follows) or good-quality mayonnaise, preferably Japanese

8 small Bibb or other crunchy lettuce leaves

Sliced pickled cucumbers (see page 39) or fresh cucumber, preferably Japanese or Persian

1 To make the burgers, in a large bowl, mash together the ground lamb and beef with the heel of your hand until well combined. Pour in the bacon drippings and the anticucho sauce, and sprinkle the salt on the meat. Keep mashing the meat mixture together with your hands for several minutes. Really get in there with the heel of your hand. The ground meat should become almost silky in texture.

2 Separate the meat mixture into 8 equal portions. Slap each portion back and forth quickly between your hands a good 15 times, like you are slapping a baseball firmly into a glove (see sidebar, page 131). You should hear the meat slap against the palms of your hands as the air is removed from the patties. Shape each portion into a patty 4 to 5 inches wide, depending on the size of the burger buns. Use your thumb to make a small indention in the center of each patty.

RECIPE CONTINUES

3 Prepare a regular or hibachi grill for direct, medium-high-heat cooking. Season the patties with salt. Grill the burgers until they are nicely charred on the bottom, about 5 minutes. Do not lift the burgers as they cook. Flip the burgers (use a spatula to loosen the patties if they stick to the grill) and grill until the burgers are medium to medium-well, usually 5 to 8 minutes more if your grill is really hot.

4 To assemble, in a medium bowl, mash together the avocados with as much juice from the lime as you'd like. Spread both cut sides of each bun with the ají amarillo–cumin yogurt sauce and top the bottom bun with a few spoonfuls of mashed avocado, a lettuce leaf, and a burger patty. Arrange the cucumbers on top, close the burgers up, and serve any remaining ají amarillo–cumin yogurt sauce on the side.

AJÍ AMARILLO–CUMIN YOGURT SAUCE

Makes 1 generous cup

This spicy yogurt makes a great spread for pita sandwiches, especially with leftover grilled flank steak or chicken, or even just a dip for crispy vegetables. Make it as spicy as you would like by adjusting the amount of ají amarillo paste.

1 cup whole-milk plain yogurt

1 tablespoon plus 1 teaspoon ají amarillo paste, store-bought or homemade (page 34)

2½ teaspoons ground cumin

Whisk together all of the ingredients in a medium bowl. Cover and refrigerate for up to 3 days. Whisk again before serving.

THE "BASEBALL BURGER" METHOD

A Japanese chef taught me how to make burger patties so they stay really moist and juicy. The technique is the polar opposite of the loosely packed patties on most American burgers. You slap the raw meat patties back and forth between the palms of your hands several times to remove most of the air, like tossing a baseball into a mitt—back and forth, back and forth. The process compacts the meat so the moisture stays inside the patty. The meat is pretty tightly packed, so the texture is a little denser than American-style burgers, but I really love the flavor and texture.

GRILLED SHORT RIBS WITH BBQ SAUCE

SERVES 5 OR 6 AS A MAIN DISH

In Peru, anticucho sauce is usually the only sauce used for grilling, but I love all types of barbecue sauce. With the mirin and tamari, this one is more of a Japanese-style sauce that is really good on beef.

Boneless short ribs are sold either as a slab of meat or already divided into individual pieces. When they are grilled this quickly instead of slow cooked, the ribs need to be very good quality—"sashimi" quality, as I like to say—with very little fat with tender meat, not the tough, fatty ribs you find at most grocery stores. You also need to remove the white connective tissue in the meat and any fat or they will be tough (ask your butcher to do it or trim the ribs well yourself). Or, if they are too difficult to find, use skirt steak or flank steak instead of ribs. Even tenderloin would be very good with this sauce. Spoon the sauce on the meat toward the end of the grilling time so the sugars in the sauce caramelize, but don't burn.

2 to 2½ pounds boneless short ribs, connective tissue removed, or skirt or flank steak
About ½ cup Japanese-Style BBQ Sauce (recipe follows)

1 Prepare a regular or hibachi grill for direct, high-heat cooking. Trim the short ribs into individual serving pieces about 3 inches long and 2 inches thick (some trimmed pieces may be smaller). Pat dry with paper towels. Set aside about 3 generous tablespoons of the barbecue sauce in a small dish to use as a finishing sauce. Put the remaining barbecue sauce in a medium bowl by the grill.

2 Grill the meat until the bottom side is nicely charred, 4 to 5 minutes. Let the meat rest on the grate without lifting it. Use tongs to transfer the meat to the bowl with the barbecue sauce, toss it around in the sauce a few times, and return the meat to the grill with the opposite side facing down. Sear until the bottom blackens in spots, about 2 minutes. It shouldn't take as long as the first side because the sugary sauce will cook more quickly.

3 Transfer the meat to the bowl again, toss it around in the sauce, and return it to the grill with the first side you grilled face down. Sear the meat for another few minutes, or until medium-rare (check with a knife; the meat should still be ruby red in the middle). Brush the meat generously with the barbecue sauce, flip one more time, and immediately transfer to a serving platter.

4 If using skirt or flank steaks, slice the steaks before serving. Drizzle the reserved barbecue sauce on top of the beef.

JAPANESE-STYLE BBQ SAUCE

Makes about 1 cup

Make the sauce at least one day before you plan to grill so the flavors have time to develop. Mixing together soy sauce and tamari gives the sauce a richer flavor than soy sauce alone, but if you only have one or the other in your pantry, don't let that stop you from making this sauce.

¼ cup soy sauce (or more tamari)
2½ tablespoons tamari (or more soy sauce)
¼ cup mirin
⅓ cup sugar
1 tablespoon light corn syrup or honey
¼ small red onion, finely grated (about ¼ cup)
2 tablespoons pureed ginger (page 37) or finely grated ginger
2 tablespoons pureed garlic (page 37)
¾ teaspoon freshly ground black pepper

Whisk together all of the ingredients in a medium bowl or food storage container. Cover and refrigerate the sauce overnight, or better still, 2 to 3 days, before using. Refrigerate the barbecue sauce for up to 1 week.

ANTICUCHOS DE CORAZÓN (CLASSIC GRILLED BEEF HEART SKEWERS)

To Peruvians, there's nothing like the pure flavor of corazón, *or beef heart. It tastes almost like a really good steak only without the fat getting in the way, and has a slight chewiness. It's the most traditional, and popular, anticucho in Lima.*

In high school, I would sometimes make *anticuchos del corazón*, traditional beef heart anticuchos, to sell for pocket money. One weekend, I went a little overboard and rented the entire first floor of an old building where I could have an *anticuchada*–basically, an anticucho pop-up party. I knocked on all the doors around our neighborhood, thinking I'd maybe sell a few dozen tickets, and somehow managed to sell more than one hundred. *¡Chevere!*

I boiled up big pots of potatoes and recruited friends to help me skewer all of the beef heart and made sure to have plenty of beer around. (Everyone is happy if there is enough beer.) It turned out to be a really fantastic party with plenty of great food and fun.

I am always surprised to find that beef heart is often unchartered giblet territory to many people in the United States. It's really very easy to cook–and delicious–just avoid cooking it too long, or it will become tough. You can buy the heart whole or already cleaned and cut into large pieces, like any other beef cut (I recommend the latter if you've never cooked with beef heart before). If you find a whole heart from your local butcher (also check Latin markets), you need to clean and trim it well before marinating the meat. If you've never done it, it's pretty eye-opening to saw off the arteries and sinew from the giant muscle that gives us all life. After a while, it becomes sort of therapeutic, and you really appreciate how much work goes into living.

To make Anticuchos del Corazón:

1 If you bought a whole heart (usually 4 to 6 pounds), use a very sharp knife to trim off all of the fat, sinew, and veins, including inside the heart. It's a big job, so be patient. When you finish, the heart should look like a nice, bright red piece of beef steak. If you manage to find trimmed heart from a fancy butcher, count on about 3 pounds to equal a trimmed heart. Slice the heart into small strips about 2 inches long by ¾ inch thick.

2 Put the meat in a single layer in a casserole dish and make a double batch (about 2 cups) of Anticucho Sauce (page 112). Pour about 1½ cups of the sauce on top so the meat is completely covered (reserving the remaining ½ cup sauce for serving). Cover and refrigerate the heart for at least 1 day, 2 days if you can, and flip the meat once while it marinates.

3 Remove the meat from the refrigerator a good 1 to 2 hours prior to grilling. Prepare a regular or hibachi grill for direct, high-heat cooking. Weave 3 or 4 strips of beef heart like ribbon candy onto the end of about 12 long or 24 shorter metal or bamboo skewers, or however many you need. The meat should be tightly bunched around the skewer.

4 When the grill is very hot, cook a few skewers of meat at a time. The bottom side should get nice and seared after 3 to 4 minutes. Flip the skewers and continue to grill the heart until it is seared on the other side but still medium-rare, about 2 minutes more. You don't want to overcook the meat, or it will be tough. When you finish grilling all of the heart, serve it with the reserved anticucho sauce.

SERVES ABOUT 12

KOREAN-STYLE BARBECUED LAMB WITH QUINOA SALAD

SERVES
5 OR 6

One of my chefs came up with the idea of adding *gochujang*, the Korean fermented red chile paste, to my Japanese-style barbecue sauce. I love the sauce with grilled lamb; the extra hit of spice and concentrated flavor from the gochujang really works well with game meats, especially with a side of quinoa salad. You can find gochujang at well-stocked grocery stores or Asian markets.

12 small (3-ounce) lamb rib chops (about 2¼ pounds)
About 1 cup Japanese-Style BBQ Sauce (page 132)
⅓ cup gochujang (Korean chile paste; see page 264)
Warm Vegetable Quinoa Salad (page 198) or steamed rice

1 Prepare a regular or hibachi grill for direct, high-heat cooking. Pat the lamb chops dry with paper towels and stack them on a platter. Whisk together the barbecue sauce and the gochujang in a small bowl. Set aside about 3 generous tablespoons of the barbecue sauce in a small dish to use as a finishing sauce. Put the remaining barbecue sauce in a large baking dish (a 9 x 13-inch dish fits the chops well) by the grill.

2 Grill the lamb chops until the bottom side is nicely charred, 4 to 5 minutes. Let the meat rest on the grate without lifting it. Use tongs to transfer the chops to the baking dish with the barbecue sauce, toss them around in the sauce a few times, and return the meat to the grill with the opposite side facing down. Sear until the bottom blackens in spots, about 2 minutes. It shouldn't take as long as the first side because of the sugary sauce.

3 Transfer the chops to the baking dish again, toss them around in the sauce, and return them to the grill with the first side you grilled face down (since it didn't have sauce when first seared, it won't be as dark). Sear the meat for another minute or two, or until medium-rare. The lamb should be firm but still give slightly to the touch. Brush the chops generously with the barbecue sauce, flip them one more time, and immediately transfer them to a serving platter.

4 Drizzle the reserved barbecue sauce on top of the chops and serve the chops with the quinoa salad.

SALTADOS Y ESTOFADOS

STIR-FRIES & STEWS

I'LL NEVER TURN DOWN A GOOD CEVICHE OR STREET-SIDE ANTICUCHO SNACK,

but *saltados*, the Peruvian version of stir-fries, and homey, slow-cooked estofados (stews) are the really good, belly-filling food you want to—and do—eat most nights. At my house, at least.

Stir-fries are especially popular in Lima, where Chinese restaurants are on every other corner. Estofados and secos, another type of slow-cooked, stewlike dish, are on tables all over the country, from the cities to the ancient Andean mountaintops, in both mom-and-pop and high-end restaurants.

For home cooks, these are the sort of dishes you cook from memory, the way your mom or grandmother taught you. I like my saltados to hold their own against traditional stir-fry sides like potatoes or rice and my secos to take on a big hunk of crusty bread, so I give all of my recipes in this chapter big mouthfuls of flavor.

SALSA DE SALTADO
SALTADO SAUCE

A saltado "sauce" doesn't really exist in traditional Peruvian cooking. It's what I call the base seasoning that we use at my restaurants to make saltados. Instead of prepping and adding seasonings like ají amarillo, ginger, and red wine vinegar as you fry the other ingredients, my saltado sauce does the work for you in one or two spoonfuls. Make the sauce ahead, keep it in the fridge, and you're ready to go. The pureed garlic is worth taking the time to make. It melts into the sauce and can take the heat required to stir-fry without burning. Substitute tamari for the soy sauce if you'd like to make a wheat-free version.

The secrets to a really good stir-fry are your sauce and a really hot pan. That's it. It wasn't until I opened my first restaurant, Mo-Chica, that I realized how easy it was to unintentionally mess up those two very simple components—even in a restaurant kitchen. My chefs tried hard, but most weren't Peruvian, and something was always off. Too much garlic one time, not enough ají amarillo heat at the back of your throat on another try. The same thing was happing with big pots of estofados, or stews made with different aderezos, mixes of seasonings that are the most important flavor base of the dish. Cooking is a lot like learning a new language. When you learn something from the time you are born, it is second nature. As an adult, you have to really pay attention, and sometimes turn your thinking inside out to get to a new place.

My solution was to make a stir-fry "sauce" that my chefs could spoon up and drop into the saltado and several braise bases for the stews. They're essentially my personal aderezo (see sidebar, page 152) for each dish, the Peruvian version of a cook's secret cooking sauce.

2 tablespoons pureed garlic (page 37)

2 tablespoons pureed ginger (page 37) or finely zested ginger

1 tablespoon ají amarillo paste, store-bought or homemade (page 34)

2 teaspoons freshly ground black pepper

2 tablespoons soy sauce, preferably a good-quality Japanese brand, or 1½ tablespoons tamari

5 tablespoons red wine vinegar

Shake up all of the ingredients in a small jar, or stir them together in another storage container. Cover and refrigerate the sauce for up to 1 week.

BEET STIR-FRY WITH GREEN BEANS & PEAS

SERVES 2

You can use whatever vegetables you like in this stir-fry, but I love the way the sugar in beets caramelizes when you blast them at very high heat. Add the less-moist vegetables, like the beets, onion, and green beans, toward the beginning of the cooking time and save the juicier tomatoes for last. As with Lomo Saltado (page 140), serve this with your favorite style of cooked potatoes or rice, or rewarm leftover potatoes or rice.

About 1 cup baby fingerlings or roughly chopped potatoes, 2 handfuls of homemade or good-quality frozen french fries, or about 1½ cups rice

1 large or 2 small beets, roasted and peeled (see page 176)

½ medium red onion

Small handful of green beans or haricots verts, steamed

Small handful of frozen peas, thawed

1 ripe medium heirloom, beefsteak, or other juicy tomato, or 2 plum tomatoes

2 scallions

3 or 4 sprigs fresh cilantro

1½ tablespoons Saltado Sauce (page 138)

1 tablespoon soy sauce, preferably a good-quality Japanese brand, or 2 teaspoons tamari, or more to taste

2 to 3 tablespoons canola or other vegetable oil

1 Prepare your potatoes or rice, or rewarm the leftovers. You can roast baby fingerlings, go all-out and confit them in olive oil (page 163), make homemade french fries, or even fry up good-quality store-bought fries. The same goes for rice: Use leftovers, or make your favorite style of white or brown rice to serve with the saltado.

2 Next, prep all of your ingredients (keep each in a separate pile). Halve the beets, or quarter them if large. Put the red onion half, cut side down, lengthwise on a work surface. Cut off both ends, then cut the onion into lengthwise strips about ½ inch thick, moving the knife at a slight angle as you work around the onion globe. Your knife should be almost parallel to the cutting board along the sides of the onion and upright at the top. Put the green beans and peas in a pile together. Cut the tomatoes in half lengthwise and cut each half into several large, chunky wedges. Finely chop the scallions, including about halfway up the green stalk, or chop them roughly for more texture, if you'd like. Finely chop the cilantro leaves and the top half of the stems. Have your saltado and soy sauces measured and ready.

3 Heat a wok or large sauté pan over high heat until hot—a good 2 minutes. Pour in the oil to lightly coat the bottom of the pan and heat the oil for 2 to 3 minutes, until very hot. The oil shouldn't be smoking, but close to it. Swirl the oil around the pan, toss in the beets, and shake the pan or use tongs to flip and sear them on all sides for a few seconds. Add the onion, toss again, and then add the green beans and peas. Fry the saltado until the edges of the onions and green beans color in a few spots (you want them crunchy in the center), another few seconds, then add the tomatoes and cook until they barely begin to soften, about 30 seconds. The total cooking time shouldn't be more than 90 seconds at this point.

4 Immediately drizzle the saltado and soy sauces along the edges of the wok or pan, not on top of the stir-fry ingredients. You should smell them caramelizing. Scatter the minced scallions and cilantro on top of the stir-fry, and toss everything together one more time. Taste, and add another drizzle of soy sauce, if you'd like. The saltado should be really juicy, with big flavors that the potatoes or rice can sop up.

5 Spoon the saltado straight out of the pan into serving bowls. Pile the potatoes on top or serve the rice alongside.

PERUVIAN BEEF STIR-FRY WITH RED ONIONS, TOMATOES, SCALLIONS & CILANTRO

SERVES 2

Lomo saltado is probably on every mom-and-pop Peruvian restaurant menu. The classic beef stir-fry is easy to make from inexpensive ingredients. When I'm having a rough day, lomo saltado is still the comfort food dish that does it for me. The best taste like a big, warm and cozy salad. You get a little crunchiness, but also something satisfying in your belly. Problem is, there are a lot of bad versions out there. It's hard not to be disappointed when a saltado has steamed, instead of seared, ingredients. That's a stew, not a stir-fry.

The key is to fry everything at very high heat so you get a good sear on the ingredients, but you don't cook out all of their freshness (see sidebar, page 142). A few years back, I watched a lomo saltado cookoff on television when I was visiting family in Lima. The fastest competitor clocked in his saltado at just under ninety seconds. You don't need to go that fast—I'll be generous and give you an extra thirty seconds. But you should never spend more than two minutes from the time your beef hits the pan to when the scallion and cilantro garnishes are ready to scatter on top of the finished dish. The meat should be medium-rare, the tomatoes juicy, and the onions barely softening on the edges but still crunchy in the center. Make sure your tomatoes—heirlooms or juicy beefsteak—are really ripe, or let plum tomatoes sit out on the counter for several days until they soften up a little. These days, you see a lot of lomo saltados made with less expensive cuts of meat, but I prefer filet mignon (*lomo* means "filet," the cut traditionally used in Peru); it's so tender and flavorful, but you can use any cut from the tenderloin.

Traditionally, the stir-fry is served on top of deep-fried or skillet-fried potatoes, but you could also serve this with leftover rice. I usually pile potatoes on top or on the side of the plate so they stay crispy, like they just came out of the fryer basket or pan. And so you can dip them into the saltado sauce—Peruvian ketchup.

About 1 cup baby fingerlings or roughly chopped potatoes, 2 handfuls of homemade or good-quality frozen french fries, or about 1½ cups rice

8 to 10 ounces filet mignon or tenderloin, thinly sliced into 2-inch-long strips

Kosher salt and freshly ground black pepper

½ teaspoon pureed garlic (page 37)

½ medium red onion, halved from stem to root end

1 ripe medium heirloom, beefsteak, or other juicy tomato, or 2 plum tomatoes

2 scallions

3 or 4 sprigs fresh cilantro

1½ tablespoons Saltado Sauce (page 138)

1½ tablespoons soy sauce, preferably a good-quality Japanese brand, or more to taste

2 to 3 tablespoons canola or other vegetable oil

1 Prepare the potatoes or rice, or rewarm the leftovers. You can roast baby fingerlings, go all-out and confit them in olive oil (page 163), make homemade french fries, or even fry up good-quality store-bought fries. The same goes for rice: Use leftovers, or make your favorite style of white or brown rice to serve with the saltado.

2 Next, prep all of your other ingredients, so they're ready; this dish cooks quickly. (Keep each in a separate pile.) Sprinkle the beef lightly with the salt and pepper and rub the pureed garlic all over the meat with your hands. Put the red onion half, cut side down, lengthwise on a work surface. Slice off both ends, then slice the onion into lengthwise strips about ½ inch thick, moving the knife at a slight angle as you work around the onion globe. Your knife should be almost parallel to the cutting board along the sides of the onion and upright at the top. Cut

RECIPE CONTINUES

the tomatoes in half lengthwise and cut each half into several large, chunky wedges. Finely chop the scallions, including about halfway up the green stalk, or chop them roughly for more texture, if you'd like. Finely chop the cilantro leaves and top half of the stems. Have your saltado and soy sauces measured and ready.

3 Heat a wok or large sauté pan over high heat until hot—a good 2 minutes. Pour in the oil to lightly coat the bottom of the pan and heat the oil for 2 to 3 minutes, until very hot. The oil shouldn't be smoking, but close to it. Swirl the oil around the pan, then toss in the beef and quickly sear both sides for a few seconds each until it begins to brown, about 30 seconds total. Add the onion and shake the pan or use tongs to flip them a few times, then add the tomatoes right away. Fry the saltado until the edges of the onions color in a few spots and the tomatoes barely begin to soften, about 30 seconds. The total cooking time shouldn't be more than 90 seconds at this point.

4 Immediately drizzle the saltado and soy sauces along the edges of the wok or pan, not on top of the stir-fry ingredients. You should smell the sauces caramelizing. Scatter the scallions and cilantro on top of the stir-fry and toss everything together one more time. Taste and add another drizzle of soy sauce, if you'd like. The saltado should be really juicy, with big flavors that the potatoes or rice can sop up.

5 Spoon the lomo saltado straight out of the pan into serving bowls. Pile the potatoes on top or serve the rice alongside.

STIR-FRYING

My chefs know how picky I am when it comes to saltados. I don't curse all that much, but they will probably tell you that I can say the word *Focus!* at an impressive decibel. These are the saltado, stir-frying, rules of my kitchen:

1. Be prepared. All of your ingredients need to be prepped and accessible, including the beef and sauces. No chopping or measuring while you are stir-frying!

2. Turn up the heat. You need a very hot pan to quickly sear your ingredients and lock in flavor in less than two minutes. Don't make more than two stir-fry servings at once, unless you have a giant wok and a huge heat source and are very experienced. An overpacked wok causes the ingredients to steam, not fry.

3. Timing is key. Start with "dry" ingredients like meats and firmer vegetables. Add soft vegetables like tomatoes toward the end, so they don't "melt" into the sauce. (If you are new to stir-frying and to making a lomo saltado, you may want to sear the beef, then take it out of the pan, so you don't overcook the meat.) When the saltado is almost ready, drizzle the saltado and soy sauces alongside the edges of the wok or pan, not on top of the ingredients, so the sauces caramelize as they hit the hot pan.

4. Trust your nose. Don't just go by the recipe cooking times. You really need to "feel" a saltado, or the stir-fry won't have any character. The stir-fry should smell very aromatic. If you're not sure, use a spoon to quickly taste the stir-fry (be careful—the sauce will be very hot). Cook the ingredients a little less or longer if you think they need it.

SHRIMP WITH TOMATOES, RED ONIONS & PASTA

SERVES
3 OR 4

There is a style of Peruvian stir-fry with noodles called *tallarines saltados*, usually made with beef or shrimp and Chinese egg noodles or Italian pasta. It's classic chifa, or Peruvian-Chinese cooking featuring a mix of local ingredients with foods that Europeans brought to the Americas. My version is not a true saltado, but more like a shrimp and pasta stew flavored with my stir-fry sauce. Instead of searing the ingredients, I cook them down more slowly, like an aderezo, so the pasta stays very moist. And with lower heat, you can make more servings at the same time, and use butter, which is so good with shrimp.

Instead of only shrimp, you could also make this like a cioppino with mixed seafood—mussels, shrimp, and firm white-fleshed fish—whatever you have. We make our own pastas for the restaurant, but at home, I use really good store-bought pasta. Because the pasta goes back into the stew pot, be sure to cook it no more than al dente on its own. For a really nice presentation, I butterfly jumbo shrimp (remove the skin but leave the tail attached), but you can use smaller shrimp and simply peel them. If you don't have ají amarillo butter already made, mix together 4 tablespoons of room temperature unsalted butter and 1½ teaspoons (or a little more, for a spicier flavor) of ají amarillo paste.

About 12 ounces good-quality linguine, fettuccine, or other dried long pasta

Kosher salt, for cooking the pasta

¼ cup extra-virgin olive oil

½ medium red onion, coarsely chopped into ½-inch chunks

1 teaspoon pureed garlic (page 37) or finely minced garlic

2 medium ripe heirloom or beefsteak tomatoes, or 4 plum tomatoes, roughly chopped

1 bay leaf

½ cup homemade fish or chicken stock (page 40) or low-sodium store-bought chicken broth

4 tablespoons ají amarillo butter (page 38)

1½ pounds peeled and deveined shrimp with tails intact, butterflied if extra-large (see page 123)

4 tablespoons soy sauce, preferably Yamasa

4 tablespoons Saltado Sauce (page 138)

2 scallions, finely chopped

3 or 4 sprigs fresh cilantro, finely chopped

1 small wedge Parmesan, for garnish

1 Cook the pasta according to the package directions until al dente. Drain and rinse the pasta under cold running water until cool. Let drain in the colander.

2 Heat the oil in a large Dutch oven or stockpot over medium-high heat until hot, a good 2 minutes. Add the onions and sauté until they begin to soften and are nicely browned along the edges, a good 5 minutes. Add the garlic, sauté another minute, then stir in the tomatoes and bay leaf. Gently push the aderezo (flavorings) back and forth on the bottom of the pan with the spoon until the tomatoes have slightly softened, a minute or two more, then add the stock.

3 When the stock is bubbling hot, add the butter, a few chunks at a time, and stir to emulsify the sauce. When all of the butter has melted, add the shrimp and sauté until the flesh just begins to turn white all over, usually no more than 90 seconds for jumbo shrimp (less if the shrimp are smaller). Drizzle the soy and saltado sauces along the edges of the wok or pan, not on top of the stir-fry ingredients. You should smell them caramelizing, then toss the pasta in the sauce.

4 Divide the pasta and sauce among four bowls, sprinkle the scallions and cilantro over the pasta, and shave a little Parmesan on top. Serve right away.

QUINOA FRIED RICE WITH SHRIMP & PICKLED RADISHES

SERVES
2

There's something about making dinner with leftovers that is relaxing, like you are just messing around in the kitchen. The Peruvian version of Chinese fried rice is called a *chaufa*. It comes, or so I've always been told, from Spanish-speaking locals mispronouncing the Cantonese name for fried rice, *chau fan*. Chaufas are some of the closest Peruvian dishes to authentic Cantonese, with some kind of meat, poultry, or seafood, onions, and often eggs cooked at high heat in a soy-based stir-fry sauce. The main Peruvian components are a little fiery ají pepper paste and local ingredients like red onions (instead of green or white) and often organ meats. You can use any leftovers you have, or fry up some chicken or beef instead of shrimp. I prefer to use quinoa instead of rice because it has a lighter texture and flavor.

This version doesn't have any saltado sauce, but like any stir-fry, have your ingredients prepped and ready to go. Unlike leftover rice, when you stir-fry quinoa, you need to add it to the hot wok or pan toward the end of the cooking time, or it can break down and fall apart. If you are frying eggs instead of using leftover scrambled eggs, have your frying pan hot and ready to go when you start cooking to fry the eggs quickly.

2 to 3 tablespoons canola or other vegetable oil

2 teaspoons pureed ginger (page 37) or finely zested ginger

2 teaspoons pureed garlic (page 37)

12 ounces peeled and deveined shrimp with tails intact, butterflied if extra-large (see page 123)

2 to 2½ cups leftover cooked quinoa, drained on paper towels if moist

About ⅓ cup leftover scrambled eggs, or 2 eggs for frying

2 scallions, finely chopped

2 tablespoons soy sauce, preferably a good-quality Japanese brand, or 1½ tablespoons tamari, or to taste

¼ cup (2 ounces) homemade fish, chicken, or vegetable stock (page 40) or low-sodium store-bought broth

¼ bunch fresh cilantro, leaves and tender top stems finely chopped

About ¼ cup ají amarillo aioli or Sriracha aioli (page 38) or a blend of the two

¼ cup thinly sliced pickled radishes (see page 39) or store-bought pickled ginger, drained (optional)

1 Heat a wok or large sauté pan over high heat until hot—a good 2 minutes. Pour in the oil to lightly coat the bottom of the pan and heat the oil for 2 to 3 minutes, until very hot. The oil shouldn't be smoking, but close to it. Swirl the oil around the pan, toss in the ginger, garlic, and shrimp, and shake the pan or use tongs to flip and sear them on all sides until they just begin to turn pink along the edges, 30 to 45 seconds, depending on their size. Add the quinoa, toss again, and fry the chaufa until the grains begin to lightly brown and smell toasty, about 1 minute, stirring often.

2 Toss in the scrambled eggs and about half the scallions, mix well, then drizzle the soy sauce along the edges of the wok or pan (not on top of the stir-fry ingredients) so the sauce sizzles, and cook for a few seconds. (If frying eggs, heat up a separate pan to fry them in; cook and hold them to place on top of the stir-fry.) Next, pour in the stock around the edges of the wok, then add the cilantro. Toss everything together one more time, taste, and add another drizzle of soy sauce, if you'd like. The chaufa should be really flavorful.

3 Spoon the chaufa straight out of the pan into serving bowls, and sprinkle the remaining scallions on top. Top each serving with a generous spoonful of the aioli and the radishes (if using).

STEWED MUSSELS WITH AJÍ AMARILLO BUTTER

SERVES 2

Olive oil is usually my go-to fat for cooking, but when I do cook with butter, I make sure there is plenty. I want to taste all of that incredible flavor. This is more of a French-style version of stewed mussels, only with ají amarillo peppers to spice up the butter. The mussels are good with bacon or a fresh, meaty Argentinean- or Spanish-style fresh chorizo.

If you don't have any ají amarillo butter already made, mix together 6 tablespoons unsalted room temperature butter and 2 to 2½ teaspoons ají amarillo paste, depending on how spicy you like it.

2 large slices crusty bread, toasted

2 tablespoons extra-virgin olive oil

3 or 4 meaty slices bacon, sliced into ½-inch-thick pieces, or 1 (4- to 5-inch) uncured link sausage, such as chorizo

1½ to 2 pounds mussels (depending on how hungry you are), scrubbed and debearded

1½ cups (12 ounces) homemade fish or chicken stock (page 40) or low-sodium store-bought chicken broth

1 bay leaf

½ medium shallot, finely chopped

1 teaspoon kosher salt, or more to taste

6 tablespoons ají amarillo butter (page 38), cut into chunks

1 lemon or 2 limes, or more to taste

3 or 4 sprigs fresh cilantro, finely chopped

2 scallions, finely chopped

1 Put the toasted bread in the bottom of two large soup bowls. Heat a large Dutch oven over medium-high heat until hot, add the oil, and heat for another minute. Fry the bacon until the meat is just cooked but still very tender, about 5 minutes.

2 Add the mussels, stock, and bay leaf to the pot. Cover and cook the mussels until about half the shells have opened, usually only 1 to 2 minutes. Sprinkle the shallots and salt over the mussels, and then stir in the butter. Cook the mussels, uncovered, stirring occasionally, until the rest have opened, 1 to 2 minutes (discard any mussels that do not open).

3 Squeeze the juice of ½ lemon or 1 lime over the mussels, taste, and season the broth with the juice from the other lemon half or the lime and some salt, if you'd like. Sprinkle the cilantro and scallions on top and divide the mussels among the bowls with the bread. Pour any leftover broth over the mussels and serve immediately.

"PERUVIAN MARIJUANA"

I use a mix of cilantro and scallions to finish so many stir-fries, stews, and other dishes that the garnish has become a running joke in my kitchens. When you chop the scallions (including the green stem) and cilantro really finely, the mixture releases incredible aromas. You just want to stick your nose in the bowl and take a big whiff (why I started calling it "Peruvian marijuana"). Now, everyone in my kitchens does the same. It's amazing how many dishes take on a whole new life when they are garnished with a little of the good stuff.

ROASTING & BRAISING MEATS

SERVES 6 TO 8 OR 10 OR MORE AS SANDWICHES

Any house that smells like braised meats is one that I want to be in; I just don't always want to stand around the stove for hours doing the braising myself. Oven-roasting fattier meats and poultry at a high temperature gets you an even better caramelized brown crust on the outside of the meat or game than stovetop searing, and the oven does all of the work. Afterward, a long, slow braise on the stovetop gets you to that fall apart-tender texture that is so good, and after slowly reducing over several hours, the braising liquid turns into an incredibly rich sauce. Everything happens virtually on its own, leaving you with time to do whatever else you want around the house.

You can use this technique with any braising liquid that you create—just be mindful of how much salt, sugar, and spices you add, because flavors will intensify as the broth cooks down into a more concentrated sauce. Roast meats and poultry like duck with the fatty side up, so all of that good flavor trickles down into the flesh. Afterward, if you come up short on braising liquid, try changing the size and shape of the cooking pot or roasting pan, or add a little more stock to almost cover the meat or poultry. The flavors will only be better if you make everything a day or two ahead.

And, if you suddenly find yourself with a few extra mouths to feed, as often happens at my house, shred the meat for sandwiches. Those flavorful braising juices get all up in the nooks on crusty sandwich bread. Chopping a few red onions so you can slather some Salsa Criolla (page 44) on top would be very Peruvian of you.

LAMB SHANKS
5½ to 6 pounds; 2 to 3 large hind shanks, if you can find them, or 6 to 8 foreshanks

WHOLE DUCK LEGS
3 to 3½ pounds; 6 drumsticks attached to the thighs

BONE-IN SHORT RIBS
4 to 4½ pounds; 6 to 8 of the big English-cut ribs, or 12 to 16 smaller American-cut ribs

OXTAIL
3½ to 4 pounds; look for the big, 3-inch chunks from the rump end

BRISKET OR CHUCK ROAST
4 pounds or so, bigger if you want leftovers

Kosher salt and freshly ground black pepper
About 1 tablespoon pureed garlic (page 37), or 2 whole cloves garlic, smashed
Canola or olive oil

1 Preheat the oven to 450°F and place a rack in the bottom of the oven. Dry off all sides of the meat or poultry well with paper towels and put them fatty side up on a rimmed baking sheet or in a roasting pan. (If roasting duck legs, use a high-sided roasting pan to catch the fat drippings and leave 2 or 3 inches of breathing room between each piece.)

2 Sprinkle the meat or poultry lightly with salt and pepper. Go lighter than you usually do on the salt; as the braise cooks down, the saltiness intensifies. You can add more at the end. Rub the seasonings into all sides of the meat along with a dollop of pureed garlic and a good drizzle of oil. If using smashed garlic, rub it on all sides of the meat or poultry and discard the cloves.

3 Roast the meat or poultry for a solid hour, until golden brown with a few charred bits. Flip the meats halfway through the cooking time to brown on the opposite side; leave the duck legs fat side up. Transfer the meats to a clean roasting pan or baking dish, depending on their size (if using duck, save the duck fat for roasting potatoes). You can oven braise the meats right away, or let cool, cover, and refrigerate overnight.

BRAISED LAMB WITH
SECO SAUCE & CANARIO BEANS

SERVES
6 TO 8

Seco, a misnomer that literally means "dry" in Spanish, is actually a very juicy, flavorful, stewlike dish made from slowly cooking down meat or poultry with aderezos, flavorings and seasonings, in plenty of liquid, usually stock. I usually add a little beer for an even richer flavor. Secos are traditionally served with white *frijoles canarios*, canary beans, which are also called mayocoba or Peruano beans (despite the name, they are native to Central America). I love the rich flavor and creamy texture of canario beans, but you can also substitute smashed potatoes or rice. It's really worth the time to cook up dried beans: The texture and flavor are so much better than canned (and dried are much more economical). But this is one case where all of those incredible flavors in the seco sauce will even make canned beans taste good (drain them before reheating). You can also use this braising technique with small or larger lamb shanks.

5 to 6 pounds lamb foreshanks or hindshanks, oven-roasted
     (see page 149)
About 8 cups Cilantro-Beer Seco Braise (recipe follows)
Homemade chicken stock (page 40) or low-sodium store-
     bought broth, if needed
Kosher salt
1 pound dried canario (mayocoba) beans or other white
     beans, cooked (see page 213) and drained if needed,
     for serving

1 Preheat the oven to 350°F and place a rack at the bottom of the oven. Arrange the roasted lamb shanks snugly in a large Dutch oven or stockpot and pour the cilantro-beer braising liquid over them. A few bones poking out the top is fine, but the meat should be mostly covered by the liquid. If needed, add a few cups of chicken stock. Cover the pot with a lid, or tent loosely with foil if using giant hindshanks that poke out of the pot.

2 Bake the lamb until the meat is fall-apart tender, 3 to 3½ hours for smaller pieces, up to 4 hours for large hindshanks. (Check smaller pieces after 2½ hours and larger lamb shanks after 3 hours.) Transfer the shanks to a platter with tongs and set them aside until cool enough to handle. Use your hands to break the lamb meat into small chunks and discard the bones. Skim off some of the surface fat from the braising liquid (it should have reduced to a jus-like sauce), but don't worry about skimming it all away—a little fat is always tasty. Taste the meat and sauce, season with salt, if needed, and return the meat to the sauce. If you are not serving the lamb right away, let cool completely, cover, and refrigerate the meat in the seco sauce for up to 2 days.

3 To serve, pile the beans onto a serving platter or individual plates, arrange the lamb on the beans, and spoon some of the seco sauce on top (or serve it alongside, like gravy).

CILANTRO-BEER SECO BRAISE

Makes about 8 cups

This is another of my base sauces—here, more of a braising liquid—that I came up with to keep the flavors consistent in my restaurant kitchens. Were you to taste all of these ingredients together before the braise cooks down, it would be terrible. But magic happens as they are heated and meld slowly, and all of the ingredients cook down into an almost currylike cilantro sauce.

I also use this braise to make *seco de pato*, braised duck (you can substitute chicken—see page 154). It would be excellent on brisket—just roast it the same way as the other meats, and use the same quantity of braising liquid as for the lamb. You could even use it on firm white-fleshed fish, as this is truly a multipurpose cooking base, but simmer the smaller quantity of sauce on its own for a solid hour before adding the fish, and cook the fish until just tender (15 to 25 minutes, depending on how thick your cut of fish).

If you are making the Arroz con Pato duck recipe (page 154), which also features this sauce, cut the recipe in half.

6 cups packed fresh cilantro leaves and stems (2 large or 3 medium bunches)

1 head garlic, cloves separated, peeled, and lightly smashed

2 (12-ounce) pilsners or other light beers

3 cups homemade chicken stock (page 40) or low-sodium store-bought broth

1 teaspoon kosher salt, or to taste

In a blender, puree the cilantro leaves and stems, garlic, and beer in batches until smooth. Transfer to a bowl or the cooking pot and stir in the broth and salt. Use the seco braise right away, or cover and refrigerate for up to 1 day.

SECOS Y ESTOFADOS

Secos are a style of slow-cooked meat or poultry stews that you find all over Peru. The word *seco* means "dry," but the stews are completely the opposite—and no one I know, at least, seems to know how the name came to be. You'll also hear some stews called *estofados*, which is the literal Spanish word for "stew." The word *seco* goes back to the *comida criolla*, the hybrid style of cooking that evolved in northern Peru when the Spanish arrived. A seco usually refers to a specific style of estofado that is built around cilantro, but you can have a seco without cilantro in it, too.

STEWED SHORT RIBS WITH TOMATO–AJÍ PEPPER SAUCE & POTATOES

SERVES
8

This estofado is my version of the Peruvian staple. In Peru, slowly cooking short ribs in a stewlike sauce is a classic Sunday supper. It's the sort of dish your mom put on the stove in the morning that made the house smell so incredible, you were never late to the table. Some versions have raisins, a Spanish or maybe Italian addition, and whatever seasonings the home cook in charge wants to throw in the pot. In mine, the tomatoes and ají peppers cook down into a rich sauce spiced with cumin, and the fall-apart-tender meat sops up all of those flavors. This estofado braise would be good with any big, meaty cuts of beef like a chuck roast or brisket. Smash, mash, or roast your favorite potatoes to serve along with the ribs, and open a really good bottle of wine.

3½ to 4 pounds meaty bone-in short ribs, oven-roasted (see page 149)
Tomato–Ají Pepper Braise (recipe follows)
Homemade chicken stock (page 40) or low-sodium store-bought broth, if needed
1 bay leaf
Kosher salt, if needed
Smashed, mashed, or roasted potatoes, for serving

ADEREZO

In Peruvian cooking, everything starts with the aderezo. The aderezo is the *sabor,* flavor, the backbone of many traditional dishes, especially slow-cooked stews and braises; it provides their unmistakable Peruvian character or personality. It is a lot like a Spanish sofrito, only the ingredients you use are not as rigidly defined and change depending on the dish and the cook's preference. In many, the aderezo includes some kind of pepper, and often garlic and onions, but it might be just garlic and onions fried in some kind of oil for the simplest rice preparations. The only consistency is that, like any good Peruvian dish, the aderezo always varies.

1 Preheat the oven to 350°F and place a rack in the bottom third of the oven. Arrange the roasted short ribs snugly in a large Dutch oven or a baking dish with 3- to 4-inch sides, and pour the tomato–ají pepper braise over them. If the ribs are not fully covered, try a different size pot, or add a cup or two of chicken stock. Add the bay leaf and cover the pot with a lid or foil.

2 Bake the short ribs until the meat is fall-apart tender, a solid 3 hours. If you are roasting a pot roast or brisket, bake the meat a little longer, 3½ to 4 hours. Use a large spoon to skim off as much of the surface fat from the braising liquid as possible (although a little fat is always tasty). Taste the meat and braising liquid (it should have reduced to a jus-like sauce) and season with salt, if needed. If you are not serving the short ribs right away, let them cool completely in the sauce, cover, and refrigerate for up to 2 days. Rewarm the ribs and sauce slowly over medium-low heat or in a preheated 300°F oven. Add a splash of chicken broth, if needed, to keep it from burning, and stir regularly.

3 To serve, pile the potatoes onto a serving platter or individual plates, arrange the short ribs on the potatoes, and spoon some of the sauce on top (or serve it alongside).

TOMATO–AJÍ PEPPER BRAISE

Makes 7 to 8 cups

Give me a hunk of beef, and the first thing I want to do is make a really good sauce. As in so many other slow-cooked Peruvian dishes, the bright, spicy ají amarillo and mellow, almost smoky-sweet ají panca pepper pastes work together to balance the flavors of the braise. The ají panca pepper paste is more like a smoky tomato paste, so it adds flavor depth and color more than heat.

1 large or 2 small red onions

1 large red bell pepper, stemmed, seeded, and veins removed

2 medium carrots, peeled

Cloves from ½ head garlic, separated

¼ cup olive oil

1 bay leaf

1½ tablespoons ají panca paste, store-bought or homemade (page 36)

1 tablespoon ají amarillo paste, store-bought or homemade (page 34)

4 plum tomatoes, stem ends trimmed, quartered

1½ teaspoons ground cumin

⅓ cup dry red wine, like Beaujolais, or whatever you have around

3 cups homemade chicken stock (page 40) or low-sodium store-bought broth

1 Chop the onion, bell pepper, and carrots into big chunks, roughly 1 inch or so. Peel and lightly smash the garlic. Heat the oil in a large saucepan or Dutch oven over medium-high heat until hot, a good 2 minutes. Add the chopped vegetables and garlic and sauté, stirring occasionally with a wooden spoon, until the vegetables begin to soften and the edges color, 8 to 10 minutes. Add the bay leaf and ají panca paste and sauté, stirring every so often, for 2 minutes more. The aderezo (flavorings) should smell deliciously smoky from the pepper paste.

2 Stir in the ají amarillo paste, reduce the heat to medium-low, and sauté for another minute or two, moving the aderezo back and forth on the bottom of the pot with the spoon. Add the tomatoes, cook for another minute or two so they release their juices, then add the cumin and scrape up any browned bits from the bottom of the pan. Cook the tomatoes until they start to break down and look juicy, 3 to 4 minutes, deglaze the pan with the wine, and reduce the liquid for another few minutes. Add the chicken stock and scrape up any browned bits from the bottom of the pan one more time. Remove the pan from the heat.

3 When cool enough to handle, discard the bay leaf and puree everything in a blender in batches until smooth. Use right away, or cool the tomato–ají pepper braise completely, cover, and refrigerate for up to 2 days.

BRAISED DUCK LEGS WITH SECO SAUCE & RICE

SERVES
6

There are so many different versions of arroz con pollo, rice and chicken, all over Latin America and Spain. We usually make ours with cilantro, so the braise cooks down into a jus-like sauce and turns the color of the forest. In northern Peru, native Muscovy ducks (see sidebar) are often used instead of chicken. Once you've had arroz con pato, it's hard to go back. With all of that good fat, the meat is so juicy and full flavored.

I usually cook the duck confit-style, meaning very slowly braised in oil, but the legs are also very good simply roasted in the oven. Chicken is also great, especially if you are short on time. Use bone-in thighs or whole legs, and sauté them in oil for a little color before braising them.

This recipe makes a good amount of braise that cooks down into more of a jus-like reduction than a thicker sauce. Fold a few spoonfuls into rice for a quick arroz verde (page 205). If you have the pantry ingredients to make huancaína sauce, all the better, but this duck can definitely stand alone.

6 whole duck legs, oven-roasted (see page 149), or 12 bone-in chicken thighs (do not roast)

About 4½ cups Cilantro-Beer Seco Braise (page 151)

Homemade chicken stock (page 40) or low-sodium store-bought broth, if needed

Olive oil, if needed

Kosher salt, if needed

Steamed rice or arroz verde (page 205), for serving

Generous ⅓ cup Salsa a la Huancaína (page 168; optional)

1 Preheat the oven to 350°F and place a rack in the bottom third of the oven. Arrange the roasted duck legs, fat side up, snugly in a medium Dutch oven or a baking dish with 3- or 4-inch sides, and pour the braise over them. If the legs are not fully covered, try a different size pot, or add a cup or two of chicken stock. Cover the pot with a lid or foil. (If using bone-in chicken thighs, skip the oven-braising step and brown the pieces in hot olive oil on the stovetop.)

2 Bake the duck legs until the meat is fall-apart tender, a good 3 hours. (For chicken, cut the baking time to 1¼ to 1½ hours.) Use a large spoon to skim off as much of the surface fat from the braising liquid as possible (although a little fat is always tasty). Taste the poultry and braising liquid (it should have cooked down to a jus-like reduction) and season with salt, if needed. (With chicken, the sauce will not have reduced as much; you can reduce the sauce further on its own in the pot after removing the chicken if you'd like.) If you are not serving the duck right away, let cool completely in the seco sauce and refrigerate for up to 2 days.

3 To serve, fold a little of the reduced seco sauce into the steamed rice, if you'd like to make green rice. Arrange the whole duck legs on the rice and spoon a little more of the seco sauce on top. Don't forget the huancaína sauce, if you have it. Drizzle the sauce all over everything, or serve it alongside.

MUSCOVY, THE MOCHE & MO-CHICA

The ancient city of Machu Picchu, built by the Incas into a mountainside in southern Peru some 8,000 feet above sea level, is one of the wonders of the world. The surrounding Cuzco region, the Incas' government headquarters as they expanded their control along the South American coastline, is a great place to try southern Peruvian cuisine like *rocoto rellenos*, rocoto peppers stuffed with meat, raisins, and peanuts.

But ever since I was a kid, I've always felt a stronger connection to the Moche, the pre-Incan civilization that thrived along northern Peru's river valleys from around AD 100 to 900. Building an empire in the desert between the coast and the Andes gave the Moche access to both sea and land animals, but it also meant they had to adapt to agricultural conditions in a dry, desertlike region that wasn't very friendly for farming. They developed a very intricate canal system to grow crops like corn, beans, and squash and on which to raise domesticated animals like llamas, guinea pigs, and Muscovy ducks, which they domesticated more than 1,500 years ago.

If the Moche could take the situation they were given and turn it into something much better, I know I can, too. One of my favorite phrases is "Let's make it happen." I say it so much that people I work with look at me like I'm crazy. Archaeologists sometimes refer to the Moche as Mochica, which was the name of my first restaurant in Los Angeles. At first, even opening that tiny little space seemed impossible . . . but we made it happen.

BRAISED PORK WITH SPICY AJÍ ADOBO SAUCE

SERVES
8 TO 10

An adobo is more of a curing technique than a specific recipe. The Spanish historically used a spicy, vinegary marinade to preserve meats before refrigeration; then the meats were slowly cooked in the adobo "sauce." In my version, the meat cooks into a fall-apart-tender mess with a double hit of ají panca and amarillo peppers. This is another of those sauces that makes almost anything taste good: pork in any form (shoulder, butt, chops, belly), brisket, or chicken.

A giant bone-in pork shoulder is really good but requires a pretty big pot. Pork butt with a nice layer of skin and fat is also *excelente*, and a little more manageable. You can serve the pork in the sauce on its own or with potatoes. In my house, a sandwich is always a good idea, as there's always so much of that crazy good sauce to sop up with the bread.

½ teaspoon ground cumin

¼ teaspoon ground cinnamon

1½ tablespoons kosher salt, or to taste

2 teaspoons freshly ground black pepper

1½ tablespoons sugar

Zest of 1 small orange

1 (5- to 6-pound) bone-in, skin-on pork shoulder or bone-in pork butt with a nice layer of fat

Olive oil

Spicy Ají Adobo Sauce (recipe follows)

Homemade chicken stock (page 40) or low-sodium store-bought broth, if needed

1 bay leaf

Kosher salt, if needed

Crusty bread, for serving

1 Mix together the cumin, cinnamon, salt, pepper, sugar, and orange zest in a small dish. Use a sharp knife to lightly score the pork shoulder, if using, in a crisscross diamond pattern at roughly 2-inch intervals. If you are using a pork butt that doesn't include the skin, don't score the fat. Rub the spices all over the meat, cover the pork with plastic wrap, and refrigerate overnight.

2 Preheat the oven to 450°F and place a rack in the bottom third of the oven. Pat the pork roast dry with paper towels and rub the meat with a few tablespoons of olive oil. Place the pork, skin or fattiest side up, on a rimmed baking sheet or in a roasting pan. Roast the pork until dark golden brown all over, 45 minutes to 1 hour.

3 Transfer the meat to a large Dutch oven or stockpot. Pour enough ají adobo sauce into the pot to fully submerge the pork. If the pork is not fully covered, try a different size pot, or add a cup or two of chicken stock. Add the bay leaf and cover the pot with a lid or foil.

4 Bake the pork until the meat is fall-apart tender, about 4 hours. Use a large spoon to skim off as much of the surface fat from the braising liquid as possible (although a little fat is always tasty). When cool enough to handle, shred the meat. Taste the meat and braising liquid (it should have reduced to a jus-like sauce) and season with salt, if needed. If not serving right away, let cool completely, cover, and refrigerate the pork in the sauce for up to 2 days.

5 To serve, pile the pork and sauce onto a serving platter or individual plates with plenty of crusty bread alongside, or make giant, sauce-covered sandwiches.

SPICY AJÍ ADOBO SAUCE

Makes 8 to 10 cups

I like to have plenty of this sauce around, just in case I need it.
If you are roasting a smaller cut of pork that doesn't need so
much sauce to cover, you can freeze any leftover sauce to braise
chicken or pork chops. And if you are lucky enough to have any
leftovers on the back end, spoon some of the cooked sauce into
a pot of beans—so good.

1 large or 2 small red onions

5 cloves garlic

¼ cup olive oil

2 tablespoons ají panca paste, store-bought or homemade
(page 36)

1 tablespoon ají amarillo paste, store-bought or homemade
(page 34)

2 teaspoons ground cumin

1 tablespoon fresh thyme leaves

1 bay leaf

1 (12-ounce) lager or other medium-bodied beer

2 teaspoons freshly ground black pepper

5 pounds plum tomatoes, stem ends trimmed, quartered

2 cups (16 ounces) homemade chicken stock (page 40) or
low-sodium store-bought broth

2 tablespoons red wine vinegar

2 to 3 teaspoons kosher salt

1 Chop the onion into big chunks, roughly 1 inch or so. Peel
and lightly smash the garlic. Heat the oil in a large Dutch oven
or stockpot over medium-high heat until hot, a good 2 minutes.
Add the onions and sauté, stirring every so often, until they are
nicely browned along the edges, 5 minutes, stirring occasionally
with a wooden spoon. Add the garlic, sauté for another minute,
then stir in the ají panca and amarillo pastes, cumin, thyme,
and bay leaf. Reduce the heat to medium-low and gently push
the aderezo (flavorings) back and forth on the bottom of the
pan with the spoon until the pepper pastes smell toasty and the
sauce reduces slightly, about 5 minutes. Pour in the beer and
scrape up any browned bits from the bottom of the pan.

2 Add the pepper, tomatoes, and chicken stock and bring the
mixture to a low boil. Boil until the tomatoes are very soft,
about 15 minutes, then set the sauce aside until cool enough to
handle. Remove the bay leaf.

3 If you have a very large blender, puree the adobo sauce until
smooth. Or, strain the liquid into a large bowl, puree the solids
in a food processor until smooth, then return them to the broth.
Stir in the vinegar and salt. If not using right away, refrigerate
for up to 3 days or freeze for up to 3 months.

BRAISED OXTAIL WITH SPICY HUACATAY SAUCE & MAÍZE MOTE

SERVES 5 OR 6

Chanfainita is traditionally made with beef lung. The stew dates back to when the Spanish conquistadors brought African slaves with them to Peru. The slaves supplemented the basic ingredients they had for cooking with whatever parts of an animal the wealthy landowners discarded. The Spanish didn't know what they were missing. Scraps like organ meats and an animal's hooves make the best-tasting stews. They hide such a diversity of flavors inside them (as with beef lung) or simply taste fantastically different (like chicken liver). And, I love all of their different textures. With beef lung, you get a very subtle beef flavor and an almost spongy texture, which may sound strange if you've never tried it, but is so good.

Unfortunately, you can't buy beef lung from butchers in the United States. I use oxtail, which has a big, beefy flavor that is so good with the huacatay and ají pepper beer braise. I have to say, some days I like it even more than the heart. A meaty 3- to 4-pound pot roast would also be good. If you are making the maíz mote, or Peruvian-style hominy (the classic choice), make it ahead and save the cooking broth to use as stock for the chanfainita.

3 pounds oxtails, oven-roasted (see page 149)
Spicy Huacatay Beer Braise (recipe follows)
Homemade chicken stock (page 40) or low-sodium store-bought broth, or use Maíz Mote cooking broth (page 220), as needed
Kosher salt, if needed
Maíz Mote (page 220) or canario or your favorite beans (see page 212)
Crusty bread, for serving

1 Preheat the oven to 350°F. Place the oxtails in a Dutch oven or roasting pan big enough so they fit snugly in a single layer and pour the huacatay beer braise on top. If the oxtails are not fully covered by the sauce, try a different size or add a cup or two of the chicken stock to cover. Cover the pan securely with foil, then the lid. Bake the oxtails until fall-apart tender, 3½ to 4 hours. Use a large spoon to skim off as much of the surface fat from the sauce as you can (although a little fat is always tasty).

2 When cool enough to handle, season the meat and braising liquid (it should have reduced to more of a sauce) with salt, if needed. If not serving right away, let cool completely, cover, and refrigerate the oxtails in the huacatay sauce for up to 2 days.

3 If chilled, rewarm the shredded oxtails in the huacatay sauce slowly over medium-low heat. Stir the sauce every once in a while, but be careful not to break up the meat. Pile the maíz mote into individual serving bowls or in a large serving bowl, and pile the oxtails and sauce alongside. Serve the chanfainita with the bread.

SPICY HUACATAY BEER BRAISE

Makes 6 to 7 cups

It's worth seeking out the herb huacatay (see page 31) for this dish. It gives the braise a really unique flavor. If you can't find it, the cooked-down sauce will still be very good. It will just taste more like a traditional seco stew instead of chanfainita.

3 tablespoons olive oil

1 large red onion, coarsely chopped into ½-inch pieces

6 large cloves garlic, lightly smashed

1 tablespoon ají amarillo paste, store-bought or homemade (page 34)

1½ tablespoons ají panca paste, store-bought or homemade (page 36)

1½ teaspoons ground cumin

1 cup packed fresh huacatay leaves, or ½ cup frozen huacatay, thawed

1 (12-ounce) pilsner or other light beer

3 cups homemade chicken stock (page 40) or low-sodium store-bought chicken broth

2 small bunches fresh cilantro

Leaves from 1 bunch fresh mint

Kosher salt

1 Heat a large Dutch oven over medium-high heat until hot, a good 2 minutes. Add the oil, heat for another minute or two, then add the onion and. Sauté the onion, stirring occasionally with a wooden spoon, until they begin to color on the edges, about 5 minutes. Add the garlic, sauté for another minute, then stir in both ají pastes and the cumin, reduce the heat to medium-low, and sauté for another minute or two, moving the aderezo (flavorings) back and forth on the bottom of the pan with the spoon.

2 Add the huacatay and beer, scrape up any browned bits from the bottom of the pan, then add the stock. Bring the braising liquid to a low boil, cook the liquid for 8 to 10 minutes to allow the flavors to mellow, and set aside the sauce until cool enough to handle.

3 Chop off the very ends of the cilantro stems and break each bunch into thirds. Puree the braising liquid in batches with the mint leaves and cilantro in a blender until smooth. Season the braise lightly with salt (the salt will become more concentrated as the braising liquid reduces). Use immediately, or refrigerate the huacatay beer braise for up to 2 days (rewarm before using).

INCAN POTATO, PORK & PEANUT STEW WITH MINT CHIMICHURRI

SERVES
5 OR 6

Carapulcra is a very old, and famous, dish in Peru. The stew is built around native ingredients like ají peppers and potatoes that have been dried in the sun. Papas secas (dried potatoes; see page 27) keep for months and aren't heavy to carry, and the drying process gives the potatoes a unique earthy flavor. The stew gets its fair share of European, Asian, and also African flavors with garlic, peanuts, and different spices. Everyone has his or her own variation.

Traditionally, dried jerky, usually made from pork, was added to the stew, but I make a meatless version to eat on its own, or with big, fat slices of fried pork belly (what you usually see in Peru today). The chimichurri idea I borrowed from Argentinean cooks, who serve the condiment with grilled meats. They usually use parsley, but a little mint really wakes up all of the flavors. I like my carapulcra potatoes on the chewier, al dente–pasta side instead of fall-apart soft, as my mom used to make them. Instead of pork belly, you can serve the stew with grilled sausage, or for a vegetarian version, leave out the bacon and use vegetable broth instead of chicken broth.

1 (15-ounce) bag papas secas

1 tablespoon olive oil

3 meaty slices bacon, chopped into ½-inch pieces

½ medium red onion, finely chopped

2 teaspoons pureed garlic (page 37)

3 tablespoons ají panca paste, store-bought or homemade (page 36)

2 tablespoons ají amarillo paste, store-bought or homemade (page 34)

4 to 5 cups homemade chicken stock (see page 40) or low-sodium store-bought chicken broth

1 cinnamon stick

2½ tablespoons crunchy peanut butter

2 teaspoons kosher salt, plus more to taste

½ teaspoon freshly ground black pepper, plus more to taste

5 or 6 slices fried pork belly (see page 70), or 2 or 3 meaty, grilled or sautéed link sausages, sliced

Mint Chimichurri (recipe follows)

1 Put the papas secas in a medium bowl, add enough water to cover by a good 2 inches, and soak the potatoes for at least 4 to 6 hours, preferably overnight. Drain the potatoes.

2 Heat the oil in a large Dutch oven or soup pot over medium-high heat, and fry the bacon until beginning to brown but still very tender, about 5 minutes. Add the onions and sauté until they begin to soften and are nicely browned along the edges, a good 5 minutes. Stir in the garlic and the ají panca and amarillo pastes with a wooden spoon and sauté for another few minutes, until the onions are soft, moving the aderezo (flavorings) back and forth on the bottom of the pan with the spoon.

RECIPE CONTINUES

3 Add the drained potatoes, 4 cups of the stock, and the cinnamon stick to the pot. Stir, bring the stock to a simmer, and cook the potatoes until tender, 25 to 30 minutes. Add a little more stock, ½ cup at a time, if the stew ever begins to look dry, and stir and scrape the bottom of the pot regularly to prevent the potatoes from sticking. When the potatoes are tender-crisp, stir in the peanut butter and season the carapulcra with salt and pepper.

4 Serve the stew family-style, in the cooking pot, with the fried pork belly or sausages on top, or ladle up the stew and meats into individual serving bowls. Drizzle about half of the mint chimichurri on top of the stew and serve any remaining chimichurri on the side.

MINT CHIMICHURRI

Makes about 1 cup

The mint makes the flavors in this chimichurri really pop. In addition to the stew, it would be so good with grilled or roasted lamb or chicken. I use two different types of salt for contrast. The kosher salt almost melts into the sauce, so you get a consistent flavor, and the sea salt holds its shape for more of a crunchy-fresh saltiness on the tip of your tongue.

2 tablespoons finely chopped mint leaves
½ cup finely chopped fresh flat-leaf parsley leaves and tender top stems
½ cup finely chopped shallots (about 1 large)
3 tablespoons finely chopped seeded and deveined jalapeños, or to taste
2 teaspoons Banyuls or good-quality red wine vinegar
¼ teaspoon kosher salt
½ teaspoon coarse sea salt, or to taste
1½ tablespoons fresh lime juice, or to taste

Mix together all of the ingredients in a small bowl. Taste, and add more salt and lime juice if needed. The chimichurri should be tangy, with a noticeable saltiness. Use immediately, or cover and refrigerate for 4 to 5 hours.

SALCHIPAPAS
(FRIED SAUSAGES & FRENCH FRIES)

Salchipapas is what we always hoped our moms would make for dinner when we were kids.

The name comes from *salchichas* (sausages or hot dogs) and *papas* (potatoes) that are fried up together and served with a splatter-paint mess of mustard, mayo, ketchup, and ají amarillo sauce squeezed on top. It's straight out of Lima's street food culture and eventually landed in home kitchens all over South America.

You don't really need a recipe to make salchipapas. Just slice up hot dogs or sausages and quickly deep-fry them in hot oil with a couple handfuls of cooked french fries, then pile plenty of your favorite condiments on top. The potatoes can be anything from the average fast-food fries to giant steak *frites,* depending on which street vendor, home cook, or restaurant serves your order.

If you want to make what I call a "fancy" version, try this recipe. Use good-quality sausages and confit baby potatoes in olive oil so the potatoes almost melt on the inside when you bite through the crunchy skin. Even still, this is not the time to worry about making the meal look pretty. Serve the salchipapas with good mustard and any spicy aiolis (see page 38) or whatever other condiments you have around. You could serve the condiments alongside, but making a big mess with the flavorful sauces is part of the fun. After cooking, let the confit potatoes cool completely in the oil, at least 1 hour. It helps them hold together when fried.

To make Salchipapas:

1 Put 1 pound scrubbed and rinsed baby fingerling potatoes, as small as you can find, in a medium saucepan and cover the potatoes completely with olive oil. Add 3 or 4 cloves garlic, 1 leafy sprig fresh thyme, and 1 bay leaf and heat the oil over medium heat until just warm to the touch. Reduce the heat to very low, and cook the potatoes very slowly until tender when pierced with a knife but the potatoes still hold together. The cooking process could take up to 1 hour, depending on the size of the potatoes; start checking the potatoes after 30 to 40 minutes. Don't let the oil simmer (reduce the heat if needed). Let the potatoes cool completely in the oil, at least 1 hour. Drain the potatoes and save the oil for frying, or transfer the potatoes and the confit oil to a food storage container, cover, and refrigerate for up to 5 days before frying. Let come to room temperature before continuing.

2 Heat a large sauté pan and pour in the reserved olive oil in which you cooked the potatoes. You should have a solid inch or more of oil; if not, add a little more. Heat the oil over medium-high heat until hot, a good 2 minutes, add 3 to 4 fully cooked, cured sausages, sliced on an angle into meaty 1-inch chunks. Deep-fry the sausages and potatoes for 1 to 2 minutes, until both turn golden brown in spots.

3 Pile the sausage and fried potatoes on a big serving platter and season them with salt and pepper. Spoon or drizzle plenty of ají amarillo aioli (page 38), Dijon-style mustard, rocoto aioli (page 38), Salsa Criolla (page 44), or whatever condiments you want all over everything, or serve the condiments alongside.

SERVES ABOUT 4

PIG TROTTER STEW

SERVES
5 OR 6

I hated *patitas*, pig trotter stew, when I was growing up. I would sneak my serving under the table to my brother Hugo, who loved it. When I tasted it again as an adult, I couldn't believe what I had been missing. Trotters are very gelatinous, so the stew tastes like eating a warm French terrine or pâté with a flavor similar to Italian mortadella—so good.

If you've never cooked with pig trotters, they're really not all that much different from ham hocks. Using all parts of an animal is also very sustainable (and affordable). The trotters you find in the States are sometimes cut on the leaner side. If they're not looking very meaty, ask your butcher for part of the lower foreshank to toss into the pot.

TROTTER STOCK

4 pounds meaty pig trotters, or 2 pounds trotters and 2 pounds meaty shanks

1 large red onion, halved

1 medium carrot

1 stalk celery

4 cloves garlic

2 bay leaves

2 leafy sprigs fresh thyme, or ½ teaspoon dried thyme

1 tablespoon kosher salt

STEW

1 pound bacon, cut into about ½-inch pieces

1 large or 2 small red onions, chopped into ½-inch pieces

4 large cloves garlic, minced

⅓ cup ají panca paste, store-bought or homemade (see page 36)

1 tablespoon ají amarillo paste, store-bought or homemade (page 34)

1 teaspoon ground cumin

1 teaspoon dried oregano leaves, preferably Mexican

1 bay leaf

Homemade chicken stock (page 40) or low-sodium store-bought broth, if needed

1 medium bunch fresh cilantro, leaves and top two-thirds of stems, roughly chopped

1 pint cherry tomatoes

2 pounds small red potatoes, peeled and quartered

Kosher salt and freshly ground black pepper

⅓ cup salted peanuts, lightly crushed

5 or 6 grilled sausages (optional)

1 To make the trotter stock, combine the trotters, onion, carrot, celery, garlic, bay leaves, thyme, and salt in a large Dutch oven or stockpot. Fill the pot with a good 3 quarts (12 cups) water, or as much water as you can. Bring the water to a boil, reduce the heat, and simmer the stock until the tendons are just tender enough to scoop out of the bones, usually a good hour. (Do not overcook the trotters or the tendons and too much fat will melt into the stock.) Occasionally skim off the foam at the top of the stock and add a little more water if the liquid ever reduces by more than half. Strain the stock and set aside to cool slightly. When cool enough to handle, scoop out the bones and roughly chop all of the gelatinous trotter cartilage and skin into meaty, bite-size chunks. Discard the bones and any really tough bits.

2 Wipe out the Dutch oven or stockpot, heat over medium heat, and fry the bacon until beginning to brown but still very tender, about 5 minutes. Pour off all but a thin layer of the rendered bacon fat (do not rinse the pot). Reheat the pot with the bacon, add the onions, and sauté until they begin to soften and brown, a good 5 minutes. Add the garlic, sauté for another minute or two, then stir in the ají panca and amarillo pastes, cumin, oregano, and bay leaf. Reduce the heat to medium-low and gently push the aderezo (flavorings) back and forth on the bottom of the pan with the spoon until the pepper pastes smell toasty and the sauce reduces slightly, about 5 minutes.

3 Pour in about 1 cup of the trotter stock and scrape up any browned bits from the bottom of the pot, then add another 7 to 8 cups of the stock and bring it to a boil. (Use chicken stock if you don't have enough trotter stock.) Stir in the cilantro, tomatoes, and potatoes and reduce the heat to maintain a simmer. Add the trotter meat when the potatoes are still on the firm side, about 15 minutes, and cook the stew until the potatoes are "al dente" tender when pierced with a knife, another 5 minutes or so. Add a little more trotter or chicken stock if the stew ever looks dry.

4 Just before serving, very gently fold the potatoes, tomatoes, and trotter meat together with a wooden spoon or rubber spatula. Don't stir too vigorously. You want some nice meaty potatoes to hold together. To serve, season the patitas with salt and pepper and sprinkle the crushed peanuts on top. Garnish with sliced grilled sausages, if you like.

DEL
MERCADO

FROM THE
MARKET

VEGETABLES AREN'T USUALLY THE HEROES OF TRADITIONAL PERUVIAN DISHES.

Something like *zapallo*, or kabocha squash, goes into a stew with a dozen other ingredients. Those that do go solo, like the choclo corn served alongside so many things, are usually boiled, fried, or prepared in another very simple way. Serving salads as a main course and vegetables as independent "sides" aren't really in the Peruvian mind-set. But after cooking abroad for two decades, I have come to really love salads and vegetables with big, independent personalities. In the salads and sides in this chapter, you'll see more of the influence from all of the places I've lived and the international restaurant kitchens in which I've worked—Peruvian, Japanese, British, American, and probably a few others in between.

SALSA A LA HUANCAÍNA
HUANCAYO-STYLE SAUCE

MAKES ABOUT 1¼ CUPS

Huancaína sauce is a tangy puree of *queso fresco* (fresh farmer's cheese), ají amarillo peppers, red onions, a little fresh or evaporated milk, and soda crackers to thicken everything up. The creamy dressing is generously poured over boiled potatoes, in a dish called *papas a la huancaína* (page 170). Today, the sauce has become so popular on its own that in Lima you can find premade batches at small markets and commercial packages at grocery stores to spoon on sandwiches like a flavored mayonnaise or whatever needs a tangy, creamy jolt of flavor. I drizzle huancaína sauce on Arroz con Pato (duck with green rice, page 154) and even on big bowls of rice and vegetables.

This is one case where using fresh or frozen ají amarillo peppers (both blanched) to make your own paste really makes a difference. The fresh or frozen peppers have a brighter flavor than the store-bought paste. If you can't find them, use a little less ají amarillo store-bought paste. The sauce will still be very good. I've also made the sauce with fresh or frozen rocoto peppers. Look for good-quality block feta cheese or the more traditional queso fresco. (Most crumbled feta on the market is not worth eating. It's so dry, it's almost chalky.) If you have time, make the sauce at least a day before you plan to use it. The flavors really develop as the sauce ages.

10 soda crackers, such as saltines

⅓ cup whole milk

¼ cup olive oil, or more if needed

½ medium red onion, roughly chopped

3 to 4 tablespoons homemade ají amarillo paste (see page 34)

1 (3-ounce) block feta cheese or queso fresco, cut into small chunks (about ¾ cup)

½ teaspoon kosher salt, or to taste

1 Roughly crumble the crackers into a small bowl, pour the milk on top, and mix them together with your fingers or a fork. Set the crackers aside to soak while you make the rest of the sauce.

2 Heat a large skillet over high heat until hot, about 2 minutes. Add the olive oil and heat for another minute, then stir in the onions and ají amarillo paste. Sauté, stirring occasionally with a wooden spoon, until the onions begin to soften and are nicely browned along the edges, a good 5 minutes. If the heat from the peppers gets in the back of your throat as you cook them, you're doing something right.

3 Puree the onion mixture in a blender on high speed until it has the consistency of a chunky salsa. If you have a small blender, be patient; it can take a while to get things going. (Add a little of the cracker-milk mixture, if needed.) Partially open the top of the blender (either remove the plastic window or cover the top with a kitchen towel) and, with the blender running, slowly pour in the cracker-milk mixture, then add the feta and salt. Keep the blender going until the sauce is very creamy, a good 30 seconds. The dressing should be very thick. Taste, and add more salt if needed (it should be on the salty side). Let cool completely and use right away, or cover and refrigerate the sauce for up to 5 days. Let the sauce come to room temperature before using.

CAESAR SALAD WITH SPICY HUACATAY DRESSING

SERVES
2 OR 3
AS A
MAIN DISH
OR

4 OR 5
AS A
SIDE

When I first moved to California, I felt like Caesar salads were everywhere, boxed up at takeout cafés and arranged on pretty plates in fine dining restaurants. I figured there must be something in the flavors that people really like, so I went back to my kitchen and started playing around. I love the way this whole salad turned out, especially the dressing. The huacatay, or Peruvian "black mint," and ají amarillo peppers give the dressing a big, almost mint-and-basil-like kick, and the grilled lettuce can stand up to the intense flavors in the dressing.

Boquerones, or white Spanish anchovies, are the caviar of anchovies and have a mild, lightly salty flavor. You can substitute the regular brown anchovies you find in most grocery stores, but start with half the amount—they can be pretty salty. The size of baby romaine and even the large heads varies, so let your eyes be the judge on how much you need.

4 or 5 thin slices rustic country bread, cut into 2 or 3 pieces each
Olive oil, for grilling
6 to 8 heads baby romaine lettuce, or 2 or 3 large heads romaine
Spicy Huacatay-Caesar Dressing (recipe follows)
10 to 12 boquerones or white anchovy fillets, rinsed and patted dry
Parmesan, for shaving

1 Prepare a regular or hibachi grill for direct, high-heat cooking. When the grill is hot, toast the bread for a few minutes until crispy, flipping once. Brush the bread lightly with olive oil.

2 Halve the romaine heads lengthwise and blot them dry with paper towels. Brush the leaves lightly with olive oil and grill the lettuce, cut-side down, until charred and just beginning to wilt, 1 to 2 minutes. Flip and grill the opposite sides until the leaves are charred in spots, no more than 30 seconds. Don't overcook

the lettuce or it won't hold its shape. (If using large heads of romaine, you may want to roughly chop the lettuce after it's grilled.)

3 In a large bowl, toss together the grilled romaine and about ⅓ cup of the dressing. Taste, and add more dressing if you'd like, or serve it on the side. Transfer the salad to a serving platter or individual plates and scatter the anchovies and a few generous shavings of Parmesan on top. Serve the grilled crostini alongside.

───

SPICY HUACATAY-CAESAR DRESSING

Makes about ½ cup

Remember this dressing when you have huacatay in the freezer or luck into the herb at the farmers' market. I use roasted garlic in the dressing, but you can substitute fresh garlic if you don't have any already made. Adjust the amount of ají amarillo paste to make the dressing as spicy as you'd like.

2 tablespoons fresh lime juice
2 teaspoons red wine vinegar
1½ teaspoons ají amarillo paste, store-bought or homemade (see page 34), or more to taste
½ teaspoon Worcestershire sauce
1 egg yolk
2 small anchovy fillets, rinsed
4 large cloves roasted garlic, or 1 small fresh garlic clove, smashed
1 tablespoon thawed frozen huacatay leaves (see page 31), chopped, or 2 packed tablespoons minced fresh huacatay
¼ cup freshly grated Parmesan
¼ cup extra-virgin olive oil, plus more as needed
Kosher salt

In a blender, combine the lime juice, vinegar, ají amarillo paste, Worcestershire sauce, egg yolk, anchovies, garlic, huacatay, and Parmesan and puree until smooth. With the blender on, very slowly drizzle in the olive oil so the dressing emulsifies. Taste, season with salt, if needed, and add a little more olive oil or ají amarillo paste, if you'd like. Use right away, or cover and refrigerate the dressing for up to 1 day. Let the dressing come to room temperature and shake or stir it well before using.

"PERUVIAN NIÇOISE" SALAD

SERVES 3 OR 4 AS A MAIN DISH OR 5 OR 6 AS A SIDE

Papas a la huancaína is basically the Peruvian version of potato salad with a little crunchy iceberg lettuce tucked underneath for good measure. The word *huancaína* means "woman from Huancayo," a city in Peru's central highlands. The recipe supposedly dates to when railroad tracks were being laid down, and home cooks in Huancayo would make meals to sell to hungry migrant rail workers. According to local legend, one woman's boiled potatoes in a creamy ají-cheese sauce were so popular, they eventually became the regional specialty. Today, you'll see huancaína sauce at restaurants and in home kitchens all over Peru.

The potatoes are usually drenched in huancaína sauce, not a bad thing as the sauce is so good, but I like more of a lighter, niçoise salad–like variation with leafy greens and green beans to up the vegetable and crunch factors. Keep an eye out for Peruvian Botija olives in brine. They have a unique flavor, but you could substitute cured Mediterranean olives. For a picnic, pack everything up separately, and serve any extra huancaína sauce on the side to use as a sauce for double-dipping the potatoes or a big loaf of crusty bread.

POTATOES AND GREEN BEANS

1¼ pounds mixed fingerling or other baby potatoes, scrubbed

1 teaspoon kosher salt, or to taste

3 meaty slices bacon, chopped into ½-inch pieces

½ pound (about 3 generous handfuls) green beans or haricots verts, trimmed

SALAD

About 3 tablespoons olive oil

5 to 6 cups loosely packed mixed baby greens

Coarse sea salt

Extra-virgin olive oil, for drizzling

4 hard-boiled eggs, halved lengthwise

½ cup Botija (brine-cured Peruvian black olives) or cured Mediterranean olives, drained

About 1¼ cups Salsa a la Huancaína (page 168), or more to taste

Generous pinch of shichimi tōgarashi (a Japanese pepper-spice blend) or cayenne pepper

1 To make the potatoes and green beans, place the potatoes and kosher salt in a medium pot, cover them with water by a solid inch, and bring the water to a low boil over high heat. Boil the potatoes until very tender when pierced with a knife, usually 20 to 25 minutes from the time you turn on the heat, but it depends on the potatoes and the pot. Drain the potatoes and let cool in the strainer for at least 10 minutes to dry out. Halve the potatoes lengthwise and use right away, or cool completely, cover, and refrigerate overnight.

2 Meanwhile, in a medium skillet, fry the bacon until crisp and set aside to drain on paper towels. For the green beans, fill a large bowl with ice and water (use plenty of ice). Bring a medium pot of water to a boil, reduce the heat to maintain a simmer, and blanch the green beans until tender-crisp, about 1 minute. Drain and immediately transfer the beans to the ice bath. Wait a few seconds, then drain and transfer the beans to a paper towel–lined bowl to dry. Use the beans right away, or cover and refrigerate overnight.

3 To make the salad, heat a large sauté pan over medium-high heat until hot, a good 2 minutes. Pour in about 2 tablespoons of the olive oil, heat for another minute, then add the green beans and sauté, tossing occasionally, until charred in spots, about 30 seconds. Transfer the beans to a bowl. Add the remaining 1 tablespoon oil to the skillet. When hot, sear the potatoes, cut-side down, for 1 minute, or until golden brown. Set aside.

4 Mound the salad greens onto a large serving plate or individual plates. Sprinkle the greens lightly with sea salt and drizzle lightly with the extra-virgin olive oil. Arrange the potatoes, green beans, eggs, and olives alongside the greens, and pour a generous ½ cup of the huancaína sauce on the potatoes. Scatter the bacon over the salads and sprinkle with a pinch of shichimi tōgarashi. Serve the remaining huancaína sauce on the side.

SOUTHERN PERUVIAN-STYLE SALAD WITH POTATOES, FAVAS & ROCOTO VINAIGRETTE

SERVES 3 OR 4 AS A MAIN DISH OR 5 OR 6 AS A SIDE

Solterito is a specialty in southern Peru around Arequipa, where high-heat rocoto peppers are king. The history is a little muddy, but the word *soltero* means "bachelor," so maybe the name comes from how easy this saladlike dish is to make—as in, even *un solterito* ("little bachelor") can make it to impress his friends. The salad has all of your vegetables on one plate, so it doubles as a one-dish meal or a substantial side.

Leftover boiled potatoes are traditional and very good, but roasting the potatoes is one of those extra steps that makes all of the flavors in the solterito really stand out. Other than potatoes, I usually go for a mix of fresh fava beans, spring peas, and tomatoes, but this is a good place to play around. Instead of favas (also known as broad beans), try frozen edamame or green garbanzos. If you do use fresh favas, remember to blanch and peel the beans after shelling them, or look for frozen favas that have already been peeled.

1 pound baby fingerling or other small potatoes, scrubbed

2 to 3 tablespoons olive oil, plus more as needed

½ teaspoon kosher salt, or to taste

1 cup shelled fresh fava beans (about 1 pound in the pod) or peeled shelled frozen fava beans, thawed

½ cup shelled fresh peas (about ½ pound unshelled) or ½ cup frozen petite peas, thawed

1 pint cherry tomatoes, or 2 ripe medium heirloom, beefsteak, or other juicy tomatoes, cut into bite-size chunks

About 1½ cups choclo (see page 28) or other blanched corn, drained

Rocoto Vinaigrette (recipe follows)

1 (4-ounce) block feta cheese or queso fresco, cut into ½-inch cubes (about 1 cup)

½ cup Botija or Kalamata olives, pitted and halved

Small handful of pea tendrils, or a few tablespoons of coarsely chopped fresh parsley leaves

1 Preheat the oven to 400°F. Halve the potatoes, or quarter them if large. In a medium bowl, toss the potatoes with the olive oil and salt. Spread the potatoes on a rimmed baking sheet in a single layer and roast, stirring occasionally, until tender and golden brown, 25 to 30 minutes, depending on their size. Set aside to cool.

2 Fill a large bowl with ice and water (use plenty of ice). Bring a medium pot of water to a boil, reduce the heat to maintain a simmer, and blanch the favas (fresh or frozen) for about 2 minutes. Drain and immediately transfer the favas to the ice bath. Wait a few seconds, then drain and peel the fresh favas by using your fingers to pop the beans out of their skins. (If using frozen favas, they should already be peeled.) If using fresh peas, refresh the ice bath and refill the pot. Bring the water to a boil, add the peas, and boil for 1 minute. Drain, then immediately transfer the peas to the ice bath. Wait a few seconds, then drain the peas. (If using thawed frozen peas, skip the blanching step.) Transfer the favas and peas to a paper towel–lined bowl to drain.

3 Pour a nice drizzle of olive oil into a large sauté pan, enough to coat the bottom of the pan (2 to 3 tablespoons), and heat the oil until hot, a good 2 minutes. Add the roasted potatoes to the pan and sear them for about 2 minutes, tossing the potatoes often. (If using leftover potatoes, let them come to room temperature before frying.) Add the favas, peas, tomatoes, and choclo and fry the vegetables until the edges color in a few spots and the tomatoes barely begin to soften, about 30 seconds.

4 Pour about ½ cup of the rocoto vinaigrette into the pan. Toss the vegetables in the vinaigrette, taste, and add a little more vinaigrette if you'd like. The flavors should be pretty bold. Remove the pan from the stove and gently fold in the feta. Spoon the solterito onto a large serving plate or individual plates. Scatter the olives and pea tendrils on top, and serve *inmediatamente*.

RECIPE CONTINUES

ROCOTO VINAIGRETTE

Makes about ⅔ cup

Rocoto peppers remind me of very spicy green bell peppers. They work really well in salad dressings when you have starchier vegetables like potatoes or hearty beans as a backdrop for the heat to play off. The subtle citrusy flavors in a really good Banyuls vinegar are nice in this dressing, but any balsamic vinegar would also be good.

1 tablespoon plus 1 teaspoon rocoto paste (see page 34), or to taste

1½ teaspoons pureed garlic (see page 37) or finely minced garlic

2 tablespoons red wine vinegar

1 tablespoon plus 1 teaspoon Banyuls or balsamic vinegar

½ teaspoon kosher salt, or to taste

1 teaspoon freshly ground black pepper

Generous ⅓ cup extra-virgin olive oil

Mix together the rocoto paste, garlic, red wine vinegar, Banyuls vinegar, salt, and pepper in a medium bowl. Slowly whisk in the olive oil so the dressing emulsifies. Season the dressing with more salt, if desired. Use right away or cover and refrigerate the rocoto vinaigrette for up to 3 days. Let the vinaigrette come to room temperature and shake or stir it well before using.

LOS MERCADOS

Produce is truly a part of Peru's everyday landscape.

It's sold at giant, dedicated markets like Lima's Mercado de Surquillo, piled up in homemade pushcarts in town squares, and laid out on sidewalk tarps on street corners. That daily *abundancia*, abundance, goes back thousands of years. There is an incredible biodiversity in different corners of the jungle, the deserts, and high up in the Andes. Over the years, those native fruits and vegetables intermarried with the plants brought by immigrants from Asia, Europe, and other parts of the world.

I strongly support local farmers' markets, but I also believe in supporting foods imported from other countries, particularly fair trade or conscientiously sourced produce. So much of what the world eats that is sourced globally, be it a newly cultivated potato variety or organic ginger planted near a remote village, helps the proud, hardworking people living near the farms. Money from the produce they grow can be used to build schools for their children and provide basic health care. It changes lives.

ROASTED BEET SALAD WITH BURRATA & AJÍ-ORANGE VINAIGRETTE

SERVES 2 OR 3 AS A MAIN DISH OR 4 OR 5 AS A SIDE

Roasted beet salads are on what seems like every restaurant menu these days, but the flavor combinations really work. The sweet beets and acidic tang of a citrusy vinaigrette are naturally drawn to each other, flavors that I like even better with the fruity heat of ají amarillo peppers. A fat mound of oozy, fresh burrata or creamy mozzarella cheese mellows out the spiciness and helps blend all of those flavors and textures together.

Small beets in several colors look nice on the plate, but whatever fresh beets you find will be tasty. If you are aiming to impress, brûlée the roasted beets by sprinkling one side with sugar, and then blast the sugar for a few seconds with a kitchen torch until it caramelizes, or put them under the broiler close to the heat for a minute or two. Roast the beets ahead of time and add some fresh bread to the salad for a quick, light supper.

1½ pounds baby or medium beets (8 to 10 small or 4 or 5 large), trimmed

Olive oil

Kosher salt

1 (8-ounce) round burrata or fresh mozzarella, or more, if you like a lot of cheese

Ají-Orange Vinaigrette (recipe follows)

4 or 5 handfuls of frisée or other crispy, small-leaf lettuce

4 or 5 radishes, thinly sliced

2 scallions, including the tender green stems, thinly sliced on an angle

2 medium blood oranges or 1 large orange, separated into sections (membrane removed)

Good-quality extra-virgin olive oil

1 Preheat the oven to 400°F. Put the beets in a small baking dish and toss them with a little olive oil and salt. Cover the dish snugly with foil and roast the beets until tender when pierced with a knife, about 45 minutes if very small or up to 1¼ hours if large. Use tongs to remove the foil (be careful—the steam will be hot). When cool enough to handle, peel the beets. Halve the beets if they are small or cut them into bite-size pieces if large, and let cool completely. Use the beets right away, or cover and refrigerate them for up to 2 days.

2 Cut the burrata into 2 or 3 chunks, more if making side salads, or cut the mozzarella into several meaty slices. In a medium bowl, toss together the beets with about ¼ cup of the ají-orange vinaigrette (darker beets will stain both your fingers and lighter-colored beets; if that bothers you, use a rubber spatula and toss each color separately). In another bowl, gently toss together the lettuce, radishes, scallions, and orange sections with 3 to 4 tablespoons of the vinaigrette. Taste, and add more vinaigrette if you'd like.

3 Mound the lettuce mixture on plates and arrange the beets on top. Lay the burrata off to one side of the salads, and drizzle the extra-virgin olive oil over both the cheese and salad. Serve *inmediatamente.*

AJÍ-ORANGE VINAIGRETTE

Makes a generous ½ cup

You can dial the heat up or down and use this citrusy ají pepper dressing on any mixed green salad with crispy lettuce, maybe with a little goat cheese and a few orange wedges on top.

Zest of ½ orange
¾ cup fresh orange juice
2 to 3 teaspoons ají amarillo paste, store-bought or
    homemade (see page 34)
2 teaspoons honey
2 tablespoons champagne or white wine vinegar
¼ teaspoon kosher salt, or to taste
3 tablespoons extra-virgin olive oil

Place the orange zest in a small bowl. Bring the orange juice to a boil in a small saucepan and boil until reduced by half, about 5 minutes. Pour the juice into the bowl with the orange zest and let cool for 10 minutes. Whisk in the ají amarillo paste, honey, vinegar, and salt until well incorporated, then slowly whisk in the olive oil so the dressing emulsifies. Use right away, or cover and refrigerate for up to 3 days. Let the dressing come to room temperature and shake or stir it well before using.

ANDEAN STUFFED POTATO CROQUETTES WITH ACEITUNA BOTIJA SAUCE

MAKES
8
RELLENAS

We all have moments when we can't figure out what is going wrong with a recipe. When we were prepping to open Picca, I was really suffering in the kitchen with my *papas rellenas*—you fill riced or mashed potatoes with a spicy ground beef filling, almost like an ají pepper–spiced chili, tuck a black olive and a slice of hard-boiled egg alongside, close the whole thing up, and fry the cakes. Easy—or so I thought. I guess I never made the stuffed potato croquettes that much. I used to buy them after school from street vendors when I was growing up. This is one recipe where it helps to have a good teacher to show you the ropes, like when learning to ride a bicycle.

At the restaurant, no matter how I shaped the potato croquettes—fat, thin, small, big, oval, or round—they would fall apart in the fryer. I finally called one of my mom's friends to ask for her secret: Once the cakes are shaped, you need to refrigerate them until they are cold before frying them. It's the same as with leftover mashed potato cakes. Chilling dries out the potatoes slightly so they hold together better when fried. It also means you can shape the cakes ahead for a party or a quick weeknight supper, or fry them to serve more as portable picnic snacks, at room temperature. My kids get as excited about these in their lunches as I did when I spotted the papas rellenas street vendor outside our schoolyard, waiting for the last afternoon bell to ring. (Smart guy.)

For the filling, instead of beef, you could use the same spice mixture to make a chicken version, or eggplant and tomatoes would be a good vegetable combo. Because it's easiest to cook a full pound of beef, this makes more filling than you need. Freeze the leftovers, and you're ready to go for another batch. When I'm too hungry to wait for the cakes to chill, I'll just spoon the spicy meat on top of mashed potatoes—quick, tasty, and no need to call up the old neighbors for help.

POTATOES

2½ pounds red potatoes, scrubbed and peeled

1 tablespoon extra-virgin olive oil

1 to 2 teaspoons kosher salt

FILLING

Olive oil

½ medium red onion, finely chopped

2 large cloves garlic, minced

2½ teaspoons ground cumin

2½ tablespoons ají panca paste, store-bought or homemade (see page 36)

1 tablespoon ají amarillo paste, store-bought or homemade (see page 34)

1 bay leaf

2 plum tomatoes, finely chopped

1 pound ground beef, preferably 80% lean

¼ cup raisins, cut in half if large

½ teaspoon dried oregano leaves, preferably Mexican

1 teaspoon kosher salt, or to taste

½ teaspoon freshly ground black pepper

2 cups homemade chicken or vegetable stock (see page 40) or low-sodium store-bought broth

ASSEMBLY

2 hard-boiled eggs, quartered (optional)

8 pitted Botija or Kalamata olives

2 large eggs, lightly beaten

1 cup all-purpose flour, plus more as needed

Canola oil, for frying

Frisée or other small, crispy lettuce leaves (optional)

Aceituna Botija Sauce (page 181)

RECIPE CONTINUES

1 To make the potatoes, quarter the potatoes if they are small, or coarsely chop larger potatoes into 1½- to 2-inch chunks. Place the potatoes in a medium pot, cover them with water by a solid inch, and bring the water to a low boil over high heat. Boil the potatoes until very tender when pierced with a knife, usually 10 to 15 minutes from the time the water begins to boil. Drain the potatoes and let cool in the strainer or better still, on a baking sheet, for 10 to 15 minutes to dry out.

2 While the potatoes are still slightly warm, pass them through a ricer or food mill into a large bowl or onto a work surface, or put the potatoes in a large bowl and mash them with a potato masher or the back of a large fork until few lumps remain. Mix in the olive oil and salt and use the palms of your hands to knead the potatoes for 2 to 3 minutes (see photos 1 to 3, page 183), until they become almost silky to the touch, like you are making causas (see page 183). Turn the potatoes out onto a work surface if your bowl isn't large enough. You should have about 4 cups potatoes. Use the potatoes right away, or refrigerate the potato base overnight.

3 To make the filling, heat a nice drizzle of olive oil, enough to coat the bottom of the pan (2 to 3 tablespoons), in a large Dutch oven or saucepan over medium-high heat until hot, a good 2 minutes. Add the onions and sauté, stirring occasionally with a wooden spoon, until they begin to soften and are nicely browned along the edges, a good 5 minutes. Add the garlic, sauté for another minute, then stir in the cumin, ají panca and amarillo pastes, and bay leaf.

4 Reduce the heat to medium-low and gently push the aderezo (flavorings) back and forth on the bottom of the pan with the spoon until the pepper pastes smell toasty, about 2 minutes. Add the tomatoes and beef and cook the meat until lightly browned, about 5 minutes. Mix in the raisins, oregano, salt, pepper, and stock. Bring the mixture to a vigorous simmer and cook, stirring often, until the filling looks like a juicy pasta sauce, a good 12 to 15 minutes (the broth should reduce by more than half). Season the filling with more salt, if desired. It should be nicely seasoned; the potatoes will tame the heat and seasonings. Let the filling cool completely before using, or refrigerate overnight, like the potatoes. Remove the bay leaf before assembling the rellenas.

5 To assemble the rellenas, massage the chilled potatoes a few times to work out any cracks that have formed in the potato "dough." Form about ½ cup of the potato base into a 4- to 5-inch oblong disc in the palm of one hand (see photo 4). Place about 2 generous tablespoons of the filling in the center and nestle 1 hard-boiled egg quarter and 1 olive alongside, if desired (see photos 5 and 6). Gently press the potato base over the filling to close, like you are closing a clamshell (see photo 7). Pass the rellena back and forth between your hands to shape it into an oblong shape, like a russet potato or tiny football (see photo 8). Add a little more potato "dough" to patch up any cracks on the outside, if necessary (see photo 9). Repeat with the remaining potatoes and filling to make 8 papas rellenas. Cover the rellenas and refrigerate for at least 4 hours or overnight.

6 Preheat the oven to 300°F. Line a baking sheet with a few layers of paper towels. Have the eggs and flour ready in two separate bowls. In a medium, deep saucepan, heat 2½ to 3 inches of oil until it registers 350°F on a deep-fry thermometer, or fill a deep fryer with the recommended amount of oil and set the temperature to 350°F. When hot, use a frying thermometer to test the oil's temperature, or drop a small nub of flour into the oil. It should bubble vigorously and rise to the top after a few seconds. If the oil smokes, reduce the heat.

7 To fry the rellenas, dip one at a time in the beaten eggs, letting any excess drip back into the bowl, then dredge lightly in the flour. Drop 2 or 3 at a time in the hot oil. Do not overcrowd the saucepan or fryer.

8 Cook the rellenas until golden brown, 2½ to 3 minutes. Use tongs to flip each once or twice (they should be bobbing at the top of the oil, like apples) to evenly brown them on both sides. Transfer the rellenas to the paper towel–lined baking sheet. If not serving immediately, place them in the oven to keep warm for up to 30 minutes. Fry the remaining rellenas the same way. When ready to serve, pile the rellenas onto a big platter or on individual plates with some lettuce (if using) and serve the aceituna Botija sauce on the side.

ACEITUNA BOTIJA SAUCE

Makes about 1 cup

This creamy sauce, really a flavored mayonnaise-based dressing, gets its intense and unique flavor from Peruvian Botija olives. They are worth seeking out, but you could substitute Kalamatas. You can use it as a salad dressing, or to make a killer tuna sandwich.

½ cup mayonnaise, preferably Japanese or similar aioli-like mayonnaise

¾ cup pitted Botija or Kalamata olives

2 teaspoons ají amarillo paste, store-bought or homemade (see page 34), or to taste

¾ teaspoon pureed garlic (see page 37) or finely minced garlic

1 tablespoon fresh lime juice

1½ teaspoons kosher salt, or to taste

½ teaspoon freshly ground black pepper

Combine all of the ingredients in a blender and puree until very smooth and creamy. Cover and refrigerate the olive sauce for up to 3 days.

HOW TO SHAPE PAPAS RELLENAS (ANDEAN POTATO CROQUETTES)

Once you get the hang of shaping the potato croquettes, papas rellenas are very easy to make.

1 to 3 Season the riced potatoes with salt, add the oil, and use the palm of your hands to knead the potatoes for 2 or 3 minutes, until they become almost silky to the touch.

4 Form about ¼ cup of the potato base into a 4- to 5-inch oblong disc in the palm of one hand.

5 Place about 2 generous tablespoons of the filling in the center.

6 Add an olive and quartered hard-boiled egg, if using.

7 Gently press the potato base over the filing to close, like you are closing a clamshell.

8 Pass the rellena back and forth between your hands to shape it into an oblong round the shape of a russet potato or football.

9 Add a little more potato "dough" to patch up any cracks on the outside, if necessary.

EGGPLANT PARMESAN WITH AJÍ PANCA– MISO SAUCE

SERVES 5 OR 6 AS A SIDE

Other than a few of the ingredients like ají panca paste, this dish isn't really Peruvian. It's based on *nasu dengaku*, miso-glazed eggplant, a Japanese dish that I first tasted in London when I was working for sushi chefs there. The ají panca peppers lend a subtle, smoky flavor and a brick-red color that almost makes the sauce look like marinara. Adding cheese to vegetables (or just about anything) is taboo in Japanese cooking, much as combining seafood and cheese is in Italy—but I've never liked playing by someone else's food rules. Here, I really like the way the Parmesan offsets the salty-sweet miso sauce.

I always "grill" eggplant directly on my gas range (see page 186). You get an incredibly close sear with the direct heat and a much better flavor than you get with eggplant cooked on a grill. For a quick weeknight supper or party side, pile the cooked eggplant into a baking dish with the sauce and rewarm everything in the oven.

4 medium Japanese or Chinese eggplants or 2 small globe eggplants (about 4 pounds), charred over the stove and peeled (see page 186)
About 4 tablespoons olive oil
Ají Panca–Miso Sauce (recipe follows)
Parmesan, for grating

1 If you are using Japanese or Chinese eggplants, leave them whole for a nice presentation. If using globe eggplants, coarsely chop the peeled flesh into 2-inch chunks. Lightly dry off the flesh with a paper towel.

2 Heat a large sauté pan over medium-high heat until hot, a good 2 minutes. Pour in about half the olive oil, heat for another minute, then add half the eggplant, or whatever you can fit without crowding the pan. Sear the eggplant until charred in spots, about 30 seconds, flip, and sear the opposite side.

Transfer the eggplant to a plate and repeat with the remaining oil and eggplant.

3 If serving right away, reduce the heat to medium and return all of the eggplant to the pan. Pour in about ⅔ cup of the ají panca–miso sauce and simmer the sauce and eggplant for a few minutes to rewarm both. Stir regularly, as the sugar in the sauce can cause it to stick to the pan, but be careful not to break up the eggplant if you are using whole pieces. Taste and add another few tablespoons of the sauce, if you'd like. The eggplant should be intensely flavored by the sauce. Spoon the eggplant and sauce into a serving dish, and grate Parmesan generously on top.

AJÍ PANCA–MISO SAUCE

Makes about 1 cup

Whenever I make this sauce, I can't stop dipping my finger in the bowl to taste it. It's that good. Use a small enough saucepan so the mirin and sake don't cook down too quickly, or the sauce will have the consistency of tomato paste.

½ cup mirin
½ cup dry sake
2½ tablespoons ají panca paste, store-bought or homemade (see page 36), or to taste
½ cup shiro (white) miso
⅓ cup sugar

1 In a small to medium, high-sided saucepan, bring the mirin and sake to a boil over medium-high heat and boil for 3 minutes to cook off the alcohol. If the liquid in the pot flames up (the flames will be blue), it's just the alcohol cooking off. They usually subside when you turn off the heat, but you can put a lid on the pot and turn off the heat if you'd rather.

2 Turn off the heat and stir in the ají panca paste and miso. The miso will soften up and be easier to incorporate with the back of a spoon as it warms up. Return the heat to medium and simmer the sauce for another a minute or two, then add the sugar and continue to simmer the sauce, stirring regularly, until it thickens slightly and turns a dark brick-red color, about 5 minutes. Immediately transfer the sauce to a small bowl to cool (it will thicken more as it cools). Cover and refrigerate the sauce for up to 1 week.

CHARRING EGGPLANT

"Grilling" whole eggplant directly on the gas flame of your stovetop actually creates a more intensely smoky flavor than outdoor grilling.

The key is to really char the eggplant skin until it starts to wrinkle up like the skin of an old, wise man. The outside should blacken so much that it almost looks like it is covered in ashes. Inside, the flesh will be so tender that it almost melts. For quick clean-up, line the burner with foil (make sure the flames can still get through).

Long, thin Japanese or Chinese eggplant work best, and are worth finding for this technique. The chubby oblong globe eggplants sold at most supermarkets will also work, but you'll need to be patient. With the big eggplants, there is a lot of meat to get through. It helps to par-roast them in the oven first.

To Char and Peel Eggplant:

1 Place long, slender Japanese or Chinese eggplant, one at a time, directly on the gas burner grate of your stove. Crank up the heat high enough so the flames directly touch the skin of the eggplant, even better if the flames come up the sides of the eggplant a little. Cook the eggplant like you are toasting a marshmallow over a campfire, until the skin is blackened all over and the flesh is falling-apart soft all the way to the center. The skin of the eggplant will begin to split as the flesh softens, so watch closely and move the eggplant around on the burner with tongs to firmer sides as needed. Be patient. It usually takes a good 5 minutes, sometimes longer, to cook Chinese or Japanese eggplant so the flesh is soft throughout.

2 Fill a medium bowl with ice and water. Transfer the charred eggplant to a bowl and cover the bowl loosely with plastic wrap to loosen up the skins. Let the eggplant cool for a few minutes (longer is fine if you are cooking multiple eggplants). Transfer all of the cooked eggplant to the ice bath. To remove the skins, reach into the water and run your fingers down the length of the eggplant. Hold the eggplant by the stem, and be careful not to break the flesh. Discard the skin. Use right away, or refrigerate the eggplant for up to 2 days.

VARIACIÓN:

To Char Globe Eggplants

Preheat the oven to 400°F. Halve the eggplant lengthwise, and place each half, cut-side down, on a lightly oiled baking sheet. Roast the eggplant until the flesh softens, 30 to 45 minutes, depending on how chubby the eggplant is. Flip the eggplant halves once while baking so they color evenly. Remove the eggplants from the oven.

Char each eggplant half directly over a gas flame on the stovetop, skin side facing the flame, until the skin blisters all over, 3 to 4 minutes. Use tongs to char different parts of the skin. Peel the eggplant as directed for Japanese and Chinese eggplant.

ROAST CARROTS WITH AJÍ-ORANGE BUTTER

SERVES 5 OR 6 AS A SIDE

If you use baby carrots in all different colors, this is a very pretty holiday dish, but even the everyday, weeknight variety is fantastic with the buttery citrus sauce. Carrots are sturdy and can take a lot of heat, so you can roast the carrots ahead and rewarm them at whatever temperature you already have the oven going for any other dishes to get a nice brown color. Roasted vegetables like a little breathing room, so use multiple pans, if needed, to roast the carrots.

2 pounds carrots (3 or 4 bunches baby carrots or about 12 large)

Olive oil

Kosher salt

Ají-Orange Butter Sauce (recipe follows)

2 or 3 scallions, including the tender green stems, finely chopped

2 to 3 tablespoons finely chopped fresh cilantro leaves and tender top stems

1 Preheat the oven to 475°F and place a rack in the bottom third. If using baby carrots, trim the tops so about 1 inch of the stems remain. Cut larger carrots into pieces about 2 inches long and halve the thicker, stem-end pieces lengthwise so the pieces are roughly the same thickness. Toss the carrots with a few tablespoons of olive oil and a generous sprinkle of salt on one or more rimmed baking sheets.

2 Roast the carrots until they are tender-crisp and caramelized in spots on the bottom, 10 to 15 minutes, depending on how thick they are. Reduce the temperature to 425°F and remove the carrots from the oven. Stir about ½ cup of the ají-orange butter sauce into the carrots, return them to the oven, and roast until tender, around 5 minutes more, depending on their size. Stir the carrots once or twice as they roast to incorporate any sauce that caramelizes along the edges of the baking sheet. Taste and season the carrots with salt.

3 Transfer the carrots directly to a serving dish, along with any tasty caramelized bits from the baking sheet. Drizzle the warm carrots with a few tablespoons of the remaining sauce, and scatter the scallions and cilantro on top.

4 If not serving right away, put the carrots and sauce in a large baking dish and let cool completely. Cover and refrigerate the carrots for up to 2 days. To rewarm, let the carrots come to room temperature, cover the dish with aluminum foil, and bake the carrots at 350°F (or whatever temperature your oven is already set) until warm, about 5 minutes. Stir the carrots occasionally.

AJÍ-ORANGE BUTTER SAUCE

Makes about ¾ cup

The ají amarillo peppers in this sauce are very subtle, more to play up the sweetness of the carrots and orange juice than for heat.

4 tablespoons (½ stick) unsalted butter, cut into a few chunks

¾ teaspoon ají amarillo paste, store-bought or homemade (see page 34)

1 (3-inch) sprig fresh rosemary

2 fresh sage leaves, or a pinch of ground sage

½ teaspoon ground turmeric

⅓ cup fresh orange juice

⅓ cup carrot juice

1½ teaspoons potato starch or cornstarch

1 Heat the butter in a small saucepan over medium-high heat until just melted. Stir in the ají amarillo paste. Add the rosemary, sage, and turmeric, then pour in the orange and carrot juices. Bring the mixture to a boil, reduce the heat to medium-high, and simmer until the sauce has reduced by about a quarter, a good 5 to 7 minutes. Discard the rosemary sprig and sage and strain the sauce if any rosemary leaves are left behind. Return the sauce to the pan.

2 In a small dish, mix together the potato starch and 2 tablespoons of water. Stir the starch mixture into the sauce and bring the sauce back to a low boil. Cook, stirring often, until the sauce has thickened slightly, about 2 minutes. Let cool completely and use right away, or cover and refrigerate the sauce for up to 3 days. Bring the sauce to room temperature and stir well before using.

GRILLED KABOCHA WITH HONEY-MISO GLAZE

SERVES
5 OR 6
AS A
SIDE

Kabocha squash is one of those vegetables that tastes as good as it looks. In this version, the honey-miso galze caramelizes on the grill, and all of its sweet and salty flavors penetrate the sweet kabocha flesh. It's an impressive vegetable on its own, or you could serve it with something a little bitter to balance the sweetness, like sautéed kale. I've also chopped up leftovers to use in quinoa salads. Invite some vegetarians over and see if they don't love you by the end of the night.

Roasting firmer winter squash varieties like kabocha in the oven can dry them out, so I steam the squash first, then transfer the juicy wedges to the grill for a quick blast of grilled flavor. If you don't have a steamer, it's easy to rig one up at home (see sidebar, page 190). For a crowd, you could simmer the squash in a pot of water instead, but you need to be careful and keep the heat pretty low or the squash can fall apart. Leaving the skin on each slice helps the squash stay in one piece on the grill. If you don't have time to light the grill, sear the squash in a really hot pan with plenty of butter. I love the light, almost fluffy crunchiness of fried quinoa on top, but toasted sesame seeds are also very good.

1 medium kabocha squash (2½ to 3 pounds)
About ½ cup Honey-Miso Glaze (recipe follows)
A few tablespoons crispy quinoa (see sidebar, page 201) or
    lightly toasted sesame seeds

1 Halve the squash lengthwise, then cut each section in half again. Scrape out the seeds, and cut the quarters into 4 wedges so you have 16 nice slices of squash a good ¾ inch or so thick.

2 Place the slices in a single layer in a steamer basket. If using a small basket, steam the squash in two batches. Steam the squash until it is tender but still holds together when pierced with a fork, 15 to 20 minutes. If too tender, the squash will fall apart on the grill, but they won't cook much more on the grill, either. The best way to know if they are ready is to taste one. Transfer the squash to a plate to cool completely. If not using immediately, cover and refrigerate the squash for up to 2 days. Remove the squash from the fridge about an hour before grilling.

3 To grill the squash, prepare a regular or hibachi grill for direct, high-heat cooking. Brush one side of each piece of squash with the honey-miso glaze. Grill the squash, unglazed-side down, until charred in spots, a good minute or two. Flip the squash and brush the top sides generously with the glaze. Grill until nicely charred on the bottom, another minute or two. Flip the squash one more time, brush the top side with the glaze again, and grill for just a few seconds. Transfer the squash to a plate.

4 To serve, arrange the squash on a serving platter and drizzle a few spoonfuls of the remaining honey-miso glaze on top, then sprinkle with the crispy quinoa.

5 If not serving right away, arrange the cooked squash (do not add the quinoa) snugly in a single layer in a baking dish. Cover and refrigerate overnight. To rewarm, let the squash come to room temperature, cover the dish with aluminum foil, and bake in a preheated 350°F oven until warm, about 8 minutes. Sprinkle with the crispy quinoa and serve.

RECIPE CONTINUES

HONEY-MISO GLAZE

Makes about ½ cup

The subtle flavor of saikyo miso (see page 265), a Korean variety of white miso, works really well with lighter dishes like the grilled kabocha squash, Paiche Lettuce Wraps (page 120), and quinoa salad dressing (page 198). The glaze takes all of five minutes to make, but for best flavor, you need to let the lime infuse overnight or, better still, for a few days before using it.

1 lime
⅓ cup honey
¼ cup saikyo miso, or substitute shiromiso (also known as white miso)

Cut the lime into 5 or 6 rings and discard both ends. If the honey has granulated, warm it for a few seconds in the microwave or on the stovetop. Combine the lime slices, honey, and miso in a small bowl and lightly mash together with the back of a spoon. Cover and refrigerate the glaze overnight, or up to 2 days for an even better flavor. Discard the lime slices and refrigerate the honey-miso glaze for up to 5 more days. Stir the glaze before using.

MOCK STEAMER

If you don't have a steamer, you can easily rig one up with the pots and kitchen tools you already have.

To make a steamer: Put a metal colander with a stand in a large Dutch oven so the colander doesn't sit directly on the bottom of the pot, or put the colander or strainer on top of a few metal ring molds or cookie cutters. Either way, make sure the bottom of the strainer is at least 2 inches from the bottom of the pot.

Fill the pot with an inch or two of water, just enough so the water doesn't hit the bottom of the colander or strainer. Add whatever vegetables you'd like, arranging them in a single layer. Bring the water to a boil and cover the pot with the pot lid or snugly with foil if the lid won't fit. Reduce the heat and keep the water at a simmer to steam the vegetables until they are tender. Check the water level periodically. If the water ever evaporates too much, pour in a little more.

GREEN BEANS WITH TERIYAKI SAUCE & BONITO FLAKES

SERVES
4 OR 5
AS A SIDE

The flavors and textures of these green beans are all over the place—caramelized, crunchy, and briny. The secret is to cook the beans until they are al dente, just tender-crisp. Then, sear them in an extremely hot pan, almost like making a stir-fry, so you get good color and flavor on the beans.

Serve the green beans as a side for grilled or sautéed seafood or chicken, or pile them on top of steamed rice to sop up the teriyaki sauce. When you scatter paper-thin bonito flakes on top, they dance around the beans like they are at a rock concert—maybe the best trick yet to get my kids to try a new veggie.

1 pound thin green beans or haricots verts, trimmed

2 teaspoons kosher salt

Olive oil

1 teaspoon pureed garlic (see page 37) or finely minced garlic

1 teaspoon pureed ginger (see page 37) or finely minced ginger

1 medium shallot, finely chopped

⅓ to ½ cup Teriyaki Sauce (page 119)

A generous handful (about ⅓ cup) of bonito flakes

1 Fill a medium bowl with ice and water (use plenty of ice). Fill a medium pot halfway with water, bring to a boil, and add the green beans and salt. Blanch the beans until bright green and tender-crisp, as few as 90 seconds for thin haricots verts or up to 3 minutes for thicker green beans. Immediately drain, and transfer the beans to the ice bath. Wait a few seconds, then drain and transfer the beans to paper towels to dry. Sauté the beans right away, or cool, cover and refrigerate them for up to 2 days.

2 Heat a wok or large sauté pan over high heat until hot, a good 2 minutes. Pour in a nice drizzle of olive oil, enough to coat the bottom of the pan (2 to 3 tablespoons), and heat the oil for another minute, until very hot. Swirl the oil around the pan, toss in the green beans, and shake the pan or use tongs to flip them a few times so they brown evenly. (If the beans are a little moist, the oil will sizzle and pop loudly; just be careful the hot oil doesn't jump up and sting you.) After about 30 seconds, add the garlic, ginger, and shallots, sauté the vegetables a few seconds longer, then add about ⅓ cup of the teriyaki sauce. Toss the beans in the sauce and let the sauce sizzle and cook for another few seconds. If you are serving the beans with rice, add another drizzle of teriyaki sauce so there is plenty for the rice to sop up.

3 Immediately transfer the beans to a serving platter, scatter the bonito flakes on top, and enjoy the show.

JAPANESE MUSHROOMS WITH YUZU KOSHO

SERVES
3 OR 4
AS A SIDE

Mushrooms didn't really make appearances on our family dinner table growing up. I'm not sure why. Look closely on many ancient Moche ceramics, and you will see drawings of mushrooms among the other crops and religious symbols. When I was working in Japanese restaurants in London, I was so inspired by all of the different mushroom varieties—long, skinny enoki; flowerlike maitake; short, stout bunashimeji; and the more common shiitake. You could make a meal out of mushrooms alone. They're especially good with yuzu kosho (see page 33), an incredibly flavorful Japanese green chile pepper paste with yuzu juice. The heat of the peppers is balanced by a good amount of salt, so you have all of these intense flavors playing off the charred, grilled mushrooms.

If you've already got the grill going, it takes all of a few minutes to mix together this basting sauce and toss on some mushrooms. You could also put everything briefly under the broiler, or use the same technique in a frying pan with a little more olive oil. I love maitake mushrooms, but oyster mushrooms or whatever Japanese varieties you stumble upon would all be good. If you use mushrooms with denser flesh, like sliced portobellos, you'll need to cook them a few minutes longer.

Basting the mushrooms regularly helps keep their meat moist. Shiso has a mild flavor similar to mint, which you can substitute.

2 tablespoons yuzu kosho
2 teaspoons pureed garlic (see page 37)
¼ cup olive oil
2 large maitake mushrooms (about 1 pound)
3 or 4 Japanese shiso leaves or mint leaves, thinly sliced

1 Mix together the yuzu kosho, garlic, and olive oil in a small dish.

2 Prepare a regular or hibachi grill for direct, high-heat cooking and place a fish or vegetable grate on the grill. Halve the mushrooms lengthwise through the stem so you have two meaty, steaklike slices. Brush both sides of the mushrooms lightly with the yuzu kosho sauce.

3 Grill the mushrooms until they begin to soften and char, 2 to 3 minutes. Flip them and brush the top sides lightly with the marinade. Grill the mushrooms until nicely charred on the bottom, a few minutes more. Cut into one to make sure they are cooked through. Flip the mushrooms one more time, brush them again with the sauce, and grill for just a few seconds.

4 Transfer the mushrooms to a plate, sprinkle them with the shiso leaves, and serve them piping hot.

GRANOS Y FRIJOLES

GRAINS & BEANS

MAINS & SIDES

BEANS AND GRAINS AREN'T JUST A COMPONENT OF THE PERUVIAN DIET; THEY ARE PART OF OUR CULTURE.

Some of the oldest-known cultivated beans, in the Americas at least, were found in a cave in northern Peru going back almost ten thousand years. Later, the Mochica people, typically referred to as the Moche in the United States, painted beans on their ceramics thinking they had mystical powers. (*¿Quién sabe?*—who knows? Maybe they really do.) It's probably old news by now that quinoa, so popular today, is indigenous to the Andes. Even the Spanish banning of the grainlike seed couldn't stop its production. (Because the Incas believed quinoa a powerful symbol for their own religious ceremonies, the Spaniards considered it anti-Christian.) In the late nineteenth and early twentieth centuries, when a large influx of Asian immigrants arrived in South America, rice, originally introduced by the Spanish, became more widely available and the daily grain of choice for many Peruvians (especially in Lima, where Chinese restaurants called chifas became popular and home cooks were influenced by the new Asian ingredients—see page 9). At my house, there was hardly a meal that didn't include a heaping pile of hot rice, even if the main course was already grain-based. Today, rice is still the "daily bread" of choice for many Peruvians.

Some of the grain and bean recipes in this chapter are rooted in those old stories and traditions, like my mom's restaurant-size pots of lentils or the rice and bean patties central to Afro-Peruvian cooking, a culinary influence that is still very strong today. Others, like a stir-fry I make with quinoa instead of rice, came from playing around with the ingredients I grew up eating every night. When I want something satisfying to eat, I still go back to that comforting place and fire up a giant pot of beans or a satisfying grain—or usually both.

FUNDACIÓN:

SALSA MADRE
MOTHER SAUCE

MAKES
1
SCANT
CUP

Salsa madre, mother sauce, is like a cook's "secret sauce" of proprietary seasoning and ingredients. You see the sauce more in restaurants than home kitchens. I'm not exactly sure why that is, but I'm guessing restaurants make the seasoning sauce for the same reason I developed my Saltado Sauce (page 138). Having a "mother sauce" helps the cook keep all of the different, and sometimes independently bold, flavors in Peruvian cooking balanced. I've heard some Peruvian home cooks also use the term *salsa madre*, but like so many of our Spanish phrases, they could be referring to an actual completed sauce, or more of a seasoning base like my salsa madre. In that way, my version is almost like aderezo (seasoning base; see page 152), in a more complete, full-flavored form (an aderezo is a cook's favorite mix of seasonings, like onions, garlic, maybe some pepper pastes, but is pretty basic). Along with sautéed onions, my salsa madre has both ají amarillo and ají panca pastes—which together have a spicy and smoky-sweet flavor balance—and a generous amount of spices like cumin and oregano, along with plenty of garlic.

The flavors in salsa madre are pretty intense, so you only need a small amount. Chop the onions finely so they almost melt into the sauce. Because the salsa madre already has a good amount of oil, you can start off sautéing whatever you are cooking simply with a dollop or two of the sauce. Store the sauce in the freezer in generous tablespoon-size portions or flat in a freezer bag so you can break off little chunks whenever you need it.

¼ cup olive oil

½ cup finely diced red onion

2 tablespoons pureed garlic (see page 37) or finely minced garlic

1 bay leaf

3 tablespoons ají amarillo paste, store-bought or homemade (see page 34)

½ cup ají panca paste, store-bought or homemade (see page 36)

1 tablespoon ground cumin

1½ tablespoons dried oregano leaves, preferably Mexican

2 tablespoons freshly ground black pepper

1 Heat the olive oil in a large Dutch oven or saucepan over medium-high heat until hot, a good 2 minutes. Add the onion and sauté, stirring occasionally with a wooden spoon, until it begins to soften, 3 to 4 minutes. Stir in the garlic and bay leaf, and then add the ají amarillo and panca pastes. Reduce the heat to medium-low and gently push the aderezo (flavorings) back and forth on the bottom of the pan until the pepper pastes smell toasty and the sauce has reduced slightly, about 5 minutes.

2 Add the cumin and oregano and stir for 15 seconds, or until the spices smell fragrant. Add the pepper, remove the salsa madre from the heat, and let cool completely. Remove the bay leaf, cover, and refrigerate for up to 5 days, or lay the sauce flat in a quart-size freezer bag, freeze, and break off small pieces as needed.

AJÍ-SPICED CANARIO BEANS WITH PORK, THREE WAYS

SERVES 6 TO 8 AS A MAIN DISH

You can't get much more French than a duck cassoulet—other than the most important ingredient. French flageolet and other white beans are actually the descendants of the beans that explorers took back to Europe from Peru and elsewhere in South America.

For me, throwing a few spoonfuls of ají pepper pastes into the pot was a given. I love duck, which Peruvians also appreciate (see sidebar, page 154), but pork works so well with the smokiness of ají panca. And since Europeans brought us pigs, our beans for their pork seems like a fair trade. Pork butt or a similar cut gives the stew that chunky, homey vibe, but I've also made this *elegante* with a Frenched rib rack of pork loin. Roast the meat whole (see page 149), then slice it into individual chops and nestle one on top of each serving. You could also fry up thick pork chops to lay on top.

To be honest, the beans are so good on their own, you could omit the pork butt and sausage (just use the bacon and other seasonings) and serve them as a bean stew.

12 to 16 ounces thick-cut bacon, cut into long, ½-inch-thick pieces

1 pound pork butt or other roast, chopped into bite-size pieces

½ large red onion, finely chopped

1 carrot, finely chopped

2 tablespoons pureed garlic (see page 37) or finely grated garlic

3 tablespoons ají panca paste, store-bought or homemade (see page 34)

1 tablespoon ají amarillo paste, store-bought or homemade (see page 34)

2 links Portuguese Linguiça-style sausage, Spanish chorizo, or other dry-cured, smoked sausage (10 to 12 ounces total), cut into meaty chunks

3 plum tomatoes, seeded and diced

1 to 2 cups reserved bean cooking liquid, homemade chicken stock (see page 40) or low-sodium store-bought broth

1 (15- to 16-ounce) bag canario (mayocoba) or other white beans, cooked (6 to 7 cups), strained, cooking liquid reserved (see page 212)

Kosher salt and freshly ground black pepper

1 bunch scallions, including the tender green stems, thickly sliced

1 Fry the bacon in a large Dutch oven or saucepan until the meat is just cooked but still very tender, about 5 minutes. Transfer the bacon to a paper towel–lined pan and pour off and discard all but a few tablespoons of the rendered fat in the pan.

2 Reheat the bacon fat over medium-high heat until hot, a good 2 minutes. Add the chunks of pork and sauté until golden brown, 3 to 4 minutes. Add the onions and carrots and sauté, stirring occasionally with a wooden spoon, until they begin to soften and are nicely browned along the edges, a good 5 minutes. Stir in the garlic and ají panca and amarillo pastes and reduce the heat to medium-low. Gently push the aderezo (flavorings) back and forth on the bottom of the pan for 2 to 3 minutes. Add the sausage and cook until it begins to lightly brown and the aderezo smells toasty, 2 to 3 minutes more.

3 Stir in the tomatoes to lightly deglaze the pan and simmer until they release some of their juices, about 30 seconds, then stir in 1 cup of the reserved bean cooking liquid. Mix in the cooked beans and bacon. Add another cup or so of cooking liquid if the cassoulet looks dry. You can make the cassoulet up to 1 day ahead at this point; the flavors will only improve.

4 To serve, bring the beans to a simmer so they are piping hot, and season the cassoulet with salt and pepper. Serve the cassoulet family-style, from the pot, or pile the stew into individual bowls. Sprinkle the scallions all over the top and serve *inmediatamente.*

WARM VEGETABLE QUINOA SALAD WITH MISO-LIME DRESSING

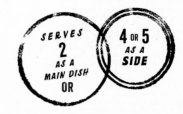

SERVES 2 AS A MAIN DISH OR 4 OR 5 AS A SIDE

Main-course salads aren't on menus all over the place in Peru like they are here. I guess we like more substantial bites with our vegetables. This quinoa "salad" is really a vegetable saltado, stir-fry, with quinoa as the base instead of rice. Like any stir-fry, you don't want to overcrowd the wok or pan with too many ingredients, so stick to no more than two servings at a time. Quinoa is more fragile than rice, so you need to add it toward the end of the cooking time. If you have red or brown quinoa, this is a good dish to use it in. The darker colored seedlike grains tend to be firmer than white quinoa and hold up well when fried. I also love the chewier texture, but white quinoa is still also very good.

I tend to use crispy quinoa (see sidebar, page 201) to contrast the chewy texture of quinoa in the stir-fry with some crunchiness (to go restaurant-style, substitute about ½ cup of the fried quinoa for steamed and fold the two together). Nuts provide a similar crunchiness and great flavor. Use whatever mix of vegetables you have around, and chop them all about the same size so they cook evenly. Keep the tomatoes a little larger so they hold their shape.

1 jalapeño, seeded and deveined
½ large red or other bell pepper, seeded and deveined
1 medium Japanese or Chinese eggplant, or ½ small globe
    eggplant
Small handful of mushrooms, any type
1 ripe medium heirloom, beefsteak, or other juicy tomato, or
    2 plum tomatoes
Miso-Lime Dressing (recipe follows)
⅓ cup plain Greek-style yogurt
Canola or other vegetable oil
2 generous cups cooked quinoa (see page 201), drained on
    paper towels if moist
8 cloves confit garlic (see sidebar, page 199) or roasted
    garlic cloves (optional)
Kosher salt
Handful of crushed walnuts, lightly toasted

1 Roughly chop the jalapeño, bell pepper, eggplant, and mushrooms into bite-size chunks, about 1 inch or so, or smaller, if you like. Halve the tomatoes lengthwise and cut each half into several large, chunky wedges. Keep the tomatoes in a separate pile or bowl. In a separate small bowl, stir together the miso-lime dressing and yogurt.

2 Heat a wok or large sauté pan over high heat until hot, a good 2 minutes. Pour in a nice drizzle of oil, enough to coat the bottom of the pan (2 to 3 tablespoons), and heat the oil for 2 to 3 minutes more, until very hot. The oil shouldn't be smoking, but close. Swirl the oil around the pan, toss in the jalapeño, bell pepper, eggplant, and mushrooms, and shake the pan or use tongs to flip the vegetables a few times. Toss the vegetables regularly until the eggplant begins to soften, about 5 minutes. Add another tablespoon or two of oil to the pan if the vegetables ever look dry.

3 Add the tomatoes, toss well, and continue to fry until the tomatoes barely begin to soften, about 30 seconds. Toss in the quinoa and confit garlic (if using) and cook for a few seconds more. Transfer the stir-fry to a medium bowl and fold in all but a tablespoon or two of the yogurt dressing. Taste, and add a little more of the dressing and salt, if you'd like. The salad should be very tangy. Transfer the warm salad to a large bowl or individual plates, sprinkle with the walnuts, and serve *inmediatamente.*

MISO-LIME DRESSING

Makes about ⅓ cup

My grilled Paiche Lettuce Wraps (page 120) and kabocha squash (page 189) are brushed with a honey-saikyo miso sauce (a specialty miso from Kyoto with a sweeter and more subtle, balanced flavor than some misos; see page 261 for sources) infused with sliced limes.

Here, this miso-lime dressing also uses the saikyo miso and honey, but the rice vinegar and ají amarillo peppers brighten and spice up the flavors. This is a dressing that works hot or cold. Add a little more oil or equal parts plain Greek-style yogurt, and you've got the kind of tangy-sweet green salad dressing that even my kids love. Or use it on a cold quinoa salad with sweet, crunchy vegetables like red bell peppers. Saikyo miso (see page 265) is worth seeking out, but more widely available shiromiso is a good substitute.

2½ tablespoons saikyo or shiro (white) miso

2 tablespoons honey

1 tablespoon fresh lime juice

1 tablespoon canola or olive oil

1 tablespoon unseasoned rice vinegar

1 teaspoon ají amarillo paste, store-bought or homemade (see page 34), or to taste

Pinch of kosher salt and freshly ground black pepper

Whisk together all of the ingredients in a small bowl until the miso is well incorporated. Taste and add a little more ají amarillo paste, if you'd like. Use right away, or cover and refrigerate the dressing for up to 5 days. Stir again before using.

CONFIT GARLIC

I love watching the faces on first-timers when they see the giant cloves of confit garlic (garlic poached in oil) that I use in the stir-fried quinoa salad. People usually taste the chunky garlic *con cuidado* (with caution), thinking the cloves will be way too intense. Before they know it, they've eaten half a head of garlic.

Slowly poaching the whole cloves in oil over very low heat really mellows their flavor. It also helps soften them but retain their shape without getting that super-soft texture that you get with overly roasted garlic cloves. Other than the quinoa salad, you can nestle a few confit garlic cloves alongside roasted vegetables, sprinkle them on top of pasta with tomato sauce, or use them as part of a crudité platter.

Try to keep the cloves whole as you peel them, so they look their best, but don't throw away any that get smashed. You can still use them for cooking. Save the garlic-infused cooking oil for salad dressings or for sautéing or roasting vegetables, fish, and meats.

To Confit Garlic: Place the peeled cloves from 1 to 2 heads of garlic (no more than will fit in a single layer) in a small or medium saucepan. Cover the cloves completely with olive oil (you will need at least 1 cup, probably more, depending on the size of the pan), bring the oil to a simmer over medium-high heat, and immediately reduce the heat to low. Gently simmer (do not boil) the oil until the garlic is very tender when pierced with a knife, about 15 minutes. If the garlic begins to turn brown in spots, turn off the heat completely for a minute or two. Let the garlic cool completely in the oil. Transfer the cloves to a jar and cover completely with the poaching oil. The garlic will keep in the refrigerator for 2 to 3 weeks. **Makes 1 to 2 heads of garlic cloves and a nice jar of garlic-infused cooking oil.**

KINÚWA (QUINOA) & KIWICHA (AMARANTH)

To the Incas, the chisaya mama, *literally "mother of all grains," was quinoa. It's not difficult to understand why they considered the grainlike seed sacred.*

The pre-Columbian crop can survive on its own high up in the *altiplano*, the frost-covered plains of the Andes, an environment that was too harsh for many other crops—and most people. Kinúwa (keen-u-wa), the Quechua name for quinoa, is still grown by small, native farmers on the altiplano stretching from Peru to Bolivia and down through Chile.

Kiwicha (kee-wee-cha), the Quechua word for "amaranth," is quinoa's Aztec cousin, only smaller and a little more tightly wound. The seeds stay closed up when you cook them, as amaranth doesn't have a sprouting "tail" (the germ of the seed) like quinoa.

Both amaranth and quinoa are "complete" proteins, pretty rare in the plant kingdom. In Peru, the seeds aren't just something you toss into a salad, but a very versatile ingredient. Think of quinoa and amaranth the next time you reach for rice, as a base for risottos and stir-fries, or added to simple broth soups or chunky stews.

Quinoa Basics

Of the hundreds of varieties of quinoa, only a few are sold commercially. There are subtle flavor and texture differences between each, but all of the dried seeds are interchangeable in almost any recipe. I recommend sticking to one color at a time. Those rainbow packs of white, brown, and red quinoa that you see on some grocery store shelves today are pretty, but each has slightly different cooking times. When you cook them together, the white quinoa may be falling apart by the time the darker-colored seeds are fully cooked.

Puffed quinoa is very different from the dried seeds. It is already cooked and popped, like popcorn, so the seeds get a light, almost rice cracker–like texture. I love it in desserts.

White Quinoa: The most common commercial quinoa is more of an off-white beige color. This is a multipurpose seed that you can really use in anything, from salads to soups to baking. It cooks up to an almost soft, creamy texture.

Red, Brown, and Black Quinoa: Darker-colored seeds usually have a chewier texture than the white seeds, almost like tiny pearls of barley, so they hold their shape better in dishes like stir-fries. Simmer them a minute or two longer than white quinoa. Any of the individually packed colored seeds (typically various shades of brown and red) are usually very good, but I really like red quinoa.

Amaranth Basics

Like quinoa, amaranth seeds are off-white to light brown, but they stay tightly closed when cooked. The seeds are so tiny that they tend to clump together when cooked. That clumpy character can be a good thing, as you get even more texture in each bite. I actually prefer amaranth to quinoa in soups, as the texture is lighter.

How to Cook Quinoa and Amaranth

I'm always surprised when I see recipes that begin by cautioning you to rinse your quinoa or amaranth very well to remove the natural, powdery residue on the seeds that tastes very bitter. I never rinse them. If I had a cooking class high up in the Andes and was using locally harvested seeds, sure, but the quinoa and amaranth available commercially have had the powdery residue washed off, even in bulk market bins in Peru. One of my first kitchen chores when I was around seven years old was to sort through and clean the quinoa and rice that my mom brought home in giant sacks from the market, but not because of any lingering residue. Vendors were notorious for slipping in extra stones to weigh down your order so they could charge more.

Toss in leftover nubs of whatever produce you have around to flavor the seeds. Or, instead of water, cooking the seeds in vegetable or chicken stock is always good. One of my most successful experiments was quinoa cooked with the leftover juice I saved from seeding a big pile of fresh tomatoes. If you're using the quinoa or amaranth for a dessert, don't use the seasonings in this recipe. Cook it the simple, Andean way—in a big pot of unseasoned water. For salads and most other dishes, you can let the seeds cool in the strainer. Whenever the seeds need to be drier, like for a stir-fry, spread out the quinoa or amaranth on a baking sheet to cool. And be sure to check in on them occasionally as they simmer. If overcooked, the seeds tend to fall apart and become mushy.

1 cup quinoa or amaranth
A mix of aromatic vegetable seasonings, such as ¼ red onion, 1 stalk celery, 1 peeled carrot, 1 smashed garlic clove
1 bay leaf
Generous pinch of kosher salt

1 Combine the quinoa or amaranth, aromatic vegetables, bay leaf, salt, and 2 cups water in a medium saucepan with a lid. Bring the water to a boil, reduce the heat to low, cover, and cook the quinoa until the seeds have sprouted (they will look like they have a little *cola*, tail) and most of the water has been absorbed, 8 to 10 minutes (amaranth seeds will not sprout). Peek in on the seeds once or twice as they cook, as some batches sprout and absorb the water more quickly. If you are cooking a darker red, brown, or black quinoa, you may need to cook the seeds for a minute or two longer. They should be chewy, but still tender.

2 Strain the quinoa or amaranth (use a fine-mesh strainer to catch the tiny seeds), and swirl a little water in the pan to get the last pieces out. Run your fingers down the vegetables to get all of the seeds off them and discard the vegetables and bay leaf. Let the seeds cool completely in the strainer, or spread them out on a parchment-lined baking sheet to cool. Use immediately, or cover and refrigerate the quinoa or amaranth for up to 5 days.

MAKES ABOUT 3 CUPS

CRISPY QUINOA

To make crispy quinoa: Spread out ½ cup to 1 cup cooked quinoa in a thin layer on a parchment-lined baking sheet to dry for 10 minutes (it can be just cooked, or precooked and refrigerated). Fill a small saucepan with a solid inch or two of canola or other vegetable oil, and heat the oil for a minute or two, until hot. Remember that you are frying a seed. The oil should be hot, but not at deep-fry temperatures (350°F or more), or the quinoa will burn. Add the quinoa and fry until golden brown, 1½ to 2 minutes. Drain through a fine-mesh strainer over a bowl to catch the oil (reserve the oil to use again, if you like), and spread out the crispy quinoa on paper towels to dry.

ANDEAN SQUASH STEW WITH QUINOA & FRIED EGGS

SERVES
4
AS A
MAIN DISH

Locro de zapallo (pumpkin stew) is a very old, very hearty Incan stew made from pumpkin, potatoes, choclo (large-kernel corn), and, since the arrival of the Spanish, chunks of fresh queso fresco. I loved it the moment my uncle Lucio, a true old-school mountain man, taught me to make it. Whenever my older brother Julio, who wasn't a fan, ribbed me for hanging out with our sisters in the kitchen, I'd make a big pot of locro de zapallo for that night's family supper, just to get back at him. I'm still waiting for him to visit Los Angeles from Japan, where he now lives, to try my version. This time, I know he's going to love it.

Instead of throwing all the ingredients together in a pot like a stew, I slowly cook the squash and potatoes confit-style, in seasoned olive oil, until they become incredibly tender and almost buttery. I also add quinoa, which isn't traditional, so you get a slightly chewy texture to contrast with the vegetables. Along with the more traditional queso fresco (or feta—see page 265), a few seared tomatoes and a fried egg on top turn the stew into an impressive dinner.

Making a confit of the vegetables makes them super moist and tender, but even roasting or sautéing the squash and potatoes gives the stew a richer flavor than simply boiling them in the stew. If you do confit the vegetables, strain and save the seasoned oil for another round of confit, or to drizzle on chicken, fish, or vegetables.

CONFIT VEGETABLES

½ medium kabocha squash (about 1¼ pounds), peeled and cut into cubes about ¾ inch wide

1 pound red or small white potatoes, peeled and cut into cubes about ¾ inch wide

4 leafy sprigs fresh thyme

1 large sprig fresh rosemary, broken in half, or 2 small sprigs

8 cloves garlic, lightly smashed

Olive oil

Kosher salt

LOCRO

¼ cup Salsa Madre (page 196)

1 cup frozen choclo (see page 28) or fresh corn kernels

About 2 cups homemade vegetable or chicken stock (see page 40) or low-sodium store-bought broth

About 3 cups cooked quinoa (see page 201)

1 (4-ounce) block feta cheese or queso fresco, cut into ½-inch cubes (about 1 cup)

½ cup freshly grated Parmesan

4 large eggs, fried as you like (optional)

4 whole Pan-Fried Tomatoes (see sidebar, page 204)

1 To make the confit vegetables, preheat the oven to 300°F. Put the squash and potatoes in separate deep baking dishes that fit the vegetables in a single layer with a little breathing room between each piece. Divide the thyme, rosemary, and garlic between the roasting dishes and generously pour enough olive oil over each so the vegetables are completely covered by a good ½ inch of oil. Cover the baking dishes snugly with foil and bake until the vegetables are very tender, about 30 minutes. Strain the vegetables through a fine-mesh strainer (it's fine to mix the potatoes and squash together) over a bowl and reserve the oil, herbs, and garlic. (When cool, transfer the oil, herbs, and garlic to a storage jar to confit vegetables again, or use as cooking oil. Store the oil in the refrigerator for up to 2 weeks.) Season the potatoes and squash with salt and use right away, or let cool completely, cover, and refrigerate for up to 3 days. Bring the vegetables to room temperature before making the locro.

RECIPE CONTINUES

2 To make the locro, heat a large Dutch oven or saucepan over medium-high heat until hot, a good 2 minutes. Add the salsa madre, stir it around with a wooden spoon for a few seconds, then stir in the choclo. Cook the corn for a minute or two, then stir in the stock, followed by the quinoa. Bring the mixture to a simmer and cook, stirring occasionally, for 2 to 3 minutes, until the quinoa soaks up most of the stock. Add a little more stock if the quinoa looks dry. Fold in the potatoes and squash very gently. Some of the squash may be so tender that it almost melts into the quinoa. It will only make the quinoa taste better. Stir in the cubed feta and remove the pot from the heat. Sprinkle about two-thirds of the Parmesan on top and turn off the heat.

3 If topping the locro with eggs, fry them now, and get your serving bowls ready.

4 Stir the locro one more time to incorporate the Parmesan, and mound the stew into the center of wide, shallow serving bowls or individual plates (the "stew" is pretty thick, more like risotto, so a plate is fine). Top each with a fried egg and nestle two pan-fried tomato halves alongside. Sprinkle the remaining Parmesan on top and serve the locro *inmediatamente*.

PAN-FRIED TOMATOES

Plum tomatoes are firm enough that they fry really well. Nestle these fried tomatoes alongside locro, risotto, or pasta, or make them the start of a warm winter salad. Make sure the pan is very hot and don't overcrowd the pan, so you get a nice sear on the tomatoes.

To make Pan-Fried Tomatoes: Halve 4 (or as many as you need) ripe but firm plum tomatoes lengthwise. Dip your finger or a spoon in a little pureed garlic (see page 37) and spread it generously on the cut flesh of each tomato (or rub each side lightly with a smashed garlic clove). Lightly season each tomato with a sprinkle of salt, pepper, and dried oregano, if you'd like. Heat a drizzle of olive oil, enough to coat the bottom of a large iron skillet or saucepan (2 to 3 tablespoons), over medium-high heat until very hot, a good 2 minutes or longer. Add the tomatoes, cut-side down, in batches if needed so you don't crowd the pan, and sear them for about 15 seconds, until they just begin to color. Flip and sear the opposite side until they just look juicy, about 15 seconds more. Transfer the tomatoes to a plate. Add a little more olive oil if the pan looks dry before cooking the remaining tomatoes. **Makes 8 tomato halves.**

GREEN RICE WITH PEAS & SECO SAUCE

SERVES 2 OR 3 AS A MAIN DISH OR 4 OR 5 AS A SIDE

With arroz verde, what ingredients go into the pot depends on the region and cook. In Peru, usually only cilantro gives the rice its namesake color (in some countries, green peppers are also used). In a lot of dishes, like Arroz con Pato (duck with green rice, page 154), the green rice is really more of a bonus than the main dish. The braising ingredients for the poultry slowly cook down to become a rich, dark green sauce to pour on top of or stir into your rice. Problem is, there's usually never enough of the reduced seco braise (the traditional sauce left over from slowly cooking meats and poultry—see page 151) to make all of the green rice you want to keep eating. To both cut down on the cooking time and have enough sauce to spare, I came up with a quick version to substitute for the traditional slow-cooked seco sauce when I don't have the time to make the classic version. It's also vegetarian. Most that you find in Peru are not. (My friends in Peru would give me a hard time about that, but hey, I get it.)

When you make the rice, the extra hit of pureed cilantro brightens up the cilantro in the seco sauce. Use medium- or long-grain white or brown rice, not sticky sushi rice. Fluffier rice soaks up all of those good aderezo juices.

⅓ large bunch fresh cilantro, cut into thirds (including the stems)

About 2 cups homemade vegetable or chicken stock (see page 40) or low-sodium store-bought broth

Olive oil

½ large carrot, finely chopped

½ red or other bell pepper, finely chopped

About 1 cup Seco Secreto (page 206)

About 2½ cups cooked white or brown rice

Generous handful (about ½ cup) of frozen petite peas, thawed

Kosher salt

1 Puree the cilantro in a blender with about ½ cup of the stock until smooth.

2 Heat a nice drizzle of olive oil, enough to coat the bottom of a large saucepan (2 to 3 tablespoons), over medium-high heat until hot, a good 2 minutes. Add the carrot and bell pepper, and sauté for a minute or two, stirring the vegetables with a wooden spoon. Stir in the seco sauce and move the aderezo (flavorings) around the pan with a wooden spoon for a few seconds, then stir in the pureed cilantro. Cook the sauce, stirring regularly, for another minute or two, or until it turns dark green.

3 Add another generous pour, about ½ cup, of the stock, bring the mixture to a simmer, and stir in the rice and peas. Continue to simmer for a minute or two, until the rice soaks up most of the stock. Add the remaining 1 cup stock and keep stirring the simmering rice until it has soaked up most of the stock, 2 minutes or so more. It should be very moist. If not, add another splash of stock. Season the rice with salt, and serve.

RECIPE CONTINUES

SECO SECRETO

Makes about 2 cups

After slowly cooking down whatever meats or poultry you have simmering on the stove, if you're doing things right, all of the leftover sauce at the bottom of the pot gets sopped up by rice or bread. It's always gone way too soon. With this independent seco sauce (the "secret" ingredient), I can make green rice and so many other dishes quickly, whenever the craving strikes.

This makes enough sauce to freeze half, so you're ready to go for a quick weeknight supper. Other than rice and tamales, spoon the sauce on chicken or pork, or stir it into smashed potatoes. I pour a little beer into the sauce, but you can use more broth to keep it kid-friendly, or use vegetable broth to make a vegetarian version.

Olive oil
1 large red onion, coarsely chopped into smallish chunks
1½ medium carrots, coarsely chopped into smallish chunks
1 teaspoon ají amarillo paste, store-bought or homemade (see page 34)
1 tablespoon ají panca paste, store-bought or homemade (see page 36)
1 teaspoon pureed garlic (see page 37) or finely minced garlic
1 bay leaf
½ cup lager or other medium-bodied beer, or use more stock
½ cup homemade vegetable or chicken stock (see page 40) or low-sodium store-bought broth
½ teaspoon ground cumin
1 large bunch fresh cilantro, very tip of stems trimmed and cut into thirds (including the stems)
1 teaspoon kosher salt, or to taste

1 Heat a nice drizzle of olive oil, enough to coat the bottom of a large saucepan (2 to 3 tablespoons), over medium-high heat until hot, a good 2 minutes. Add the onion and carrots and sauté, stirring occasionally with a wooden spoon, until they begin to soften and are nicely browned along the edges, about 5 minutes. Add the ají amarillo and panca pastes, pureed garlic, and bay leaf, reduce the heat to medium-low, and gently push the aderezo (flavorings) back and forth on the bottom of the pan with the spoon until the pepper pastes smell toasty and the sauce reduces slightly, about 5 minutes.

2 Pour in the beer and stock and scrape up any browned bits from the bottom of the pan. Simmer until the broth has reduced by almost half, a good 5 minutes. Stir in the cumin, then the cilantro, and remove the pot from the heat. Let the sauce cool slightly.

3 When cool enough to handle, transfer the sauce to a blender and puree until smooth in batches, if necessary. Season the sauce with salt and use immediately, or let cool completely, cover, and refrigerate for up to 2 days. Or freeze for up to 3 months in two batches (about 1 cup each) so you're ready to go with the right amount of seco sauce whenever you need it.

PERFECT (AND EASY) STEAMED RICE

I've made steamed rice every which way, in fancy steamers and on the stovetop, and I still go back to this simple method. The steam releases through the parchment paper and edges of the lid so you get a nice, sticky, steamed rice. If you want to mimic a steamer more literally, you could use foil as the lid and poke a few holes in it, but both methods work very well. Short-grain, sushi-style rice makes the best sticky rice, but you can also use this method with brown rice. Don't use quick-cooking rice, which cooks too quickly and becomes mushy. With this technique, you can cook up any quantity of rice.

To make Steamed Rice: Preheat the oven to 350°F. Follow the package instructions for rinsing the rice, if necessary. Combine equal parts rice and water in an oven-safe pot. Use a pot that isn't too big and fits the rice and water nicely. Cut a piece of parchment to fit inside the pot, and put the parchment directly on top of the rice and water (don't press down). Put the lid on the pot and bring the water and rice to a boil on the stovetop. As soon as you can hear the water boiling and see steam coming out beaneath the lid, like a train is coming, transfer the pot to the oven and bake for exactly 20 minutes. Don't ever open the lid.

Remove the pot from the oven (do not remove the lid) and let the rice steam on a trivet on the countertop for 20 minutes more. The rice should be perfectly cooked (if using brown rice, taste, and if needed, cover and steam the rice for 10 minutes more). Serve the rice immediately, or leave it covered for a little while longer so it stays warm while you finish whatever else you are cooking, or let cool completely, cover, and refrigerate the rice for up to 5 days.

PLANTAIN RICE CAKES WITH JALAPEÑO-HUACATAY SAUCE

MAKES 8 CAKES

SERVES 4 AS AN APPETIZER COURSE OR SIDE

Tacachos are patties made from plantains smashed between grinding stones and flecked with small pieces of fried pork. Like the *tacu tacu* on page 211, this dish is rooted in African traditions. It is especially popular in villages in the Amazon, where plantains are widely available.

Traditionally, tacacho is served as a fritterlike snack. I like a more savory version, so I fold in leftover rice and sometimes even beans like chickpeas, or I'll turn it into a vegetarian dish by omitting the bacon and using sautéed mushrooms instead.

The plantains are best when they are very ripe and the skin has blackened on the grill, but you can sear them (unpeeled) directly over the flame of a gas stove, like eggplants (see page 186), for a quick side dish. As with bananas, you can put them in a paper sack to speed up the ripening process.

2 ripe medium plantains, unpeeled

6 to 8 slices thick, meaty, smoky bacon, coarsely chopped, or 1 portobello mushroom cap, halved and cut into ½-inch-thick strips plus 1½ to 2 cups sliced mushrooms

Olive oil

2 tablespoons Salsa Madre (page 196)

About 2 cups cooked white or brown rice (not sushi rice), or more as needed

Kosher salt and freshly ground black pepper

Canola or other vegetable oil

Jalapeño-Huacatay Sauce (recipe follows)

1 Grill or sear the plantains. To grill, prepare a grill for medium-high-heat cooking. Put the plantains on the grill or directly on a stovetop gas range over high heat (on the stovetop, the flames should kiss the flesh; see charring eggplant, page 186). Sear the plantains until the skin blackens all over and begins to split, about 5 minutes on the stovetop or a few minutes longer on the grill. Flip the plantains with tongs occasionally so they blacken evenly. Let the plantains cool slightly, peel, and smash them with a potato masher or in a large mortar and pestle (I use a Japanese grinding stone) until the flesh has broken down but is still chunky. You should have about 1 cup (refrigerate or freeze any excess for later).

2 Preheat the oven to 250°F. Line a baking sheet with a few layers of paper towels. To make the bacon version, sauté the bacon in a large sauté pan over medium-high heat until golden brown, 4 to 5 minutes. Pour off the rendered fat into a small bowl, leaving a thin layer of fat in the pan. To make the mushroom version, in a large sauté pan, heat about 2 tablespoons of olive oil over medium-high heat until hot, about 2 minutes. Add the sliced portobello cap and sauté, stirring often, until the pieces are golden brown on all sides and tender, about 6 minutes. (Break one open if needed to make sure it is fully cooked.) Use tongs to transfer the portobellos to an ovensafe plate. If the pan looks dry, add another tablespoon of olive oil, heat the oil for about a minute, and add the sliced mushrooms. Sauté, stirring often, until the slices are golden brown on all sides and tender, 4 to 5 minutes. Transfer the sliced mushrooms to a small bowl.

3 Return the pan to the heat, add the salsa madre, and sauté, stirring continuously, until it smells aromatic, about 30 seconds. Add the rice, scrape up any brown bits, and transfer to a medium bowl.

RECIPE CONTINUES

4 Add the smashed plantains, about half the bacon or all the sliced mushrooms (whichever you are using; if mushrooms, save the portobello strips for garnish), and mix well to combine. If the mixture feels wet, add a little more rice. Taste and season the mixture with salt and pepper if needed. Lightly oil your hands with the bacon fat or vegetable oil and shape the mixture firmly into patties the shape of small hamburgers.

5 Heat a few tablespoons of oil in a skillet (preferably nonstick) over medium-high heat for 2 to 3 minutes, until very hot. Fry the patties a few at a time (do not overcrowd the pan) and cook until they are golden brown, about 2 minutes per side, flipping once with tongs halfway through the cooking time. Transfer the patties to the lined baking sheet. If not serving immediately, put the baking sheet in the oven while you continue to fry the remaining patties the same way.

6 To serve, spoon about ¼ cup of the huacatay sauce on the bottom of each of four small plates. Place 2 patties on each plate and arrange a few pieces of bacon or portobello mushroom caps on top of each. Or pile the cakes onto a large platter, sprinkle the bacon or portobellos on top, and serve the huacatay sauce in a bowl alongside, for dipping. Serve *inmediatamente*.

JALAPEÑO-HUACATAY SAUCE
Makes about 1 cup

This is one of my favorite sauces. The funny thing is, other than a few of the ingredients like ají amarillo paste and huacatay, an herb that tastes almost like a mix between basil and mint, it's not even all that Peruvian. It took me a while to figure out what people were talking about when they said they loved the "green sauce" they had at Peruvian restaurants in the United States that is served on top of all sorts of dishes, from choclo corn to roast chicken. We don't really have such a thing, other than some of the seco sauces we use on stews like seco de cordero (braised lamb with seco sauce, page 150). That is a cilantro, ají pepper, and sometimes huacatay-based braising sauce, yes, but it's traditionally only served with certain dishes, and everything cooks down together with the meat or poultry.

When I finally tried this mysterious Peruvian-American "green sauce," I liked it so much, I decided to make my own. Other than the tacacho, I mix the sauce into rice, quinoa, or other grains, or spoon it on top of corn or potatoes. Whatever you serve it on is even better topped with more queso fresco, or, my favorite with this sauce, a tangy goat cheese. To make a vegan version of the sauce, use tofu instead of cheese.

1 to 2 medium jalapeños, seeded and deveined
1 medium bunch fresh cilantro, leaves and top two-thirds of stems
1 teaspoon pureed garlic (see page 37) or finely minced garlic
1½ tablespoons ají amarillo paste, store-bought or homemade (see page 34)
¼ cup crumbled goat cheese, queso fresco, or tofu
5 tablespoons red wine vinegar
2 tablespoons packed fresh huacatay leaves, or 1 tablespoon frozen huacatay, thawed
½ cup extra-virgin olive oil
1 teaspoon kosher salt, or more to taste

Puree all of the ingredients in a blender until smooth. Season with more salt and add another jalapeño, if you like. Cover and refrigerate the sauce for up to 5 days.

RICE & BEAN PATTIES WITH SPICY TUNA

MAKES
24
BITE-SIZE
PATTIES
OR

8
LARGER
ROUNDS

When I make dishes like this, it reminds me what I love about cooking the food of my country. Tacu tacu is rooted in Afro-Peruvian traditions. There is such a rich history there, and it is also a very humble one. Slaves had to piece together whatever leftover ingredients they had to stretch a meal, and many of those dishes, like these rice and bean cakes, were incredibly good and creative. The spicy tuna topping is my addition, and very much the influence of my days working the sushi line in London restaurants. I love the contrast in flavors and textures, with the comforting rice and bean cakes and the light, spicy chilled tuna on top. These are very nice for a party, as you can make the cakes ahead and serve them at room temperature.

You can use virtually any beans in this dish, and almost any type of rice or quinoa. I've made these with garbanzos, canarios (mayocoba beans), and pallares, lima beans, as here. Even canned beans are good here for a quick weeknight supper (leftovers are even better). The only trick is to make the cakes small enough so they hold together, and chill them for several hours before frying them up. I use sushi molds, which are pretty easy to find, or you could use small round cookie cutters.

I usually blast the top of the rocoto aioli with a cooking torch for a few seconds so it gets caramelized in spots, but you can just add a dollop of the aioli on top, al fresco–style.

1 cup homemade chicken or vegetable broth (see page 40) or low-sodium store-bought broth

3 tablespoons Salsa Madre (page 196)

About 2½ cups cooked rice

About 1½ cups cooked lima, canario (mayocoba), great northern, or other white beans (recipe follows), drained well

Kosher salt and freshly ground black pepper

Olive oil

About 1 cup spicy tuna (see page 73)

Rocoto aioli (see page 38)

1 serrano chile, thinly sliced

2 or 3 scallions, finely chopped

1 Heat a large sauté pan over medium-high heat until hot, a good 2 minutes. Add the stock and cook until reduced by half (about 5 minutes), then add the salsa madre and sauté, stirring continuously, until the sauce smells aromatic, about 30 seconds. Add the rice and beans and continue to cook, stirring regularly, until the broth has been absorbed by the rice and beans, about 5 minutes. (If any excess broth remains, strain the rice and beans.) Season the rice mixture with salt and pepper and let the mixture cool completely.

2 Preheat the oven to 250°F. Line a baking sheet with a few layers of paper towels. Shape the rice mixture into 8 medium patties or twenty-four 1 x 2-inch rectangles by pressing them firmly into ring molds or sushi molds. Make sure to press the mixture into the molds firmly with your hands so the patties hold together when pan-fried. Remove the patties from the molds and arrange them on a plate. Repeat the shaping process with the remaining rice mixture.

3 Heat 2 to 3 tablespoons of olive oil in a large skillet (preferably nonstick) over medium-high heat until hot but not smoking, about 2 minutes. Add a few of the tacu tacu patties (don't overcrowd the pan) and sauté until very light golden brown on the bottom, about 2 minutes. Use a spatula to gently flip the patties and fry the opposite side until light brown, about 1½ minutes more. (If the patties fall apart as you fry them, press the remaining patties together firmly with your hands before frying and be careful when flipping.) Transfer to the lined baking sheet. If not serving immediately, put the baking sheet in the oven while you continue to fry the remaining patties. You can leave the fried patties at room temperature for up to 2 hours before topping and serving.

4 To serve, spoon about 2 teaspoons of spicy tuna on top of each sushi-size patty or divide the tuna among the larger patties. Drizzle each with a little rocoto aioli, and place a serrano slice or two on top. Sprinkle the minced scallions all over the tacu tacu and the serving platter and serve *inmediatamente*.

PALLARES (LIMA BEANS) Y CANARIOS (MAYOCOBA BEANS)

Beans, native to the Americas, have been part of the Peruvian diet for thousands of years, from ancient times through today.

Different varieties of the beans have been grown along the coast since at least 2000 BC, probably earlier. The two you probably see the most in Peruvian cooking are large, dried white lima beans and small, creamy-yellow canario beans.

In Peru, we call lima beans *pallares*. *Pallar de la oreja* is one of a few Spanish names for earlobes, a pretty obvious reference if you take a close look at the shape of a lima bean. When they were first exported to Europe, the boxes were supposedly labeled "Lima," as in, from Lima, which was mistaken as the name of the beans. Some people also call them butter beans because of their starchy yet tender texture and mild but rich, almost buttery flavor. Today, you find lima beans all over Peru, but especially in the southern parts of the country, in both fresh green and dried forms. Limas are eaten on their own (sometimes pureed into a smooth soup), and because they hold up well when fried, they are often used in dishes like Tacu Tacu (rice and bean patties, page 211).

Canarios, also called mayocobas in other Latin American countries, are native to the Andes region. They grow very well, almost on their own, so you can usually find them at both the smallest outdoor village markets and in Lima supermarkets. They are so central to the Peruvian diet, you sometimes hear them simply referred to as *frijoles Peruanos* (Peruvian beans). The canario, canary, name comes from their almost creamy yellow color, like the bird (or, to my eye at least when dried, a somewhat beige canary). The beans both absorb other flavors well and tend to hold their shape. In Peru, people use them in all kinds of dishes, anything really, or just eat them on their own. They are my go-to bean for stews, cassoulets, or just any time I'm craving a big, satisfying bowl of beans.

Cooking Dried Beans

I've focused here on lima and canario (mayocoba) beans, but you can use this method for any beans. Adjust the cooking time as needed so the beans are tender but still hold their shape. Like many of the beans you commonly find in the United States, including similar great northern beans, canarios are simple to cook. Limas are a little different. The mature white beans hold on to their firm texture better than many dried beans, so they usually don't become fall-apart tender, and the cooking time varies greatly depending on the size of the beans. I've bought *pallares grandes*, or extra-large lima beans, that are the size of a quarter from Peruvian importers, and others from American companies called "large" that aren't much bigger than a penny.

1 (15- to 16-ounce) bag dried canario (mayocoba) or lima beans (about 2 cups canarios or 2½ to 3 cups limas), soaked overnight in cold water to cover the beans by 3 inches and drained

A mix of aromatic vegetables: ½ red onion, sliced lengthwise; 1 celery stalk, halved; 1 coarsely chopped carrot; and/or 3 peeled cloves garlic

1 bay leaf

2 teaspoons kosher salt, or more to taste

1 Combine the beans, aromatic vegetables, and bay leaf in a large Dutch oven or stockpot, cover the beans with a good 3 inches of water, and bring the water to a boil. Reduce the heat to maintain a simmer and cook the beans, uncovered, until tender. The cooking time will vary depending on the type and freshness of beans. (Unlike other beans, limas will retain a slightly firm texture.) If the cooking liquid ever recedes below the beans, add enough water to cover them by about 1 inch, and occasionally skim off the white foam that accumulates on top of the liquid. Season the cooked beans with the salt.

2 Allow the beans to cool completely in their cooking liquid, then fish out and discard the aromatic vegetables and bay leaf. If you'd like a creamier texture, scoop up about 1 cup each of the beans and their cooking liquid, puree them in a blender until smooth, then stir them back into the beans. Serve the beans right away, or let cool completely, cover, and refrigerate the beans in their cooking liquid for up to 5 days.

MAKES 6 TO 7 CUPS

BARLEY RISOTTO WITH MUSHROOMS

SERVES 4 OR 5 AS A MAIN DISH

I don't know of a risotto tradition in Peru, but I am sure there are some Italian Peruvians who could point out dozens of examples for me. Barley, a grain that arrived with the Conquistadors, is one of the main ingredients in *emolientes*, the herbal tea remedies going back to the Spanish occupation that you still find on the streets of Lima today (see page 30). Barley has a nutty flavor and chewy texture that works really well in a risotto, and together with the mushrooms, you get an intensely flavored dish that almost tastes meaty, even though it's vegetarian.

I use a mix of Japanese mushrooms like oyster mushrooms and shimeji, but you can use any mushrooms; portobellos and shiitakes will give the risotto an even meatier mushroom flavor. The sour cream is like gravy—you probably don't need it, but it makes the dish richer. Whole-grain barley soaked overnight cooks up more quickly. If you substitute pearl barley, cook it according to the package directions.

1 cup (about 7 ounces) whole-grain barley, soaked overnight in cold water to cover by 3 inches and drained

¼ cup olive oil

½ medium red onion, finely chopped

1 teaspoon pureed garlic (see page 37) or finely minced garlic

2 teaspoons ají amarillo paste, store-bought or homemade (see page 34)

About 12 ounces mixed mushrooms, stems saved for broth, halved or coarsely chopped if large

About 1½ cups Mushroom Broth (recipe follows)

⅓ cup sour cream (optional)

About ½ cup freshly grated Parmesan (from a 2- to 3-inch wedge)

Kosher salt and freshly ground black pepper

1 Put the barley in a large Dutch oven or soup pot, add enough water to cover by a solid 3 inches, and bring the water to a boil. Reduce the heat to maintain a simmer and cook the barley, uncovered, until tender, about 35 minutes, give or take 15 minutes, as whole-grain barley can be a little unpredictable. Drain the barley.

2 Heat the olive oil in a medium Dutch oven or saucepan over medium-high heat until hot, a good 2 minutes. Add the onion and garlic and sauté until the vegetables begin to soften, stirring occasionally with a wooden spoon, 2 to 3 minutes. Stir in the ají amarillo paste, then the mushrooms, and sauté until the mushrooms start to shrink and darken, about 3 minutes. Stir in 1 cup of the broth and scrape up any browned bits from the bottom of the pan. Cover the pan, reduce the heat to medium-low, and simmer the mushrooms until tender, a few minutes more (depending on their size). Stir in the barley and bring the broth to a simmer, uncovered. Cook, stirring often, until the barley soaks up most of the broth. Stir in the remaining broth, if needed, so the risotto looks very juicy.

3 Just before serving, stir in the sour cream (if using) and about two-thirds of the Parmesan. Season the risotto with salt and pepper, and pile it into a serving dish or individual bowls. Sprinkle the remaining Parmesan on top, and serve *inmediatamente*.

MUSHROOM BROTH

Makes about 3 generous cups

Dried mushrooms always make a good broth, but I usually save the stems of fresh mushrooms, or any whole mushrooms that aren't so good looking, to make broth. They make a lighter broth with a more subtle mushroom flavor that doesn't compete with whatever else you have going on in a dish.

Use white wine to deglaze the pan, if you have it, and the broth will taste even better. If my mom ever made anything like this, she'd definitely save the simmered mushrooms and vegetables to pile on top of steamed rice with a little of the broth and soy sauce. Since these aren't cooked very long, they still retain some really good flavor.

1 tablespoon olive oil

2 tablespoons unsalted butter

½ red or white onion, coarsely chopped

1 medium carrot, coarsely chopped

1 celery stalk, coarsely chopped

6 cloves garlic

5 to 6 ounces mushrooms or stems, any variety or a mix, cut into chunks (about 3 cups)

1 bay leaf

A splash of white wine, if you have it

1 leafy sprig of fresh thyme

1½ teaspoons kosher salt, or to taste

1 Heat the olive oil and butter in a large Dutch oven or saucepan over medium-high heat until just hot, about 1 minute. Add the onion, carrot, and celery and sauté until the vegetables begin to soften, stirring occasionally with a wooden spoon, 3 to 4 minutes. Stir in the garlic, mushrooms, and bay leaf and sauté until the mushrooms begin to color and slightly soften, 3 to 4 minutes. They don't need to be fully softened, like you would when serving them.

2 Deglaze the pan with a splash of white wine or water and scrape up any browned bits from the bottom of the pan. Add the thyme and pour in 4 cups water. Bring the water to a boil, reduce the heat to maintain a simmer, and cook the broth for 25 minutes. Set the broth aside until cool enough to handle, or better still, let it cool completely. Strain out the vegetables and herbs, discard them, and season the broth with the salt. If not using immediately, let cool completely, cover, and refrigerate the broth for up to 5 days, or freeze for up to 3 months in two batches (about 1½ cups each) so you're ready to go with the right amount of broth whenever you need it.

BELUGA LENTILS WITH GRILLED ROMAINE

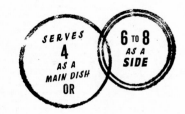

SERVES 4 AS A MAIN DISH OR 6 TO 8 AS A SIDE

When we got lucky and my mom had enough grocery money to buy a chicken—one bird for the fifteen of us—she would make a big pot of lentil stew to go with it. Lentils aren't native to South America, but they are so affordable, filling, and tasty, they have become very popular in Peru. The little bits of chicken (when dispersed among the whole family) would become *el adorno*, as we called it, on top of the stew, like the pretty little garnishes you get at high-end restaurants. We loved every bite.

Beluga lentils are tiny and tasty like the caviar they are named after, so they seemed a fitting tribute to my mom's lentils. You can use any variety of lentils; just adjust the cooking time according to the package (some lentils cook very quickly), and dice all of the vegetables very finely so they disappear into the lentils. Stirring a few tablespoons of plain Greek-style yogurt into the lentils just before you serve them lends a subtle tanginess that I really like, but you can skip the yogurt and Parmesan cheese to make the dish vegan. The grilled romaine is my own adorno.

If not serving the lentils right away, strain out the hot broth and allow them to each cool completely (so the lentils don't become mushy), then return the lentils to the broth. For a more substantial version, add leftover roasted chicken or sliced, cooked link sausages.

¼ cup olive oil, plus more as needed
½ medium red onion, very finely chopped
½ large stalk celery, very finely chopped
1 medium carrot, very finely chopped
3 large cloves garlic, minced
3 tablespoons Salsa Madre (see page 196)
1 bay leaf
2 leafy sprigs of fresh thyme
1 (15- to 16-ounce) bag beluga lentils (about 2 cups), rinsed
7 cups homemade chicken or vegetable stock (see page 40), low-sodium store-bought broth, or water
Kosher salt
6 to 8 heads baby romaine lettuce, or 2 or 3 large heads romaine
3 to 4 tablespoons plain Greek-style yogurt, or to taste
Parmesan, for grating

1 Heat a nice drizzle of olive oil, enough to coat the bottom of a medium Dutch oven or pot (2 to 3 tablespoons), over medium-high heat until hot, a good 2 minutes. Add the onion, celery, carrot, and garlic and sauté, stirring occasionally with a wooden spoon, until the vegetables begin to soften, about 5 minutes, then add the salsa madre and sauté, stirring continuously until the sauce smells aromatic, about 30 seconds. Stir in the bay leaf and thyme, then add the lentils and stock. Bring the stock to a boil, reduce the heat to maintain a simmer, and cook the lentils for 15 minutes. Add salt to taste and continue to simmer until the lentils are tender, 5 to 10 minutes more.

2 While the lentils are cooking, prepare a regular or hibachi grill for direct, high-heat cooking. Halve the whole heads of romaine lengthwise and blot them dry with paper towels. Brush the leaves lightly with olive oil and grill the lettuce, cut-side down, until charred and just beginning to wilt, 1 to 2 minutes. Flip and grill the opposite sides until the leaves are charred in spots, usually just a few seconds longer. Don't overcook the lettuce or it won't hold its shape. (If using large heads of romaine, you may want to coarsely chop the lettuce after it is grilled.)

3 Drain the lentils, reserving the cooking liquid. Stir in enough of the cooking liquid to just moisten the lentils, then stir in the yogurt. Season the lentils with more salt, if you'd like, and pile them into a large serving bowl or on individual plates. Top each with a few grilled romaine leaves, sprinkle the Parmesan generously over the top, and serve. If not serving right away, let the lentils and reserved stock cool completely. Return the lentils to the cooled stock, cover, and refrigerate for up to 5 days.

PERUVIAN DRIED CORN WITH AJÍ PEPPERS & HIERBA BUENA

SERVES 6 TO 8

In Peru, hominy (dried corn kernels treated with mineral lime) is known as maíz mote (from the Quechua *mut'i*, meaning dried grains that must be cooked in water), or mote for short, only the corn kernels we use are usually bigger. The dried kernels from the Cusco region are actually called *maíz mote gigante del Cusco*.

Making mote is a lot like making a big pot of beans. You need to soak the dried corn in water for a long time and then cook them patiently. The corn gets an almost chewy texture that with the broth turns into more of a stew. It's used in rustic dishes like Chanfainita (page 158), but a big bowl of maíz mote on its own with a little queso fresco or feta on top is pretty hard to beat. Don't substitute canned hominy, which becomes almost mushy in the can. *Hierba buena* is an herb in the mint family, so mint is a good substitute.

MOTE

1 (15-ounce) bag maíz mote pelado or dried hominy, soaked in plenty of cold water overnight and drained

About 6 cups homemade chicken or vegetable stock (see page 40) or low-sodium store-bought broth

1 cup pilsner or other light beer (optional)

STEW

Olive oil

1 medium red onion, coarsely chopped into ½-inch pieces

4 cloves garlic, minced

1 tablespoon ground cumin

1 teaspoon dried oregano leaves, preferably Mexican

1 teaspoon kosher salt, or to taste

3 tablespoons ají panca paste, store-bought or homemade (see page 36)

1 tablespoon ají amarillo paste, store-bought or homemade (see page 34)

1½ to 2 tablespoons frozen huacatay, thawed, or about ¼ cup fresh huacatay leaves, coarsely chopped, to taste

Homemade chicken or vegetable stock (see page 40) or low-sodium store-bought broth, if needed

½ cup hierba buena or mint leaves, chopped

1 (8-ounce) block feta cheese or queso fresco, cut into ½-inch cubes (about 1 cup), optional

1 To make the mote, combine the mote, stock, and beer (if using) in a medium Dutch oven or saucepan and bring to a boil. Reduce the heat to maintain a simmer and cook the corn, uncovered, until the kernels pop open and break apart, a good 2 hours. If the liquid level ever recedes beneath the corn, add water to cover. Drain the mote, reserving the cooking liquid. Use the mote right away, or let cool completely, cover, and refrigerate overnight.

2 To make the stew, heat a nice drizzle of olive oil, enough to coat the bottom of a medium Dutch oven or saucepan (2 to 3 tablespoons), over medium-high heat until hot, a good 2 minutes. Add the onion and garlic and sauté, stirring occasionally with a wooden spoon, until the vegetables begin to soften, about 5 minutes. Stir in the cumin, oregano, and salt, then add both ají pastes and the huacatay.

3 Reduce the heat to medium-low and gently push the aderezo (flavorings) back and forth on the bottom of the pan for 2 to 3 minutes more. Add a few spoonfuls of the reserved cooking liquid and scrape up any browned bits on the bottom of the pan. Stir in the mote and enough of the mote cooking liquid to almost cover the corn (if you don't have enough cooking liquid, add a little stock or broth), bring the stew to a boil, reduce the heat, and simmer for about 10 minutes to meld the flavors. Season the mote with salt to taste. If not serving right away, let the mote cool completely, cover, and refrigerate for up to 5 days. (To rewarm the mote, heat it slowly over medium heat, stirring occasionally, and add a little more stock or broth if the corn seems dry.)

4 Stir in all but a few tablespoons of the hierba buena, then add the feta. Pile the mote into a large serving bowl or on individual plates. Sprinkle the few remaining tablespoons of the chopped hierba buena on top, and serve.

TORREJITA DE ARROZ (MINI RICE OMELET)

In my house growing up, a *tortilla de arroz*, the Peruvian version of a *tortilla Espanola* (Spanish omelet), was like a grilled cheese sandwich. It's a quick, hot, and delicious meal that fills your belly, and is easy to make with a few basic ingredients.

Instead of using potatoes like the Spanish version, in Peru (or at least at my house growing up) we used leftover rice and filled it out with pantry ingredients or whatever leftovers are in the refrigerator. When I lived in London and was still working the dishwashing shift at my first restaurant job, I would come home and make it with canned tuna as a quick, inexpensive late-night snack. That classic version is always good, but I really love the omelet with vegetables. It's a great late-night snack, or serve the *torrejitas* as part of a brunch.

Today I like to make mini torrejitas with the leftovers from prepping other recipes, like the fried hearts of red onions (see page 45), crispy scallions, leftover nubs of juicy tomatoes, and the steamed little bits of cauliflower that break off when you slice the whole head. I quarter the omelets and serve them on a tangy pool of homemade ponzu sauce (see page 37) that I already have in my restaurant refrigerator (if you don't have ponzu, don't skip the recipe; the torrejitas are also good on their own). Sprinkle a little chopped parsley on top and add a dollop of mayo or a spicy Sriracha aioli (see page 38) and it's an impressive five-minute vegetarian tapas plate. Not bad for leftovers.

To make Torrejita de Arroz:

1 Put about ½ cup leftover rice in a bowl, crack 2 eggs over the rice, and add a small handful (⅓ to ½ cup) of whatever mix of vegetables you would like. Finely chopped tomatoes, jalapeños, red onions or scallions, and leftover cooked and chopped broccoli, cauliflower, and carrots are all good. (A mix of fresh tomatoes and scallions, along with cooked cauliflower, is one of my favorite combinations.) Mix everything together with your fingers or a spoon. The mixture should be very moist, like an omelet.

2 Heat a tablespoon or two of olive oil in a medium skillet—nonstick works best if you have one. When the oil is very hot, use a serving spoon to scoop about 2 tablespoons of the egg mixture into the pan like pancake batter to create a mini omelet. Add another two or three spoonfuls of batter to the pan to make 4 or 5 mini omelets, whatever you can fit in the pan. Cook the omelets on one side until firm and golden brown on the bottom, about 1 minute. Use the spatula to quickly flip the omelets, like you would with pancakes. Cook the opposite side until golden brown and the firm to the touch, a minute or two more. Remove the omelets from the pan and repeat with the remaining batter.

3 Transfer the omelets to a serving plate with a few spoonfuls of ponzu sauce on the bottom, if you would like. Add a dollop of mayonnaise or spicy Sriracha aioli (see page 38), or sour cream, and sprinkle a little chopped cilantro, parsley, or scallions on top.

SERVES 1–2, MAKES 6–8

LA HORA LOCA Y DULCE

THE CRAZY & SWEET HOUR

STRUCTURALLY, COCKTAILS AND DESSERT ARE VERY SIMILAR.

With both, you need to find that sweet-tart balance. And though they're usually served at opposite ends of a meal, in a restaurant kitchen, they often appear at the same time. As the last desserts go out from the pastry station, the rest of the kitchen staff is usually cleaning up and sometimes, after a really long night, popping open a beer or mixing up a cocktail (and if we're lucky, getting a taste of the pastry chef's *dulces*, sweets, maybe leftover cake trimmings or misshapen cookies). It might not be *la hora loca*, or "the crazy hour," as we call late night-partying in Lima, but after a long night on your feet, sometimes it's the only time all of the kitchen staff has to relax together.

It's a given that in Peru, a *coctél* bar at home or in a restaurant has to include pisco, and I'll never turn down a really good sipping pisco or a classic pisco sour (or *chilcano*, my favorite pisco cocktail). But now that I live in the country where cocktails originated, I really appreciate the creativity of a fresh, unexpected flavor combination in my drinks. (I have all of the great mixologists who have worked at my restaurants to thank for that.)

Sweets are more typically eaten on the go in Peru, bought from pushcart vendors who fry up *picarones*, sweet potato–squash fritters, or neighborhood kids selling marcianos, what we call ice pops (back in the day, that kid was me). In this chapter, I've upgraded many of those classics so they are more sit-down-dessert friendly, but some, like homemade ice pops, are always meant to be eaten straight up.

FUNDACIÓN:

CHICHA MORADA
PURPLE CORN PUNCH

MAKES ABOUT 4½ QUARTS

SERVES 16 DEPENDING ON HOW THIRSTY YOUR CHICHA DRINKERS ARE

Chicha morada is the Peruvian version of an ancient drink used in ritualistic ceremonies by the Incas. It's made from maíz morado, a variety of dried purple corn that was and still is used both as food and a natural food dye (see page 28). It's almost the color of the midnight sky, so fantastically inky that it will stain your T-shirt like crazy if you're not careful (never a problem at my house). In the summer, families keep giant jugs of chicha morada in the fridge—Incan Kool-Aid.

Every home cook has his or her own secret recipe for the punch, but the basic components are the same. You slowly steep maíz morado with leftover pineapple rinds (save them in the fridge for a few days after you slice up the fruit), apples, and spices like cinnamon and cloves. Whatever else goes in the pot is up to you, but I always throw in one of my favorite spices, star anise. The dark purple juice gets livened up with plenty of fresh lime juice and a little sugar or honey.

One bag of dried corn makes a big batch, but the punch goes fast, no matter what your age. When friends come over during the summer, I'll sometimes pour in a bottle of pisco to make a bowl of (adult) punch for a big batch of ready-made cocktails. Use leftovers of the alcohol-free version to make Marcianos (ice pops, page 236), or Mazamorra Morada (purple corn pudding, page 243).

1 (15-ounce) bag maíz morado (2½ or 3 ears)

Core and rind of 1 pineapple, both top frond and bottom discarded

2 large Granny Smith or other tart apples, quartered

2 cinnamon sticks

4 whole cloves

2 star anise

½ teaspoon whole black peppercorns

¾ cup sugar, honey, or agave syrup, or to taste

¾ cup fresh lime juice, or to taste

1 Put the maíz morado, including the cobs and any loose kernels, into a large pasta pot or stockpot. Add the pineapple rinds and core, apples, cinnamon sticks, cloves, star anise, peppercorns, and 5 quarts water. (If your pot is too small for so much water, a little less is fine.) Bring the water to a boil and cook until the liquid has reduced by a solid inch, about 1 hour.

2 Turn off the heat, stir in the sugar, and let steep for 30 to 45 minutes. Strain the punch into a pitcher and discard the solids. Stir in the lime juice. Taste and add more lime juice and/or sugar, if you'd like. Refrigerate the chicha morada for up to 1 week. Serve the punch over ice.

PASSION FRUIT CAIPIRINHA

MAKES
1
CÓCTEL

A caipirinha is Brazilian, not Peruvian, but I'm a friendly cocktail neighbor—especially when the cocktails are really good. And like other neighboring countries in Latin America, we share many of the same tastes and ingredients.

A classic caipirinha is made with lime juice, sugarcane syrup or sugar, and cachaça, the local spirit distilled from cane sugar that has a very fresh, almost fruity flavor. Deysi Alvarez, one of the mixologists I've been lucky to work with, came up with this variation with passion fruit. If you find whole passion fruit, throw the seeds into the shaker. They give you even more of that really good jungle flavor.

1 passion fruit, halved, or 1 tablespoon frozen passion fruit pulp, thawed

1 lime, halved and each half quartered

½ ounce (about 1 tablespoon) sugarcane syrup, such as Martinique, or simple syrup (see page 235), or to taste

2 ounces (about 4 tablespoons) good cachaça, such as Leblon

1 Scrape the passion fruit seeds and pulp into a cocktail shaker. Save one lime section for garnish and add the rest to the cocktail shaker along with the sugarcane syrup. Mash the fruits together with a muddler or large spoon.

2 Fill the cocktail shaker with ice, pour in the cachaça, and shake for a solid 10 seconds. Add a dash more sugarcane syrup, if you'd like. Strain into an ice-filled rocks glass, and squeeze the remaining lime wedge into the cocktail.

PISCO SOUR

MAKES
1
CÓCTEL

Other than good pisco, the secret to Peru's most famous cocktail is el limón Peruano (see page 33). Peruvian limes are tangier than the everyday variety of limes you find in the United States. You can get really close to the flavor with an equal mix of lemon and lime juice, which is what I use.

2 ounces (about 4 tablespoons) good-quality pisco, such as Portón
1 large egg white
Scant ½ ounce (about 2½ teaspoons) fresh lime juice
Scant ½ ounce (about 2½ teaspoons) fresh lemon juice
¾ ounce (about 1½ tablespoons) simple syrup (see page 235)
Angostura bitters

Combine the pisco, egg white, lime and lemon juices, and simple syrup in an ice-filled cocktail shaker. Shake to the beat of good salsa music until the egg white is very foamy, a solid 10 seconds. Strain into a rocks glass and top the pisco sour with a dash of bitters.

LA HISTORIA DEL PISCO SOUR

The original pisco sour recipe was developed in the 1920s at a bar owned by Victor Morris, an American businessman living in Lima, back when whiskey sours were popular. Or so the story has long been told, until mixologist Franco Cabachi of Lima's Pitahaya Bar tweeted a photo of a recipe he found in *Nuevo Manual de Cocina a la Criolla*, a Peruvian-Creole cookbook dating to 1903 that was printed in Lima. In Peru, "creole" refers to *criollos*, or those born in Peru with mainly Spanish colonial ancestry. Though called simply a "cocktail," it sounds a lot like a pisco sour, and even includes the egg white missing from earlier recipes. Who knows . . . maybe the cocktail is even more *Peruano* than people once thought.

RHUBARB-GINGER PISCO COCKTAIL

MAKES
1
CÓCTEL

Give me a *chilcano* on a hot summer day, and I'm happy. The classic Peruvian version is simple to make: Pour pisco over ice with a nice squeeze of lime juice and top the cocktail off with ginger ale and a dash of bitters. This is a little more *glamoroso* version with ginger syrup and rhubarb-cardamom marmalade that our first mixologist at Paichē, Deysi Alvarez, created. My old friends in Peru would probably give me a hard time, but the traditional roots are all there—and this is one good cocktail.

1½ ounces (about 3 tablespoons) Rhubarb-Cardamom Syrup (recipe follows)
1 ounce (about 2 tablespoons) fresh lime juice (1 to 1½ limes)
½ ounce (about 1 tablespoon) Ginger Syrup (page 235)
2 ounces (about 4 tablespoons) good-quality pisco, such as Portón
1½ ounces (about 3 tablespoons) club soda, chilled, or to taste
Angostura bitters
Small wedge of lime

Combine the rhubarb-cardamom syrup, lime juice, ginger syrup, and pisco in an ice-filled cocktail shaker. Shake to the beat of good salsa music for a solid 10 seconds and strain into a tumbler or tall, narrow Collins glass. Top with club soda and a dash or two of bitters. Squeeze the lime wedge on top and drop it into the glass.

RHUBARB-CARDAMOM SYRUP

Makes 1 to 1¼ cups (for about 6 cocktails)

For a cocktail party, double or triple the rhubarb marmalade and ginger syrup, and you're ready to shake the night away. Since the consistency is almost as thick as marmalade, it doubles as a morning-after toast spread.

1 generous tablespoon whole green cardamom pods
1 pound rhubarb (about 4 large stalks), ends trimmed and coarsely chopped into ½-inch pieces
2 cups sugar
6 ounces (¾ cup) fresh lemon juice
2 tablespoons red wine vinegar

1 Lightly crush the cardamom pods using a mortar and pestle, or place the pods on a flat work surface and press on them lightly with a heavy skillet to break open the shells. Heat a medium saucepan over medium-high heat for 1 minute. Add the cardamom and toast, shaking the pan occasionally, until the pods just begin to darken, about 1 minute. Add 1 cup water (it will sizzle when it hits the pan), the rhubarb, and the sugar, stir well, and bring to a boil. Reduce the heat to low and simmer until the rhubarb is very tender, like stewed apples, about 20 minutes. Remove from the heat, stir in the lemon juice and vinegar, and set aside to cool for about 30 minutes.

2 Strain the syrup into a medium bowl. Use a spoon to press the rhubarb pulp to release as much juice as possible, and wipe any accumulated juices off the bottom of the strainer. You should have about 2 cups of syrup.

3 Return the strained syrup to the saucepan, bring to a boil over medium-high heat, and cook until the syrup has reduced by half, 10 to 15 minutes. Remove the syrup from the heat and let cool completely. The syrup will thicken to have a more jamlike consistency as it cools. Cover and refrigerate for up to 1 week.

PISCO

In ancient Quechua, the word pisco *refers to coastal birds, but like
so many Peruvian words, there is more to the story.*

Piskos (or *pishkos*) is the name of the caste of potters who made *botijas*, the giant, almost amphora-looking clay storage jars the Spanish used to cure Botija olives, and later wine and grape-based spirits—the first rudimentary piscos. (They were called *aguardiente de uvas*, grape firewater; *aguardiente* is still a generic term for moonshine in some Latin countries.) The name pisco finally stuck when the port in Ica, the main grape-growing region south of Lima, became the main portal where the grape spirit was exported around the world. It was called the port of Pisco.

Pisco has also been a player in cocktail history closer to my current home in California. Peruvian pisco was firmly planted in San Francisco culture by the mid to late 1800s, when gold brought hundreds of thousands of thirsty fortune seekers to the Bay Area. The spirit was one of many souvenirs brought by seamen returning from trading expeditions in South America. Pisco punch, of all things, a very famous house cocktail first mixed up by barman Duncan Nicol, soon became the city's unofficial cocktail. Bars all over town made the pineapple and lime punch according to their own unscripted formulas, at least until pisco, like so many other good spirits, all but disappeared from the States during Prohibition. It would be almost seventy-five years until imported piscos would get the same kind of cocktail respect again. I like to think that there is still some of pisco's original aguardiente passion deep down in the top-quality versions available today.

The Pisco Distilling Process

In Peru, pisco is tightly regulated, down to the eight grape varietals that can be used and the way the spirit is distilled (for starters, no flavors, other than pure grapes, can be added at any point during distillation).

Some piscos in other parts of Latin America are made more like European-style grappas, another grape-based spirit, in which leftover pressed grapes from the winemaking process are recycled. Peruvian *mosto verde*–style piscos, considered the highest quality and the style typically found in the United States today, are instead distilled from pure grape must (grape juice) that has been partially fermented. That mosto verde, literally "green must," is very high quality. In a way, the Peruvian pisco-making process is more similar to top-quality winemaking (which begins with the best grapes) rather than the distilling method for some other spirits (with some, more emphasis is placed on the ingredients and flavorings added after distilling). Some distillers, including Pisco Portón, grow their own grapes, as a winemaker might, to ensure that they are the highest quality.

The result is a spirit with a very clean, bright flavor and a broad range of grape aromatics, like you might find in wine. Look for those mosto verde piscos, the style mainly found in the United States, which can be made from one grape or many (those made from a blend of grapes are often considered more complex and are highly sought after). The best piscos have incredibly complex aromas and a smooth, food-friendly finish.

AVOCADO DAIQUIRI

MAKES
1
CÓCTEL

In South America, people eat avocados in and on everything, but also out of hand like any other fruit. Thick, buttery avocado slices on a hunk of bread with a good sprinkling of salt was one of my favorite snacks when I was little. When I moved to Los Angeles, I was surprised that I'd seen so few that weren't mashed up and on a tortilla chip. When Julian Cox, whom we were fortunate to have as our consulting mixologist at Picca, came up with this cocktail, I wasn't convinced people here could get past the whole guacamole thing. The sticky-sweet impression most daiquiris left (thanks to the poor-quality versions of the overly sweetened lime and rum cocktails at one too many beach dive bars) didn't exactly help. This was so far from either. We were never able to take the daiquiri off the menu.

When you shake the cocktail really well and strain the liquid through a kitchen strainer, the avocado almost melts into the rum. What's left is more the essence of avocado that has been very lightly sweetened, so a good rum can take its rightful place as the dominant flavor (use your favorite). Those kitschy giant daiquiri-size glasses are way too big here; use elegant, old-school Champagne coupe glasses, if you have them.

3 tablespoons Pureed Avocado (recipe follows)
1 ounce (about 2 tablespoons) fresh lime juice, or to taste
¼ ounce (about 1½ teaspoons) agave nectar or honey, or to taste
1½ ounces (about 3 tablespoons) lightly aged golden (not white) rum

Combine the avocado, lime juice, agave nectar, and rum in an ice-filled cocktail shaker. Shake longer than you usually would, a solid 15 seconds. The mixture should be very frothy and the pureed avocado nicely incorporated. Taste and add more lime juice and/or agave, if you'd like. Strain through a fine-mesh sieve into the "dry" half of the shaker, then strain again into a shallow coupe glass. Serve *inmediatamente*.

PUREED AVOCADO

Makes about ¾ cup, enough for 3 or 4 cocktails

A good squeeze of lime or lemon juice keeps the mashed avocados from turning brown for several hours, so you can make a big batch of this puree for drinks ahead. Omit the agave nectar or honey and you can use the same technique to make a big batch of smashed avocados for sandwiches like pan con tuna (page 73). Use a creamy variety like Hass.

1 large or 1½ small ripe Hass avocados
¾ ounce (about 1½ tablespoons) agave nectar or honey
½ lime or ¼ lemon

Puree the avocado flesh, agave nectar, lime juice, and 1 tablespoon water in a blender until smooth (a few small chunks are fine). If you don't have a high-powered blender, you may need to give the thick mixture a good stir once or twice. Use right away, or cover and refrigerate for up to 4 hours.

¿QUE PALTA?

Avocados are native to the central swath of the highlands stretching from Mexico down along the coast through Central America. Eventually, they made their way down to ancient Peru and Chile. Incas called avocados *paltas*, based on the Quechan word for the fruit, which is what we still call them in Peru.

Most other Spanish-speaking countries call them *aguacates* or *ahuacates*, a descendant of the Aztec word *ahuacatl*, which means "testicle." I'm guessing it's obvious that the name comes from the shape of the fruit (*sí*, it was a symbol of fertility). In the early 1900s, a group of California farmers who wanted to grow the "exotic" fruit didn't think Americans would go for the reference. (The Peruvian slang term *¿Que palta?*—"how embarrassing"—seems like the thing to say right now.) The growers introduced the fruit by the tamer name avocado.

"THE PERUVIAN REMEDY" WITH LEMON, GINGER & PISCO

MAKES
1
CÓCTEL

Peru doesn't have a cocktail tradition like the Bloody Mary, at least that I know of. We do have emolientes, herbal teas that pushcart vendors make with toasted barley, medicinal herbs, and honey to cure your ills any time of day, a tradition that the Spanish brought over (thank you). Fine for some ailments, but sometimes after a late night, a boozy brunch really does seem to cure a few ills.

This martinilike version (it's pretty strong) is definitely eye-opening. You can feel the heat of the rocoto-spiced pisco and the tanginess of the icy cold lemon juice soothing your throat as it goes down.

2 ounces (about 4 tablespoons) Rocoto-Spiced Pisco (see sidebar), or as much as you'd like

¾ ounce (about 1½ tablespoons) fresh lemon juice

¼ ounce (about 1½ teaspoons) agave nectar or honey, or to taste

¼ ounce (about 1½ teaspoons) Ginger Syrup (recipe follows)

Thin slice of lemon

Combine the spiced pisco, lemon juice, agave nectar, and ginger syrup in an ice-filled cocktail shaker. Shake vigorously for 8 to 10 seconds, or as long as you can early in the morning. Taste and add more agave, if you need a little more at this hour. Strain into an ice-filled rocks glass and garnish with lemon. Serve *inmediatamente*.

GINGER SYRUP

Makes a generous ½ cup

To make unflavored simple syrup for a Pisco Sour (page 226) and other cocktails, leave out the ginger and boil the water for only a minute or two.

½ cup sugar

1 (2-inch) piece ginger, peeled and thinly sliced

In a small saucepan, bring the sugar, ½ cup water, and the ginger to a low boil over medium-high heat. Boil for 5 minutes, until slightly thickened, turn off the heat, and steep the ginger for 30 minutes. Strain through a fine-mesh sieve into a small bowl or jar and discard the ginger. Refrigerate for up to 2 weeks.

ROCOTO-SPICED PISCO

I usually leave a good spirit alone. Still, some mornings, a smoky-hot pisco is a *bienvenida*, welcome, infusion. For a brunch, make a big batch ahead. Or, on those unanticipated days when you need a morning remedy, you can mix up as few as two cocktails' worth of infused pisco.

To make Rocoto-Spiced Pisco: Pour 1 (750ml) bottle pisco into a large pitcher (save the bottle) and stir in 2 tablespoons rocoto paste (see page 34). Let the pisco infuse for 30 minutes, or up to 1 hour if you like your cocktails really spicy (a good excuse to taste the pisco). Strain through a fine-mesh sieve into another pitcher, or use a funnel to pour the pisco back into the bottle and seal. Keeps indefinitely. **Makes 1 (750ml) bottle.**

To make enough for 2 cocktails, decrease the pisco to 4 ounces (½ cup) and the rocoto paste to 1 teaspoon.

MARCIANOS

ICE POPS

MAKES 8 SMALL OR

4 LARGE ICE POPS

PER TYPE OF FRUIT

We call ice pops *marcianos*, martians, in Peru. I'm not sure why, but maybe it has something to do with the antennalike way they look. Vendors sell their homemade push-up pops all summer long in coolers along the sidewalks, which seemed like fair game to an eight-year-old, so I started making my own after school. Before long, I figured out that I liked making the ice pops a whole lot more than selling them. I put a sign on our front door with my daily menu, my friends knocked, and all I had to do was grab one from the freezer. *Fácil*—easy.

Since you just mix everything together, it's easy to play around with different flavors. Adjust the amount of sugar to taste, but keep in mind that the pops won't taste as sweet frozen as at room temperature. You can find long plastic ice pop bags (ice candy bags) at Latin markets or online. Freeze the pops on their side so the ingredients stay evenly distributed.

LUCUMA CLASSICO

1 cup fresh or frozen lucuma pulp (see sidebar, page 240)
1 cup whole milk
5 to 6 tablespoons sugar
½ teaspoon vanilla extract

MANGO-COCONUT

2 very ripe mangos
1 cup unsweetened coconut milk
5 to 6 tablespoons sugar
6 small fresh mint leaves

SPICY ROCOTO-WATERMELON

3 cups cubed fresh watermelon, seeds removed
½ teaspoon rocoto paste (see page 34), or to taste
6 to 8 tablespoons sugar

CHICHA MORADA

2 cups Chicha Morada (page 224), strained
3 to 4 tablespoons sugar, or more if your chicha morada isn't very sweet

DULCE DE LECHE

2 cups whole milk, warmed
6 to 8 tablespoons Dulce de Leche (page 252)

1 Puree all of the ingredients in a blender. (Or, if making the chicha morada or dulce de leche, you can whisk the ingredients together in a stand mixer or bowl.) If your blender is too heavy to pour from, transfer the ice pop base to a liquid measuring cup and divide the filling among as many ice pop bags as you are making (a funnel helps).

2 Seal the ice pop bags with a twisty tie as close to the liquid as possible. Or twist the bag (remove the air) and tie the bag snugly. The less air in the bag, the better, so you get a symmetrical ice pop cylinder shape. Lay the ice pops flat on the bottom of a baking dish and freeze until very firm, at least 8 hours or overnight. To serve, remove the twisty tie or snip off the plastic knot.

CREMOLADAS

Churn a marciano as you would ice cream, and you've basically got a *cremolada*. The texture is between a sorbet and a fruit slushy. In the summer, a *cremoladeria* menu is an advertisement for all of the fruits that grow in Peru: *camu camu*, cherimoya, *guanábana*, passion fruit, tamarind, and definitely *lúcuma*. Fruits are the most common flavors, but you can churn almost any ice pop base, or drinks like chicha morada or even a pisco sour. You could use an ice cream maker, but I'm loyal to the old hand-stirred days of cremoladas.

To make Cremoladas: Freeze the marciano base in ice cube trays or in a baking dish large enough so that it freezes in a layer no more than 1 inch thick. Puree the ice cubes (or break the ice into chunks) a little at a time in a high-powered, professional blender until smooth. (If you don't have a high-powered blender, let the marciano base thaw for up to 15 minutes, until slightly softened.) Pour the slushy into a bowl and return it to the freezer, and stir every 15 minutes, until it thickens to the consistency of a thick slushy, 30 minutes to 1 hour.

FRUTAS (FRUITS)

When you live in a country with a true jungle like the Amazon, it seems like there are always new fruits to taste. Some, like tumbo, *a tangier variety of passion fruit, and camu camu, another acidic native fruit that is cooked down in sauces or used in baked desserts, should be added to your list to try in Peru. These are a few of my favorites that are usually easier to find in the United States.*

Caigua

Technically a fruit, caigua has been eaten more like a vegetable at least since the Moche era. Look closely, and you will see the fruit depicted in their artworks and ceramics alongside corn and other produce. It resembles a long green chile pepper and tastes somewhat like a mix between a cucumber and a bell pepper. Caigua are usually pickled and used in salads, sautéed, or stuffed (the fruit conveniently has a generous cavity in the center, which is why it is sometimes referred to as *pepino de rellenar*, or "stuffing cucumber"). Your best bet for finding caigua in the United States is usually Latin markets, but I've also seen them at my local farmers' markets. I really love them stuffed and baked or steamed. Cut a few inches off the tip and scrape out the seeds and veins so you can stuff the whole caigua with whatever you like (papas rellenas filling, page 179, is very good), then bake the *caiguas rellenas* in homemade tomato sauce until tender, or steam them and serve them with the sauce on the side.

Chirimoya (Cherimoya)

The fruit may not look so pretty on the outside, with light green, scaly skin, but when mature, the soft, cream-colored flesh of cherimoya is beautiful—and so good. It tastes like a mix of strawberry, banana, and tropical flavors that are difficult to describe. (Guanábana, soursop, another jungle fruit that has become popular outside of Peru recently, is in the same family.) The Incas considered the fruit, which they called *chirimuya*, an aphrodisiac, and some of the first Europeans to taste it called cherimoya the "pearl of the Andes." For a long time, you couldn't find the the fruit very far from where it was grown because it bruises very easily, but today, you can find cherimoya individually wrapped in a protective Styrofoam "cages" at good grocery stores and some farmers' markets in winter through early spring. Let the fruit ripen at room temperature until almost as soft as

an avocado, then refrigerate the cherimoya (unpeeled) for a few days before peeling.

Lúcuma (Lucuma)

The sweet and slightly starchy fruit known as "the lost gold of the Incas" looks like a large avocado, complete with a pit. Beneath the green skin is bright orange flesh that, when ripe and pureed into ice cream, tastes almost like a tropical version of maple syrup, only not so creamy and perfect. Pureed into a pulp for puddings or ice cream, the gold reference is *claro*, clear. It's not always easy to find fresh; if you find the frozen pulp, check the ingredients to make sure it's just the pureed fruit. The fruit is grown all over northern South America and Central America, with many of the exports simply labeled "lucuma," which could refer to the pureed fruit or to derivatives like sorbets with sugar.

Maracuyá (Passion Fruit)

Native to the Brazilian Amazon, the fruit of the "climbing plant" has a unique, tart-yet-sweet pulp. It tastes like a tropical mash-up of guava, pineapple, and lime juice. You don't usually need much, a good thing, as the fruits only have a good spoonful or so of pulp in the center. Most passion fruits that you find in the States are the purple variety, and should be good and wrinkly on the outside. The wrinkles are a sign that the fruit pulp is at its peak. Other, larger varieties are usually processed for pulp. Slice open the fruit over a bowl to catch all of the juices, and save the crunchy, greenish-black seeds with any of the remaining tangy pulp clinging to them to sprinkle on yogurt or ice cream. If you can't find the fresh fruit at your local supermarket or specialty grocer, look for the pure, frozen pulp without added sugar. One tablespoon of the frozen pulp is about the equivalent of the strained pulp of one passion fruit.

Platanos (Plantains)

Native to Africa, plantains spread all over Latin America after arriving with slaves brought by explorers and European settlers. The fruit adapted well to its new home both agriculturally and within the country's various cooking styles. Plantains are used at various stages of ripeness. When the skin is still green and the flesh very firm, they are usually fried, as in plantain chips. When the skin turns black, the soft, creamy flesh is very tender and sweet. In Peru, we usually mash it up to make dishes like Tacacho (page 207), fried plantain cakes that are sold by street vendors.

PURPLE CORN PUDDING WITH PINEAPPLE

SERVES
6 TO 8

Take chicha morada (page 224), thicken it into a pudding and add dried fruit, and you have mazamorra morada. It's a popular, homey stovetop pudding that cooks make during the winter, and vendors sell the dark purple corn-and-fruit pudding on the streets. This is the dessert to make if you've got a mixed crowd of kids and adults, dairy and gluten lovers and avoiders, and carnivores and vegans. If you don't have anyone at the table with dietary issues, I love the warm pudding with a drizzle of heavy cream or vanilla ice cream. The chilled leftovers make a good breakfast.

Prunes and apricots are traditional and get nice and plump in the pudding, but you can use a mix of any dried fruit, including raisins, cherries, or even strawberries. Some dried fruits are very moist straight out of the bag, others need a good soaking. Use your own judgment.

Harina de camote, or sweet potato starch, doesn't leave the off-taste that cornstarch can in large quantities, so it works really well as a thickener in desserts. It can be tricky to find sweet potato starch in the States, but you could substitute any potato starch. With this recipe, even cornstarch works, if that's all you have.

1½ cups mixed dried apricots and pitted prunes, or a mix of your favorite dried fruits

6 cups Chicha Morada (page 224), made with the recommended ¾ cup each sugar and lime juice

⅓ cup harina de camote (sweet potato starch) or other potato starch, plus more as needed, or substitute cornstarch

1 medium Granny Smith or other tart apple, peeled and cut into bite-size chunks

1 cup bite-size fresh pineapple chunks

1 lime, halved

Ground cinnamon

1 Halve the apricots and prunes and place them in separate small bowls. Pour simmering water over the fruit to cover, and soak until very plump and soft, as few as 30 minutes for soft fruit or up to 2 hours for stiffer fruit (usually the apricots).

2 In a small bowl, whisk together about ½ cup of the chicha morada and the potato starch until no lumps remain. In a medium to large saucepan, bring the remaining chicha morada to a boil over medium-high heat. Reduce to a simmer and whisk in the potato starch mixture. Bring the chicha morada back to a simmer, and cook for a minute or two, then stir in the dried fruits, apple, and pineapple. Cook until the pudding thickens somewhat (it will not be as thick as American-style puddings) and has a delicious fruity aroma, a solid 5 minutes.

3 Turn off the heat and squeeze in the juice of one half of the lime. Taste, and add the juice from the remaining half, if you'd like. Let the pudding cool for at least 15 minutes (it will thicken a little more as it cools) before spooning it into serving bowls and sprinkle each serving with cinnamon. If not serving immediately, cover and refrigerate the pudding for up to 5 days, and serve it chilled.

CHOCOLATE QUINOA PUDDING WITH SABAYON & PUFFED QUINOA ICE CREAM

SERVES 6

Chufla is the dish that made me want to be a chef. My mom usually did the cooking (and she was a great cook), but my dad sometimes took over the lunch duty to feed the youngest of the thirteen kids. Rice and milk were inexpensive and filling, so he would make a big pot of chufla, a creamy Peruvian rice pudding. What little kid doesn't love dessert for lunch? It was the first dish I learned how to make when I was around six or seven years old.

These days, I like to make the pudding with quinoa, because it has such a great texture, and a good hit of dark chocolate. You can serve the pudding on its own (the way my kids like it), or to make it fancy, top it with puffed quinoa ice cream balls, sabayon, and even edible flowers. For a party, you can make all of the components ahead. (The ice cream balls coated in quinoa are also fun to try on their own.)

QUINOA ICE CREAM BALLS

About 1 cup puffed quinoa (see page 200; optional)

1 pint good-quality vanilla ice cream

CHOCOLATE QUINOA PUDDING

¼ cup canned regular or light coconut milk (not coconut water)

⅓ cup sugar

1 cinnamon stick

4 ounces dark chocolate (60 to 70% cocoa), coarsely chopped, or bittersweet chocolate chips

2 cups whole milk, plus more to rewarm pudding

2½ cups cooked quinoa (see page 201)

LEMON SABAYON

4 large egg yolks

½ cup sugar

1 teaspoon ají amarillo paste, store-bought or homemade (see page 34)

1 tablespoon fresh lemon juice

ASSEMBLY

Sugar, for garnish (optional)

Edible flowers, for garnish (optional)

1 To make the quinoa ice cream balls, place a small baking pan in the freezer for 10 minutes. Place the puffed quinoa in a small bowl. Scoop six approximately 2-inch rounds of ice cream with an ice cream scoop and transfer to the chilled pan. Freeze the ice cream balls for about 15 minutes, then roll each in the puffed quinoa and return to the freezer pan. Chill for at least 30 minutes, or cover and freeze for up to 3 days.

2 To make the pudding, in a large saucepan, bring the coconut milk, sugar, and cinnamon stick to a simmer over medium heat. Stir until the sugar has dissolved. Add the chocolate and stir continuously until the chocolate has completely melted, about 2 minutes. Add the whole milk and quinoa, bring to a simmer, and cook, stirring often, until the pudding has thickened slightly, 6 to 8 minutes. Remove the cinnamon stick. If not serving right away, transfer the pudding to a bowl and let cool to room temperature. Cover and refrigerate for up to 3 days. Before serving, rewarm the pudding over low heat and add additional milk (up to ½ cup) to thin it to approximately the original consistency.

RECIPE CONTINUES

3 To make the sabayon, fill a medium saucepan about one-third full of water and choose a medium metal bowl that fits snugly on top (it should not touch the water; if it does, choose a different bowl or remove some of the water). Remove the bowl from the saucepan. In the bowl, vigorously whisk together the eggs and sugar until the consistency of mayonnaise, 3 to 5 minutes, then whisk in the ají amarillo paste.

4 Bring the water in the saucepan to a simmer. When the water simmers, place the bowl with the egg mixture on top of the saucepan. Use a rubber spatula to stir continuously in a circular motion, scraping the bottom and sides of the bowl (to keep the eggs from curdling), for 3 to 4 minutes. The egg mixture should look almost silky (the eggs should never be hot to the touch or bubble; if they are, briefly remove the bowl from the heat and reduce the heat). Whisk in the lemon juice. If not serving immediately, transfer the sabayon to a clean bowl and whisk every few minutes. When cool, cover with plastic wrap and set aside at room temperature for up to 2 hours or refrigerate overnight. Bring to room temperature and whisk again just before serving.

5 To assemble, divide the chocolate pudding among six serving bowls and top with the sabayon. (If you'd like to brûlée the top, sprinkle the sabayon lightly with sugar and use a torch to caramelize the sugar.) Place a quinoa ice cream ball on top of each serving and a few edible flowers, if you have them, and serve immediately.

AJÍ AMARILLO CHEESECAKE

SERVES
10 TO 12

The first time I tasted an American-style cheesecake, it was at a famous national chain restaurant known for the cake. I'd never tasted anything like it. I have to admit, I thought it was pretty great, if too sweet. I started experimenting with a version that I could serve at events—cheesecakes are often a hit at parties, judging by the number of requests I get.

In this Peruvian-style version, the sugar is so subtle, the cake is almost savory. I think that's why it works so well with the spicy ají amarillo peppers, which are pretty tame in this cake, so you can add a sauce without going into sugar or spice overdrive. Warm up a good-quality jar of jam, maybe some orange marmalade, and stir in a teaspoon of ají amarillo paste.

I realize I wasn't born in the land of cheesecakes, but I don't understand why some bakers get worked up about cheesecakes that crack in the center. To me, those cracks look like the *tierra*, earth, and are part of the cake's beauty. It's also a sign that the cream cheese and eggs where whipped enough to keep the cake from becoming too dense.

CRUST

8 tablespoons (1 stick) unsalted butter, melted, plus more for the pan

20 individual graham cracker squares, finely ground in a food processor (about 1¾ cups)

1 tablespoon sugar

Pinch of kosher salt

FILLING

4 (8-ounce) packages cream cheese, at room temperature

2 tablespoons ají amarillo paste, store-bought or homemade (see page 34), or to taste

1¼ cups sugar

⅓ cup heavy cream

Zest of 1 medium orange

5 large eggs

1 To make the crust, preheat the oven to 375°F and place a rack in the middle. Rub a little butter on the bottom and up the sides, all the way to the rim, of a 9-inch spingform pan. Cut a piece of parchment to fit the bottom, place it in the pan, and lightly butter the top.

2 Mix together the butter, graham cracker crumbs, sugar, and salt in a medium bowl. Press the cracker mixture firmly into the bottom and about 1 inch up the sides of the pan with your hands. Be sure to press into the corners. Bake the crust for 10 minutes and set aside. The crumbs won't color much, mainly just on the edges.

3 Meanwhile, to make the filling, in the bowl of a stand mixer fitted with the paddle attachment, combine the cream cheese, ají amarillo paste, and sugar mix on medium speed until fluffy, like soft-serve ice cream, about 5 minutes. Turn off the mixer, add the cream and orange zest, and mix on the lowest speed for a few seconds (to keep the cream from splashing out of the bowl). Raise the speed to medium-low and whip for another minute, then add the eggs, one at a time, waiting until each is well incorporated before adding the next. Scape down the sides of the bowl and mix the filling for 30 seconds more.

4 Pour the cream cheese filling into the prepared crust (it will come almost all the way to the top) and bake for 10 minutes. Reduce the oven temperature to 325°F and bake for 1 hour. The edges should be golden brown, but the cake should still be jiggly when you gently shake the pan. Crack the oven door about 2 inches and leave the cake in the oven for 15 minutes more.

5 Transfer the cake to a baking rack to cool completely, about 3 hours. Wrap the cake pan in plastic wrap and refrigerate the cake for at least 8 hours or overnight, or up to 1 week. To serve, remove the sides of the springform pan and cut the cake into wedges. Serve the cake with your favorite fruit sauce, or a lightly ají-spiced marmalade, if you'd like.

VANILLA-PISCO FLAN WITH STRAWBERRY–PASSION FRUIT SAUCE

MAKES
8
FLANS

A splash of pisco gives this classic South American custard kick. Flan already has a built-in caramel sauce, but the strawberry–passion fruit sauce is like the *cereza*, cherry, on top. Good as it is, don't put too thick a layer of caramel sauce on the bottom of the flan, as it tends to stick to the bottom. And cover the pan snugly so the flans steam as they bake to help the custards set properly and also make them easier to unmold. When making the caramel, the trick is not to overbrown the sugar. You want a nice golden color, but if the caramel gets too dark, it will remain hardened even after baking.

2 cups heavy cream

¾ cup whole milk

¼ teaspoon kosher salt

1 vanilla bean, split lengthwise and seeds scraped

Canola or other vegetable oil

Caramel Sauce (see sidebar, page 250)

4 large eggs

3 large egg yolks

½ cup sugar

1½ tablespoons pisco

Strawberry–Passion Fruit Sauce (see page 250)

Fresh mint, for garnish (optional)

1 Put the cream, milk, salt, and vanilla bean pod and seeds in a medium saucepan and bring the mixture to a simmer. Remove the pan from the heat, cover with plastic wrap, and let steep for about 30 minutes.

2 Preheat the oven to 350°F and place a rack in the middle of the oven. Rub eight small (4-ounce) ramekins lightly with a paper towel dipped in oil and fill them with the caramel sauce. Place the caramel-filled ramekins in one or two high-walled baking dishes, arranging them so they have a little breathing room between each. Whisk together the eggs, egg yolks, sugar, and pisco in a medium bowl. Very slowly pour the warm vanilla cream into the eggs, whisking continously so the eggs don't curdle. Strain the mixture through a fine-mesh sieve (you may need to push down on the egg solids) into a heatproof pitcher or large measuring cups so the custard base is easy to pour into the ramekins. (Save the vanilla beans to infuse milk or cream.) Pour the filling almost to the top of each ramekin.

3 In a kettle or saucepan, heat several cups of water until steaming hot. Pull out the oven rack slightly so you can set the baking dish easily on it. Pour the hot water into the baking dish so the water comes about halfway up the sides of the ramekins. Carefully cover the pan with plastic wrap and then with foil, and bake for about 25 minutes, or until the custards are set but still jiggle in the very center when you shake the ramekins with tongs. Remove the baking pan from the oven and use tongs to transfer the ramekins to a wire rack to cool. Let cool completely, 1 to 2 hours, return the ramekins to the baking dish, and cover the dish with plastic wrap. Refrigerate until very cold, at least 5 hours, preferably overnight.

4 To serve, run a knife around the edges of each flan. Place individual serving plates, face-down, on top of each ramekin and flip both upright. Top the flans with the strawberry–passion fruit sauce and garnish with mint, if using.

RECIPE CONTINUES

STRAWBERRY–PASSION FRUIT SAUCE

Makes about 1¾ cups

This is one of those sauces that you can spoon on anything that needs a little unexpected flavor—vanilla ice cream, fruit salad, or the simplest vanilla cake. If you can't find passion fruit, add another squeeze of lemon juice. Don't use too big of a roasting pan or all of the good sauce juices will evaporate.

1 tablespoon honey

2 tablespoons sugar

2 tablespoons pisco or other brandy

Pinch of kosher salt

Zest of ½ lemon

2 pints (about 1½ pounds) strawberries, hulled and halved lengthwise

1 passion fruit, or 1 tablespoon frozen passion fruit pulp, thawed

1 tablespoon fresh lemon juice, or to taste

1 Preheat the oven to 375°F. Mix together the honey, sugar, pisco, salt, and lemon zest in a large bowl. Toss the strawberries in the honey sauce and spread out the strawberries and sauce in a small baking dish (8 x 8 inches or smaller). The berries should be pretty snugly arranged but still in a single layer. Roast the berries until they have turned a rich ruby red color, 20 to 25 minutes. Transfer the berries and pan juices to a medium bowl.

2 Halve the passion fruit lengthwise over a small bowl and scoop the seeds and pulp into a fine-mesh strainer. Press down firmly to strain out as much juice as you can and add any chunks of pulp to the juice (save the seeds for a yogurt or ice cream topping). Mix in the lemon juice, and toss the strawberries in the juice mixture. Taste and add more lemon juice, if you'd like. Let cool, cover, and refrigerate for up to 5 days.

SALSA DE CARAMELO (CARAMEL SAUCE)

I'm always surprised when I hear cooks in the United States say making caramel sauce scares them. In South America, you grow up hearing that if you can boil water, you can make caramel sauce. You just need to watch the pot closely for the last few minutes so the sauce doesn't overbrown, or it won't incorporate into the flan (if too caramelized, the sauce will remain candylike instead of "melting" into the flan). Squeezing in a tiny amount of tart lime or lemon juice at the end subtly balances out all of those good caramelized sugar flavors.

To make Caramel Sauce: If you are making flan, have your lightly oiled ramekins (step 2) at the ready. Combine ½ cup sugar and 1 tablespoon water in a medium saucepan. Stir and bring the sugar mixture to a boil over high heat. Boil until the syrup turns the medium-amber color of a caramel-milk candy, about 5 minutes. Occasionally swirl the pan as the caramel darkens, but don't stir (you may indirectly add water, and the sugars can stick to your spoon). Watch the sugar closely for the last few minutes, when it starts to caramelize quickly. Remove it from the heat when it turns light brown (the caramel will continue to cook off the heat).

Carefully squeeze in the juice from 1 wedge of lime or lemon and swirl the pan to incorporate the juice. Immediately pour a very thin layer of caramel, about ⅛ inch thick, into the bottom of each ramekin. The sauce will harden as it cools.

PERUVIAN SANDWICH COOKIES WITH DULCE DE LECHE & ROCOTO GANACHE

MAKES
18 TO 20
COOKIES

Alfajores arrived in Peru by way of the Spanish colonists, who borrowed the recipe idea from Arabic bakers sometime during the Middle Ages. Today, you'll find the sandwich cookies all over Latin America. The common link is the cornstarch in the dough, which makes the cookies crumbly (the Spanish version is very different and made from flour, almonds, and honey).

I like my alfajores really, really crumbly—so crumbly that they almost dissolve into a powder on your tongue, or even better, all over your fingers. That also means that even if you spread the filling onto the cookies very gently, you may lose a few cookies along the way. (Give the crumbs a dollop of filling and scoop it all up with a spoon for a snack—baker's *suerte*, luck.) I roll the sides of the cookies in puffed quinoa (see sidebar, page 200). It's not essential, but it looks nice and gives the alfajores a light, airy crunchiness that plays off the already crumbly cookies and creamy filling.

1 cup (2 sticks) unsalted butter, at room temperature

½ teaspoon kosher salt

2¼ cups cornstarch

1¼ cups all-purpose flour

¾ cup powdered sugar, plus more for dusting

1 teaspoon baking powder

2 tablespoons pisco or other brandy

1½ teaspoons vanilla extract

About 1 cup Manjar Blanco (dulce de leche, see sidebar; page 252) or Rocoto Ganache (recipe follows)

About ⅓ cup puffed quinoa (see sidebar, page 200; optional)

1 In the bowl of a stand mixer fitted with the paddle attachment, combine the butter and salt. In a medium bowl, sift together the cornstarch, flour, powdered sugar, and baking powder and add about half to the bowl of the stand mixer. Cover the top of the mixer bowl with a kitchen towel (to avoid a kitchen snow flurry) and mix on low speed for about 1 minute. Add the remaining cornstarch mixture, cover the bowl, and mix for 30 seconds more. The mixture will look very dry, almost like pie dough without the water. Pour in the pisco and vanilla and mix for a minute or so more, until a dough forms.

2 Shape the dough into two chubby logs about 6 inches long and about 2 inches wide. Wrap each snugly in plastic wrap and twist the ends tightly to close. Roll each dough log back and forth a few times on a flat work surface with your palms to smooth out the sides (try to keep the logs about the same length). Refrigerate the dough for at least 4 hours or overnight.

3 Preheat the oven to 350°F and place both racks toward the middle of the oven. Line two or three baking sheets with parchment paper.

4 Slice each log of dough in half to make four smaller logs, and slice off the ends of the dough where they're crinkly from the plastic wrap. Cut each log into about ten ¼-inch-thick rounds so you have about 40 discs. Place them on the parchment-lined baking sheets, spacing them about an inch apart. Bake until the bottoms barely begin to turn light brown (lift one up with a spatula to check), 15 to 18 minutes. Rotate the baking sheets from top to bottom and front to back halfway through the baking time. Let the cookies cool for 5 minutes on the baking sheets, then carefully transfer them to a wire rack to cool completely.

RECIPE CONTINUES

5 Line up the cookies in pairs on a work surface so each is close to the same size. If the manjar blanco or ganache has been refrigerated, rewarm it on the stovetop for a minute or two, or in the microwave for a few seconds. The filling should be very easy to spread or the cookies will break.

6 Dollop a spoonful (about ¾ tablespoon) of filling gently on each cookie half. Put the filling-topped cookie in the palm of one hand and gently spread the filling toward the edges of the cookie with your finger or the back of the spoon. Gently nestle a partner cookie on top of the filling to make a sandwich. Don't push down on the top cookie too firmly, or it will crumble. Repeat with the remaining cookies. If desired, place the puffed quinoa on a large plate and very gently roll the sides of the alfajores in the quinoa. Or, if your filling doesn't go all the way to the edges, press the quinoa on the sides. Use a sifter to dust both sides of the alfajores with powdered sugar.

7 Store the cookies with parchment paper between each layer in a sealed container at room temperature for up to 3 days, or refrigerate the cookies for up to 1 week. They will soften a bit in the fridge. Dust the cookies with a little more powdered sugar before serving if they need some sprucing up.

ROCOTO GANACHE

When I play around with different alfajores fillings, it's usually something spicy, like this rocoto ganache. You can vary the amount of rocoto paste depending on your cookie crowd's heat tolerance.

To make Rocoto Ganache: Warm ⅓ cup heavy cream in a small saucepan over medium-high heat (do not boil) and stir in 6 ounces (1 generous cup) bittersweet chocolate chips or chunks. Cook until the chocolate starts to looks sludgy, less than 1 minute. Remove the pan from the heat and keep stirring until the chocolate has melted completely. Stir in 1 teaspoon vanilla extract, 1½ teaspoons rocoto paste (see page 34), or to taste, and a pinch of salt. Stir 1 cup sifted powdered sugar into the chocolate until completely incorporated and let the ganache cool. Taste and add more rocoto paste for more spiciness, if you'd like. Cover and refrigerate for up to 5 days. **Makes about 1 cup.**

MANJAR BLANCO (DULCE DE LECHE)

Give the milk plenty of cooking time to get a really rich caramelized flavor in dulce de leche—or *manjar blanco*, as it's known in Peru. Oven-baking the milk in a water bath or cooking it in a double boiler is faster than the old-school stovetop method (boiling the milk in the unopened can), plus you can gauge how dark the caramel gets. When you're not cooking the milk in the can, you also don't have the problem of the caramel sauce shooting out at rocket speed if you open the can while it's still warm. These things are loads of fun when you're an eight-year-old, not so much when you're the parent of one.

To make Manjar Blanco: Preheat the oven to 400°F. Pour 1 (14-ounce) can condensed milk into a 7- or 8-inch glass or ceramic baking dish and cover it with aluminum foil. Make a water bath by putting the dish inside a larger baking dish with a solid inch or more to spare on all sides, and pour hot water into the baking dish to come about halfway up the sides of the interior pan. Bake until the milk has turned a *toastado*, toasty, caramel color, 40 minutes to 1 hour, depending on the size of the pan. Remove the interior pan, let the sauce cool, cover, and refrigerate for up to 1 week. **Makes about 1 cup.**

ANISE-SESAME WREATH COOKIES

MAKES
16
COOKIES

I've never been exactly what you would call *tímido*, shy. Once, when I was nine or ten, I walked past a rickety abandoned warehouse that smelled like freshly baked cookies (unlicensed bakeries weren't uncommon finds). The door was partly open, so I walked right in. After a while, the owner of the bakery saw me poking around and started yelling at me. I guess he thought this little kid was there to steal cookies. The guy was covered head to toe in flour, like some giant snow monster. At first I was scared, then I told him I was there to do business. He laughed and turned away until he realized I was serious.

Selling the bakery's anise-spiced rosquitas became a pretty good after-school gig for the next couple of months. The braided, crisp, biscottilike cookies are sturdy enough to survive a school bag and aren't too sweet, so they make a good snack. I stacked the rosquitas neatly in plastic bags, one on top of the other, tied them off, and took them to school in a big basket. (For the record, I sold them all the next day.) This version is my tribute to the classic cookies that I still love.

2 tablespoons aniseeds
About 3 tablespoons white sesame seeds
1 teaspoon kosher salt
¾ cup (1½ sticks) unsalted butter, at room temperature
3 cups all-purpose flour
½ cup sugar
½ teaspoon vanilla extract
1 large egg yolk

1 Heat a small saucepan over medium-high heat until good and hot. Add the aniseeds and toast, stirring or shaking the pan regularly, until just beginning to smell fragrant, about 45 seconds. Transfer the seeds to a mortar and pestle. Right away, put about 2 tablespoons of the sesame seeds into the hot pan and toast, stirring continuously, until half or more turn light brown, about 1 minute. Transfer the seeds to a small dish. You may need to use a folded paper towel or rubber spatula to nudge the last stubborn seeds out of the pan. Add the salt to the mortar and pestle and coarsely grind the aniseeds until you can smell all of their good flavors. Many of the seeds will still look whole, which is fine.

2 In the bowl of a stand mixer fitted with the paddle attachment, combine the butter, flour, sugar, anise, and sesame seeds. Cover the top of the mixer bowl with a kitchen towel (to avoid a kitchen snow flurry) and mix on low speed until the butter is crumbly and the mixture looks like dry pie dough, about 1 minute. Or, to make the cookies by hand, put everything in a large bowl and mix the butter into the dry ingredients with your fingers.

3 Pour ¼ cup plus 2 tablespoons water and the vanilla on top of the dough and mix again until the dough just starts to come together. If using a stand mixer, you may need to turn it off and reach in and use your hands to pull the dough together into a round. Add another tablespoon of water if you need to, but the dough shouldn't be super moist. Cover with plastic wrap or a kitchen towel and let the dough rest at room temperature for 30 minutes to 1 hour.

4 Preheat the oven to 350°F and line two baking sheets with parchment paper. Mix together the egg yolk and 2 teaspoons water in a ramekin or small dish. Shape the dough into 2 logs about 10 inches long and cut each log into 8 equal pieces. To shape the rosquitas, follow the instructions in the sidebar.

5 Arrange 8 rosquitas on each parchment-lined baking sheet with a solid inch of breathing room between each cookie. Brush the cookies with the egg wash, making sure to get into all of the crevices, and lightly sprinkle the remaining tablespoon or so of untoasted sesame seeds on top. Bake the cookies until light golden brown on the bottom (lift one with a spatula to check; they won't color much on the top), 20 to 22 minutes, rotating the baking sheets top to bottom and front to back halfway through. Let the cookies cool completely on the baking sheets.

6 Store the rosquitas at room temperature in a sealed container for up to 5 days. The cookies will soften up after a day or two, also very tasty, but freeze them if you prefer a crunchier cookie.

SHAPING ROSQUITAS

Rosquitas dough is on the drier side, which along with the sesame seeds tends to cause little cracks and crevices as your shape the dough. Instead of the more traditional powdered anise, I like the crunch and flavor of toasted anise seed, which adds even more texture. Fortunately, this is a very forgiving dough. If the cookies ever fall apart, just pinch everything back together with your fingers.

To shape rosquitas: Place one dough log on an unfloured work surface and tear it in half. Smash one half of the dough with the palm of your hand into a flat disc and pinch the dough into a log roughly 3 inches long with your fingers (it doesn't need to be perfectly shaped). Roll the palms of both hands back and forth over the top of the log, like you are making a snake out of clay, until it is about 7 inches long. Whenever the log breaks, just pinch the dough back together with your fingers. Do the same with the remaining half of the dough.

Line up the two strands of dough side by side and pinch the top ends together. Cross one strand on top of the other three or four times to braid them loosely together, like you are making challah bread. Form the braid into a circle and gently pinch the two ends together to make a small, wreathlike shape. You can dip your fingers into water to help pinch together the ends, if needed, but the wreath doesn't need to be perfect. Repeat with the remaining dough.

SWEET POTATO & SQUASH BEIGNETS WITH CHANCACA SAUCE

MAKES
12 TO 14
DOUGHNUTS

If you luck into a *picaronera* vendor on the streets while you are visiting Peru, change whatever plans you have and wait in line. Machu Picchu isn't going anywhere. The sweet potato–pumpkin fritter vendor, on the other hand, only sticks around as long as there is enough batter to fry up. The batter is shaped into bracelet-size loops and deep-fried, then piled into a bag or onto a paper plate and served with *chancaca*, a cane sugar sauce seasoned with cinnamon and other spices.

If you are making kabocha squash for something else, like grilled kabocha (page 189), save a chunk to make these doughnuts. In Peru, the doughnuts are usually served as a snack. But since you can also make the batter the night before, the recipe is weekend-breakfast friendly—or what you call brunch (we still consider that breakfast). Just be Peruvian about it and eat the doughnuts straight out of the fryer basket.

Instead of ricing the vegetables, you can mash the squash and potatoes by hand like my mom used to do, and then mix in the flour and other ingredients. The texture will be a little chunkier than if you use a ricer and stand mixer, but they will still taste great. And don't be tempted to skip the kabocha squash. It keeps the batter light; all sweet potato would make the doughnuts dense. The chancaca sauce is worth making, but if you can't find it, maple syrup is also very good.

¼ medium kabocha squash (4- to 5-inch-wide wedge), peeled and seeded

1 medium sweet potato or yam, peeled

1 cinnamon stick, or ¼ teaspoon ground cinnamon

2 whole cloves

1 star anise

½ cup sugar

1 generous teaspoon instant or active dry yeast

About 1½ cups all-purpose flour, as needed

Generous pinch of kosher salt

1 large egg, lightly beaten

Canola or other vegetable oil

Chancaca Sauce (recipe follows)

1 Roughly chop the peeled squash into 1-inch chunks. Do the same with the potato, keeping the vegetables in different piles. You should have about 1½ cups of each, but a little more or less of one or the other is fine.

2 Put the cinnamon, cloves, star anise, sugar, and squash in a medium saucepan. Add enough water to cover the squash by a solid inch and bring the water to boil. Reduce to a low boil and cook until tender, about 8 minutes. Strain over a bowl to reserve the spiced cooking liquid and return the liquid, cinnamon, cloves, and star anise to the saucepan. Add the potatoes, along with another ½ cup or so of water, if needed, so they are covered, and boil the potatoes until tender, about 10 minutes. Strain and reserve the cooking liquid. While still warm, pass the squash and potatoes through a ricer into the bowl of a stand mixer fitted with the paddle attachment, or into a large bowl. Or smash the vegetables with a potato masher as finely as you can.

3 Add the yeast and about ⅔ cup of the reserved cooking liquid to the stand mixer or bowl. Mix the two together on low speed for a few seconds, or by hand with a spoon, and add the flour and salt. Continue to mix until the dry ingredients are incorporated, then add the egg. The dough should be sticky, like pancake batter; if it seems dry, add another splash of the cooking liquid. Mix the dough for 1½ to 2 minutes on low speed until smooth and even stickier, or use the spoon or your hands to knead the dough really well by hand for 5 minutes.

4 Transfer the dough to a bowl lightly rubbed with oil, cover with plastic wrap, and refrigerate overnight, or set the dough aside in a warm spot to rise until more than doubled, a good hour, then refrigerate the dough for about 30 minutes before frying, or overnight if serving for breakfast.

5 Line a baking sheet with a few layers of paper towels. In a medium, deep saucepan, heat a solid 2 inches of oil to 350°F, or fill a deep fryer with the recommended amount of oil and set the temperature to 350°F. Use a frying thermometer or test the oil temperature with a small nub of batter; it should bubble vigorously (if the oil smokes, reduce the heat).

6 Place a small dish of water near the dough. To shape the fritters, dip your hands in the water and shake off the excess. Scoop up a golf ball–size round of dough (about 2 tablespoons, but exact measures aren't important). Poke a hole in the center with your thumb, then use your fingers to roughly shape the dough into a doughnut shape about 3 inches in diameter. The dough is very sticky, so the edges will be roughly finished and prickly looking.

7 Carefully drop the dough ring into the hot oil, wipe off your hands, and fry the doughnut until it browns on the bottom, about 1 minute. Flip and fry the opposite side until lightly browned, 30 seconds or so more. If either side ever becomes dark brown very quickly, reduce the heat. Meanwhile, dip your hands in water again and shape 2 or 3 more fritters. Carefully drop them in the oil, but don't crowd the pan. By the time you finish, the first fritter should be turning golden brown. As they cook, transfer the fritters to the paper towel–lined baking sheet. Serve the fritters fresh from the fryer with a big bowl of warm chancaca sauce nearby for dipping.

CHANCACA SAUCE

Makes about 2½ cups

The sauce for *picarones* is made from chancaca (see page 263), a sugar similar to Mexican *piloncillo*. The figs are authentic but optional, and I like to add a little brown sugar to give the sauce a richer color and flavor. Make the sauce several days before you plan to serve it, if you can. The flavors only get better. Save leftovers for pancakes or waffles, or to sweeten your coffee or tea for the next few weeks.

As the water boils, the thick block of chancaca will warm up and break down more quickly if you help it along by mashing the sugar up with a spoon. Look for chancaca at Latin markets, or substitute piloncillo or *panela*.

1 (10-ounce) package chancaca, banana leaves removed
⅔ cup dark brown sugar
3 whole cloves
1 cinnamon stick
Peel of ½ orange, most of the pith removed
4 fresh (preferably) or dried figs, halved (optional)

1 Combine the chancaca, brown sugar, cloves, cinnamon, orange peel, figs (if using), and 3 cups water in a medium to large saucepan. Bring the mixture to a boil, reduce the heat to maintain a simmer, and use a wood spoon to mash up the canchaca as it warms up.

2 Once the chancaca has fully melted, continue to cook the sauce, stirring occasionally, until slightly thickened to a thin syrup, about 20 minutes. Let the sauce cool completely, cover, and refrigerate for up to 2 weeks. You can strain the spices and fruit immediately, or leave them to infuse for 3 to 4 days for even better flavor. To serve, rewarm the sauce over low heat, stirring often to avoid burning the sugar.

ACKNOWLEDGMENTS

I have enormous respect for all of the people who help make the actual pages of a book happen. I didn't realize how difficult and time-consuming making a cookbook can be. (I owe each of you a really, really good dinner.) First, to the Houghton Mifflin Harcourt team in New York and Boston, for dedicating so much time of your time to this project: publisher Natalie Chapman, art director Melissa Lotfy, production editor Jamie Selzer, freelance designer Laura Palese (the book's design is amazing), copy editor Ivy McFadden, Brad Parsons on the marketing team, and especially editors Linda Ingroia and Stephanie Fletcher. Linda, thank you for making sure I met my deadlines (or got close enough?), your editing eye, advice, and especially, your never-ending trust in me.

A big thank-you is also in order for my agent, Cait Hoyt at CAA, who was always so confident and supportive of this project, along with Lisa Shotland for believing in me.

And then there is Jenn Garbee, my coauthor. I don't even know how to thank you for so many months of dedicated work. You helped me figure out what I wanted to say when I couldn't describe it (and I corrected your Spanish!), you researched Peruvian food and the history of my country like you were writing a university thesis, and you spent countless hours testing recipes and talking through the content with me—you made our book the best it could be. Even more than all of that, I've never met anyone so committed to a project that isn't truly her own. I have immense *respeto* for you that I hope is mutual, and I have gained a true friend.

When I look back, I am equally amazed at how many people dedicated themselves to making the photographs happen in this book. Ed Anderson, your images speak for themselves. You produced so many *increíble* photographs that I still get excited looking through them—and we still got to enjoy a few piscos in Peru, right? Los Angeles food stylist Valerie Aikman-Smith, you are such a pro, and we couldn't have made so many dishes without our set assistants, Sandra Cordero and Alex Galan.

The Peru photo opportunities never would have happened without the generosity of so many people. Thanks to my brother Marcos, we were able to navigate from one corner of Peru to another on our five-day photography trek in our "cozy" van (Jenn sends a hug, too), and Hector Arevalo, you were so patient to drive us all over the map. Isaac Gherson and Eddy Anderson of Amazone, a fish farm specializing in paiche, an ancient Peruvian fish, your hospitality was contagious (and Isaac, *muchas gracias* for sharing your jungle mosquito repellant). Seeing firsthand a sustainable project that helps so many local people made me very proud of my home country. Johnny Schuler, the master distiller at Pisco Portón, you opened my eyes to new tastes and styles of pisco. Publicist Ursula Vega Benavides, you are a woman who knows how to get things done, and Susana de la Puente of Lima's Hotel B, you have incredible taste. Ricardo Romero of the Peruvian Trade Commission, I am always inspired by the sophisticated ways that you promote Peru. If there were more people like you, our country would only benefit. Photojournalist Josip Curich, thank you for entertaining all of the Americans (myself included) and being our guide to all that is new, and fortunately still old, in Lima. I will always remember the anticucho vendor singing to us in what would become one of my favorite pictures in the book.

I also must send a big thank-you to the people who have made my recipes a reality every single day. This book would not have been possible without the chefs, line cooks, dishwashers, waitstaff, managers, and everyone else who has worked at my restaurants in the past, present, and future. A special thanks to the chefs who put in hours of their own kitchen time to keep this project moving along: Richie Lopez, Bryan Huskey, Tomás Mendez, Alex Carasco, Rudy Lopez, and anyone else I may be inadvertently forgetting, and for their stellar cocktails and pastry, Deysi Alvarez and Debbie Renteria. Alissa Kotick, thank you for keeping me organized, and especially Lauren Moreno, for truly "making things happen," as I like to say (and making sure that I showed up to work on the book on time). I can't wait to hear about all of your own dreams becoming a reality in the years to come.

And finally, I thank my friends and family for their

never-ending unconditional love. Friends like *los amigos del barrio* (my old neighborhood friends), Nestor and Fabio Camargo (my "Colombian brothers," as I like to say), Seamus Gallagher, and Andrea Rademan, who all gave me support whenever things weren't perfect. David Saettone, I am so grateful for all you have done, not only your help in finalizing the photo shoot details and other projects, but to have found someone who genuinely supports me in both the good and bad times. Keiko Perry, you are a friend so special, my kids call you "grandma," and Conille, you are such a good mother.

When you have twelve brothers and sisters, people always ask if you know all of their names, so I will write them here as I thank them, whether still with us or loved in memories, so I can prove it once and for all: Teresa Elvira, Marcos Antonio, Rosalinda, Ana Maria, Luis Alberto, Juan Manuel, Miguel Angel, Julio Cesar, Carlos Enrique, Victor Hugo, Luisa Luzmila, and Renzo Gustavo. *Mi mama y papá (¿cómo podré agradecerles?)*, and my grandparents, uncles, aunts, nephews, nieces, cousins, and "great" versions of the next generation, there are too many to name, but I love you all. Thank you to the entire the Zárate-Choy family for your support. I appreciate you all, whether you are still on this earth or in my heart. The moments we are together are still the happiest of my life, and I can't imagine being anywhere else.

And mostly, every single day, I thank my kids. You are the real fire of my life.

RESOURCES / SUPPLIERS

I buy many good-quality jarred and dried Peruvian pantry staples and frozen ingredients like peppers, the herb huacatay, and choclo (large-kernel corn) from these quality importers. I expect we will see more Peruvian importers and dedicated retailers in the years to come. Peruvian ingredients are available from several online retailers, at well-stocked Latin markets, and in some specialty food shops.

Look for Japanese ingredients like kombu (a dried seaweed), miso, and yuzu kosho paste at well-stocked grocery stores, Asian markets, and online from small retailers or Amazon. Also look for:

———

Jarred: Ají amarillo, ají panca, and rocoto pastes; Botija olives

Dried: Pallares (lima beans) and mayocoba (canario) beans; maíz chulpe (dried corn for popping) and maíz morada (dried purple corn); papas secas (dried potatoes); trigo (barley), kinuwa (quinoa) and kiwicha (amaranth); Mexican oregano

Frozen: Whole ají amarillo, ají panca, and rocoto peppers; huacatay; choclo corn; tropical fruits including lucuma

La Tienda (**tienda.com**), Latin Merchant (**latinmerchant.com**), and Kosmos Foods (**kosmosperu.com**) are among several online retailers specializing in Peruvian or Latin food products. Major online retailers like Amazon also carry a range of Peruvian products. Other retailers include:

———

INCA'S FOODS
incasfood.com

PERÚ FOOD
perufoodimport.com

PERUVIAN GOURMET (INCA FOOD IMPORTER)
incafoodimporter.com

T & C SPECIALTIES
tc-specialties.com

TRADICIONES ANDINAS
tradicionesandinas.com

GLOSSARY

Aderezo. A seasoning base used to flavor a dish. The aderezo, literally "to dress," varies by the cook and dish. See sidebar, page 152.

Adobo. A curing and cooking technique. Before refrigeration, the Spanish used a spicy, vinegary marinade to preserve meats, then the meats were slowly cooked in the adobo "sauce."

Agave Syrup. Mexican sweetener made from agave plants. Like honey, agave syrup is slightly sweeter than sugar, but not as thick, so it mixes well into other ingredients at room temperature or chilled. Amber agave syrup is the most commonly available grade and works well in cocktails. Substitute: honey.

Ají. The Peruvian name for native chile peppers. Of the hundreds of cultivated varieties, the three most significant to Peruvian cooking are ají amarillo, ají panca, and rocoto. For more on each type of pepper, see La Cocina, page 20.

Alfajores. Sandwich-style cookies that get their crumbly texture from cornstarch. Alfajores are traditionally filled with manjar blanco, what dulce de leche is called in Peru.

Alpaca. Llamalike animal domesticated thousands of years ago in northern Peru. Alpaca can survive at high altitudes and require less feed than many similar animals, so their meat remains popular in Peru, especially in mountain regions. The flavor is similar to lamb, only not as gamy. Ask for farm-raised alpaca at specialty butchers. Substitute: equal parts ground lamb and beef.

Amaranth. *See* Kiwicha.

Aniseed and Star Anise. Unrelated spices with a similar licoricelike flavor. Aniseeds, a Mediterranean spice, have a mild, almost floral licorice flavor and are used in Peruvian pastries in both whole or powdered form. Star anise is a Chinese spice with a more intense, but balanced, licorice flavor, so I add them whole to both savory dishes and desserts and sweet drinks like chicha morada, an Andean purple corn punch.

Anticuchos. Grilled street foods. A specialty of Lima, anticuchos are grilled-to-order skewered meats and poultry, traditionally made from gizzards or other less expensive cuts. Every vendor has his or her own special anticucho sauce, or basting glaze, and often serves the skewers with a side of choclo, Peruvian corn.

Arroz Verde. Green rice, a common dish all over Latin America. In Peru, the rice is made with plenty of cilantro as the base, so it takes on a very dark green color.

Bonito Flakes. A fish related to tuna and mackerel preserved by dry-aging, curing, and smoking. In Japanese cooking, the salty, smoky flesh is shaved into tissue-thin flakes and used to flavor bold sauces like teriyaki sauce.

Botija Olives. Dark purple descendant of a Spanish variety of olives cured in an earthenware jar with a rich, briny flavor. Botijas are worth seeking out for salads and sauces like the traditional aceituna Botija sauce for papas rellenas. Look for jarred and brine-packed Botijas, not the dried, salted olives. Substitute: Kalamatas.

Caigua. A long, green, vegetablelike fruit cultivated by the Incas, also known as a "stuffing cucumber" because of its hollow interior. Caiguas have a flavor somewhere between a cucumber and a green bell pepper and are traditionally served raw or pickled in salads, sautéed, or stuffed and baked. Available at some farmers' markets and Latin markets.

Camotes. Sweet potatoes and yams. See La Cocina, page 20.

Canarios. Canary beans. Medium-size, off-white beans with a mild flavor and tender texture that make them very versatile. Also called mayocobas and frijoles Peruanos (Peruvian beans). Substitute: great northern beans or similar firm, white beans. For more on mayocobas, see sidebar, page 212.

Cancha. Toasted and salted corn kernels made from maíz chulpe, a large-kernel variety of corn that is dried. See La Cocina, page 20.

Chancaca. Pure cane loaf sugar used all over Latin America (where it goes by different names). In Peru, the sugar is shaped into chubby cones, wrapped in banana leaves, and used as the base for the sauce for desserts like picarones, sweet potato–pumpkin beignets. Traditionally, the juice of freshly harvested sugarcane is cooked down and pounded by hand to lend a caramelized flavor; processed versions today are machine made from refined white sugar (both are suitable for making canchaca sauce). Substitutes: panela, piloncillo, or similar loaf sugar.

Canola Oil. The workhorse vegetable oil used in most Peruvian households for both chilled dishes like salads and for all types of cooking, including deep frying. For chilled dishes and most cooked dishes, I prefer the cleaner flavor of olive oil, but I do use canola oil for frying. Substitute: any vegetable oil.

Carapulcra. Incan-style stew made with papas secas (sun-dried potatoes), pork, ají peppers, and peanuts. The dish really shows the mix of influences in Peruvian cuisine, from local to European, Asian, and African flavors.

Causa. Potato salad–like dish made from mashed potatoes mixed with ají amarillo paste, lime juice, and oil (see pages 101–109). The very creamy, chilled potato mixture is pressed into casserole dishes or shaped with molds and traditionally topped with chicken or seafood-based salads, avocados, tomatoes, and other toppings.

Cebollas Rojas. Red onions. See La Cocina, page 20.

Ceviche (Cebiche). Chilled seafood dish served in leche de tigre sauce, with raw and sometimes quickly blanched seafood. Ceviche is probably Peru's most famous dish. For more information on ceviche, see the sidebar on page 79.

Chanfainita. Creole soup traditionally made with beef lung and maíz mote, Peruvian-style hominy. The soup dates to the arrival of African slaves, who used the leftover meat and vegetable scraps Spanish landowners discarded to make flavorful new dishes.

Chaufa. Peruvian-style fried rice. Chaufa is a uniquely Peruvian word that emerged in Lima, where there are many Chinese-Peruvian families, including my own.

Chicha Morada. Nonalcoholic corn punch made from maíz morado (purple corn), fruits, and spices (page 224). Popular in the summertime as a punch, chicha morada can also be served hot, or used as the base for mazamorra morada, a purple corn pudding (page 243). Chicha morada is not the same as *chicha de jora* (or simply *chicha*), a traditional beerlike drink made from corn, fruit, and sugar traditionally fermented by saliva (today, barley is used).

Chifa. Local name for Peruvian-Chinese–style cooking. One of many uniquely Peruvian words in Spanish drawing on the culture's strong Cantonese roots.

Chirimoya (Cherimoya). Large, green-skinned tropical fruit that the first Europeans dubbed the "pearl of the Andes," with sweet, creamy flesh and an almost guavalike flavor. In Peru, the fruit is enjoyed out of hand or churned into cremoladas, or creamy sorbets. For more on chirimoyas, see sidebar, page 240.

Choclo. Several starchy varieties of large-kernel corn. See La Cocina, page 20.

Chorritos a la Chalaca. Mussels steamed and served with a spicy rocoto pepper–red onion–tomato salsa with plenty of lime juice. A specialty of Callao, Peru's main seaport just west of Lima, and the inspiration behind my version of oysters a la chalaca.

Chuño. Naturally freeze-dried potatoes. See La Cocina, page 20.

Conchas a la Parmesana. Parmesan scallops with béchamel sauce. A classic dish that combines local ingredients like scallops and ají peppers with Italian Parmesan.

Criollo. Widely used term in Peru for anything involving the mix of local Quechua (the native language) and Spanish cultures. Peruvians of mixed descent (indigenous and European, African, or other immigrants) are also referred to as Criollos, or Creoles.

Estofados. General name for several Peruvian-style stews. Most begin with an aderezo, mix of seasonings, that make up the flavor base of the dish.

Gochujang. Korean fermented red chile paste. I use the paste, more of an L.A. influence, in my barbecue and other sauces. There really isn't a good substitute.

Harina de Camote. Sweet potato starch. See La Cocina, page 20. Substitute: Japanese potato starch (katakuriko) or cornstarch.

Huacatay. An herb with an almost aniselike mint flavor that is native to the Andes. See La Cocina, page 20.

Jengibre. Ginger. See La Cocina, page 20.

Katakuriko. Japanese potato starch. See La Cocina, page 20.

Kinúwa. Quechua word for quinoa, the "mother grain" of the Incas. See sidebar, page 200.

Kiwicha. Amaranth, a grainlike seed related to quinoa that has also been cultivated in the Andes for thousands of years. See sidebar, page 200. Substitute: quinoa.

Kombu. A variety of dried kelp (seaweed) that gives many Japanese soups and sauces their distinct flavor. The flat, rectangular sheets add umami to sauces like ponzu. Brush off the salty, dried white residue with a damp cloth before using. There really isn't a good substitute.

Leche de Tigre. "Tiger's milk," the base sauce for ceviche (page 78). Depending on the version, the sauce is traditionally made from fresh lime juice, ají amarillo or rocoto peppers, often ginger and/or garlic, and a small amount of pureed fish to add body and flavor.

Lima Beans. *See* Pallares.

Locro de Zapallo. Pumpkin stew. A very classic, old stew going back to the Incas made from pumpkins (or similar squash), potatoes, choclo corn, and usually queso fresco.

Maíz. Corn, both fresh and dried, is used extensively in Latin American cooking. See La Cocina, page 20, for the various types: choclo (fresh), and dried maíz chulpe, maíz morado, and maíz mote.

Manjar Blanco. A general term in Latin American countries used to described milk- and cream-based custards. In Peru, we refer to dulce de leche ("milk candy") as manjar blanco, the caramel custard made from sweetened, condensed milk.

Marcianos. Peruvian-style ice pops frozen in long, thin plastic bags and eaten like push-up pops. Flavors often include regional fruits like lucuma and cherimoya.

Mirin. Japanese cooking wine made from fermented rice. The cooking version is sweeter and has less alcohol than most rice wines or sakes meant for drinking.

Miso. Japanese paste made from fermented and aged soybeans, salt, and rice, barley, or other grains. Store open packages of miso in the freezer for up to 2 months.
　　Akamiso. Commonly known as "red" miso. Akamiso is a darker color and often saltier than shiromiso and saikyo miso. It is bold enough to stand out in sauces with other strong flavors, like ají panca.
　　Saikyo Miso. A specialty miso from Kyoto. The lightest in color, saikyo miso is also the least salty and has a more subtle, balanced flavor than many other misos, which works well with many of my dishes. Substitute: shiromiso.
　　Shiromiso. Often called "white" miso, but really more of a light tan color, and used in miso soups. Compared to other misos, it has a midlevel saltiness that is good for milder dishes.

Paiche. Jurassic-era fish native to parts of the Amazon that has been a part of the local diet for thousands of years. The white flesh holds together well yet is very tender, so it is very versatile. Substitutes: firm, white-fleshed fish like corvina, striped bass, yellowtail, or halibut.

Pallares. Lima, or broad, beans, one of many native Peruvian beans grown along the coast for thousands of years. The beans have a firm texture and hold their shape well. For more on pallares, see sidebar, page 212.

Panko. Japanese-style bread crumbs. Their larger size yet almost delicate texture makes panko ideal for breading and frying.

Papas a la Huancaína. A dish of boiled potatoes with hard-boiled eggs and olives drenched in a creamy sauce. The chilled, creamy, ají amarillo–cheese sauce is named after the city in Peru's central highlands, Huancayo, where it was introduced.

Papas Rellenas. Mashed potato cakes stuffed with spicy ground beef, hard-boiled eggs, and aceituna Botija olive sauce (page 179).

Papas Secas. Potatoes that have been boiled and dried for preservation and flavor. See La Cocina, page 20. There really isn't a good substitute.

Patitas. Traditional Afro-Peruvian stew made from slowly simmered pig trotters with ají peppers and other spices.

Picarones. Sweet potato and pumpkin squash fritters. A street vendor staple, picarones served with chancaca sauce were one of my favorite treats growing up.

Pisco. The national spirit of Peru. Authentic Peruvian pisco must be made from certain varieties of *uvas*, or grapes, and was traditionally distilled in small clay, amphora-shaped vessels similar to those used to make chicha, corn beer. For more on pisco, see sidebar, page 230.

Pollo a la Brasa. Peru's famous rotisserie chicken marinated in a flavorful mixture of smoky ají panca paste, spices like cumin, soy sauce, and vinegar.

Ponzu. A tangy, citrusy, salty Japanese sauce made from soy sauce and yuzu juice flavored with bonito flakes, kombu, and other seasonings. The store-bought versions in the States are harsh and overpower food, with none of the delicate flavors of the ocean that you get with the homemade sauce (page 37).

Pulpo al Olivo. Octopus with creamy Botija olive sauce. A traditional coastal dish that was the inspiration for my Tiradito de Pulpo al Olivo (page 99).

Queso Fresco. Fresh, Spanish-style cow's-milk cheese (known as *queso blanco* in Europe). In Peru, fresh cheese are often made with a blend of sheeps and cow's milk that gives them a very balanced flavor. The packaged queso frescos at most grocery stores are pretty poor quality. Look for fresh blocks of queso fresco in the deli counter of good grocery stores or Latin markets. Substitute: feta.

Quinoa. *See* Kinúwa.

Rocoto Pepper. *See* Ají Peppers.

Rosquitas de Anis. Aniseed cookies braided and shaped like a wreath topped with sesame seeds and anise seeds (page 254).

Salchipapas. Sausage (salchi) and potatoes (papas). Lima's famous street food-turned-fast-food dish of fried hot dogs or sausages and potatoes.

Salsa Criolla. The king of fresh Peruvian condiments. Made with freshly shaved or sliced red onions, lime juice, ají peppers, and salt. Served on sandwiches, ceviche, or with anything that needs a little crunch and tanginess.

Salsa de Soya. The generic name of soy sauce in Peru, but like Kleenex refers to tissue in the United States, we usually refer to soy sauce by the most popular brand name, Sillao. See La Cocina, page 20. *See also*: Tamari.

Salsa Madre. Mother sauce. A cook's "secret sauce" of proprietary seasonings and ingredients.

Saltado. A Chinese-Peruvian style stir-fry. The most famous version, lomo saltado, is made with lomo (beef filet), red onions, tomatoes, and ají peppers.

Seco. A Criollo-style stew from northern Peru made with various meats or poultry that includes a dark green cilantro sauce. The word literally means "dry," but slow-cooked secos are the opposite, very moist and flavorful.

Solerito. Saladlike dish from Arequipa in southern Peru traditionally made with lima beans, red onions, choclo corn, tomatoes, and ají peppers, among other ingredients. The name means "little bachelor."

Tacacho. Smashed plantains mixed with pork and formed into patties and fried. The snack is especially popular in the Amazon, where it is made to order by street and market vendors.

Tacu Tacu. Leftover rice and beans are shaped into cakes and fried in this Afro-Peruvian dish.

Tamalitos Verdes. Mini tamales that are a specialty of the northern Andes region. Instead of flourlike masa, the main ingredient in Mexican tamales, Peruvian tamales are made with fresh choclo, a large-kernel, sweet corn.

Tamari. A wheat-free alternative to soy sauce with a slightly more intense flavor. *See also*: Salsa de Soya.

Tiraditos. Sliced raw or lightly seared fish typically served sashimi-style, typically in some type of bold, ají pepper and lime juice sauce. See sidebar, page 79.

Tobiko. Flying fish eggs, also known as "poor man's caviar." See sidebar, page 88.

Trigo. Barley, an ancient whole grain that arrived in Peru several hundred years ago via Spanish colonists. See La Cocina, page 20.

Yuca (Cassava Root or Manioc). Slightly sweet and nutty tuberous root vegetable indigenous to South America (not to be confused with yucca, a desert shrub). The boiled root has been used in traditional dishes dating back to the Moche and also to make fries and yuquitas (fritters, page 61). Available frozen at well-stocked grocery stores or Latin markets. If using the fresh root, peel well before using.

Yucas Fritas. Thick-cut fries made from native cassava root. Like a potato, cassava gets crispy on the outside but has a denser, almost creamy texture inside. The fries are the stand-in for french fries at many Peruvian restaurants and cafés.

Yuquitas. Cassava root fritters, a beignetlike version of yucas fritas, or cassava root fries. They are served alongside one of my favorite soups, sopa rachi, the Peruvian version of Cantonese-style congee.

Yuzu. A Japanese citrus fruit with a complex flavor, almost like a mix of lime and orange juices with the flowery scent of orange blossoms. The fresh citrus fruit can be difficult to find outside of Japan. Look for the frozen, unsweetened and unsalted juice (do not substitute bottled juices). Substitute: lime juice, in small quantities. For sauces like ponzu that rely on a lot of the juice for a balanced flavor, make mock yuzu juice (page 37).

Yuzu Kosho. Japanese chile pepper paste made from green (sometimes red) chile peppers, yuzu citrus zest and juice, and salt. See La Cocina, page 20.

INDEX

OH, BELLA FLOR LIMEÑA!
SANTA Y PURA DONCELLA
TAN SOLO TU PRESENCIA
INFUNDE FORTALEZA.
ERES TAN SOLO PUREZA
AMOR, LUZ Y VIDA.
ERES REYNA DE LOS PUEBLOS
Y DE TODA LAS NACIONES.
ESO ERES, SANTA Y BELLA,
HERMOSA, ROSA LIMEÑA.
*
OH, BEAUTIFUL FLOWER OF LIMA!
HOLY AND PURE MAIDEN
JUST YOUR PRESENCE
INFUSES STRENGTH.
YOU ARE THE ONLY PURITY
LOVE, LIGHT AND LIFE.
YOU ARE QUEEN OF THE VILLAGES
AND OF ALL NATIONS.
THAT'S WHO YOU ARE, HOLY AND BEAUTIFUL
GORGEOUS FLOWER OF LIMA.

—ELVIRA ZÁRATE CHOY, MI MAMÁ